THE SUBJECT OF SEMIOTICS

THE SUBJECT
OF SEMIOTICS

Kaja Silverman

New York
OXFORD UNIVERSITY PRESS
1983

Library of Congress Cataloging in Publication Data
Silverman, Kaja.
  The subject of semiotics.

  Bibliography: p.
  Includes index.
  1. Semiotics.   2. Discourse analysis.
3. Psychoanalysis.   4. Communication—Sex
differences.   I. Title.
P99.S52   001.51   82-6306
ISBN 0-19-503177-6   AACR2

Printing (last digit): 9 8 7 6 5 4 3 2 1

Printed in the United States of America

For
Michael
and
Philosophy in the Kitchen

Preface

The book that follows is intended as a methodological guide to a group of semiotic writings frequently taught in advanced undergraduate courses in North America and Britain, writings that are for the most part available in English. It should therefore be viewed as a supplementary and explanatory text rather than as one that precedes the reading of any primary semiotic materials.

The Subject of Semiotics differs from other synthetic books on post-structuralism in three important ways. First, it maintains the centrality of psychoanalysis to semiotics; it proposes, that is, that the human subject is to a large degree the subject of semiotics. The chapters of this book approach the connection between psychoanalysis and semiotics in a variety of ways, but each argues that signification occurs only through discourse, that discourse requires a subject, and that the subject itself is an effect of discourse. The final three chapters also situate signification, discourse, and subjectivity within the larger symbolic order that determines their relation to each other.

Second, *The Subject of Semiotics* assumes the connections between literary and cinematic texts and theory to be at all points reciprocal, and it attempts consistently to pose one in relation to the other. Thus theoretical discussions merge into literary and cinematic explorations, and analyses of specific novels, poems, and films return us to broader speculative paths.

The third respect in which *The Subject of Semiotics* must be distinguished from its predecessors is its emphasis upon sexual difference as an organizing principle not only of the symbolic order and its "contents" (signification, discourse, subjectivity), but of the semiotic account of those things. Not only does psychoanalytic semiotics establish that authoritative vision and speech have traditionally been male prerogatives, whereas women have more frequently figured as the object of that vision and speech, but it provides a vivid dramatization of this role division at the level of its own articulation. The theoreticians most fully associated with this branch of semiotics—Sigmund Freud and Jacques Lacan—function as exemplary representatives of the paternal values they locate at the center of the existing symbolic order.

The relationship of the female subject to semiotic theory is thus necessarily an ambivalent one. That theory affords her a sophisticated understanding of her present cultural condition, but it also seems to confine her forever to the status of one who is seen, spoken, and analyzed. In order for semiotics to be of any real value to the female subject, she must somehow interrupt its "always–already"—she must find ways of using it that permit her to look beyond the nightmare of her history.

In the sections of this book devoted to sexual difference (Chapters 4 and 5), I have attempted just such a rewriting of female subjectivity. I have tried, that is, to denaturalize the condition of woman, and to isolate its cultural determinants. This project puts a certain critical distance between my discourse and those of Freud and Lacan, particularly whenever the Oedipus complex is on the agenda.

Chapter 1 of *The Subject of Semiotics* charts the path leading from Ferdinand de Saussure and Charles Sanders Peirce to that much more recent body of semiotic theory within which the categories of discourse, subjectivity, and the symbolic order centrally figure. It thus provides a context for the chapters that follow. Chapter 2 explores those signifying processes described by Freud as the "primary" and the "secondary," and which he associates with the two major areas of psychic reality: the unconscious and the preconscious. Chapter 3 accounts for the sets condensation and displacement, metaphor and metonymy, and paradigm and syntagm in terms of these processes, thereby demonstrating the impossibility of isolating even the most rudimentary of signifying formations from subjectivity. Chapter 4 outlines the two most important theories of the subject made available by semiotics—the Freudian and the Lacanian—theories that give a conspicuous place to discourse and the symbolic order. Chapter 5 uses the theory of suture to articulate the relationship between the subject and the discourse of the classic cinematic text, and to explore some of the ideological implications of that relationship. The final chapter of *The Subject of Semiotics* confronts the subject's relationship to another discourse (or to be more precise, *group* of discourses), the literary. It also outlines some of the strategies evolved by Roland Barthes for uncovering the symbolic field inhabited by the individual literary instance.

Whenever possible I have utilized English language sources, so as to facilitate ready access to those sources for as wide a range of readers as possible. The numerous literary and cinematic examples are also intended as aids to the general reader.

I would like to thank John Wright for encouraging me to write this book, and Bob Scholes and JoAnn Putnam-Scholes for intellectual and culinary support while I was doing so. I would also like to thank my students (and in particular the "Rome contingent") for their constant stimulation, and for their willingness to share my obsessions. Khachig Tololyan read a late version of this book, and offered such fine and persuasive criticism that I returned enthusiastically to the typewriter, for which I am most grateful. Thanks are also due to Leona Capeless, whose editorial suggestions untangled many syntactic knots, and helped me to say what I meant. Finally, I would like to thank Michael Silverman, who read this book at every stage of its production with the energy most of us reserve for our own work.

Hampton and Vancouver   Kaja Silverman
1981

Contents

It is in and through language that man constitutes himself as a *subject,* because language alone establishes the concept of "ego" in reality, in *its* reality which is that of the being.

The "subjectivity" we are discussing here is the capacity of the speaker to posit himself as "subject." It is defined not by the feeling which everyone experiences of being himself . . . but as the psychic unity that transcends the totality of the actual experiences it assembles and that makes the permanence of the consciousness. Now we hold that that "subjectivity," whether it is placed in phenomenology or in psychology, as one may wish, is only the emergence in the being of a fundamental property of language. "Ego" is he who *says* "ego." That is where we see the foundation of "subjectivity," which is determined by the linguistic status of "person."

Emile Benveniste

1

From Sign to Subject, A Short History

Although its origins can be traced back as far as Plato and Augustine, semiotics as a self-conscious theory emerged only at the beginning of this century, in the writings of Charles Sanders Peirce and Ferdinand de Saussure. It received fresh impetus in 1958 with the publication of Claude Lévi-Strauss's *Structural Anthropology*, which applied Saussure's principles to the study of primitive cultures, but it achieved maturity only when it was consolidated with psychoanalysis. That consolidation was effected by Jacques Lacan. However, it was implicit from 1900, when Sigmund Freud gave us *The Interpretation of Dreams*.

Semiotics involves the study of signification, but signification cannot be isolated from the human subject who uses it and is defined by means of it, or from the cultural system which generates it. The theoretical intimacy of the terms "signification," "subject," and "symbolic order" has long been apparent to readers of Freud and Lacan, but it has perhaps remained less obvious to those semioticians who trace their lineage to Saussure.

This chapter attempts to demonstrate that the theory of signification has evolved in ways which increasingly implicate the subject and the symbolic order, and that this evolution finds one of its most important culminations in the writings of the linguist Emile Benveniste. As we shall see, the central term within those writings—"discourse"—makes apparent not only

the importance of linguistics for psychoanalysis, but of psychoanalysis for linguistics.

Other important developments in the theory of signification
were engineered by Charles Sanders Peirce (who started writing well before Saussure, but whose work was assimilated much
later), by Roland Barthes, and by Jacques Derrida. Peirce in-
creases the number of signifying relationships over those
charted by Saussure, and makes the human subject their support. Barthes demonstrates that signification cannot be divorced from the operations of myth or ideology, and that it
thus always implies the larger cultural field. Derrida indicates
that certain privileged terms not acknowledged by Saussure
function to anchor and restrain the play of signification. He
also reveals the ideological basis of those terms, and in so doing
attempts to liberate signification from their dominance. All three
of these theoreticians agree that meaning is much more open-
ended than Saussure would have us believe, and that it cannot
be isolated from the symbolic order.

The sequence of the "history" which follows is dictated less
by a strict chronology than by the unfolding of a theoretical
argument which begins with Saussure and ends with Benveniste—an argument which is essentially linguistic, and which revolves around the relation of abstract signifying systems to concrete utterances, and that of signifiers to signifieds. As I have
already indicated, this argument has profound implications for
our understanding of both the subject and the symbolic order.

A) FERDINAND DE SAUSSURE

The Swiss linguist Ferdinand de Saussure died in 1913 before
putting into manuscript form the insights for which he is now
chiefly known. The *Course in General Linguistics* was subsequently compiled by several of Saussure's students from his lec-
ture notes. That book not only reconceived linguistics along
semiotic lines, but it called for the application of its semiotic
principles to all aspects of culture:

> Language is a system of signs that express ideas, and is
> therefore comparable to a system of writing, the alphabet of

deaf-mutes, symbolic rites, polite formulas, military signals, etc. But it is the most important of all these systems.

A science that studies the life of signs within society is conceivable; it would be part of social psychology and consequently of general psychology; I shall call it semiology. . . . Semiology would show what constitutes signs, what laws govern them. Since the science does not yet exist, no one can say what it would be; but it has a right to existence, a place staked out in advance. Linguistics is only a part of the general science of semiology; the laws discovered by semiology will be applicable to linguistics, and the latter will circumscribe a well-defined area within the mass of anthropological facts.[1]

Recent years have more than justified Saussure's prediction. Umberto Eco points out in *A Theory of Semiotics* that the present semiotic field consists of zoology, olfactory signs, tactile communication, paralinguistics, medicine, kinesics and proxemics, musical codes, formalized languages, written languages, natural languages, visual communication, systems of objects, plot structures, text theory, cultural codes, aesthetic texts, mass communication, and rhetoric,[2]—and one would of course want to add anthropology and psychoanalysis to this list.

The logocentricity of Saussure's model has also proven to be a general feature of semiotics; it is the common assumption of most semioticians that language constitutes the signifying system *par excellence,* and that it is only by means of linguistic signs that other signs become meaningful. In Roland Barthes's *Système de la mode,* for example, photographic signs are shown to depend upon the mediation of the linguistic "copy" which surrounds them, and to be indecipherable or at least unreliable without it. The privileged status enjoyed by language within semiotic theory has provoked some students of film to stress the image rather than the sound track, and to locate cinematic syntax at the level of shot-to-shot relationships instead of at the level of dialogue. As later chapters will attempt to demonstrate, one of the great values of Freud's writings is the very sophisticated scheme they give us for understanding the relationship between visual and linguistic signification, and the equilibrium which that scheme establishes between the two registers.

The terms "sign" and "system" receive equal emphasis both

in the passage quoted above and throughout *Course in General Linguistics*. Language, and by extension any other object of semiotic inquiry, is a "system of signs that express ideas," a network of elements that signify only in relation to each other. Indeed the sign itself is a relational entity, a composite of two parts that signify not only through those features that make each of them slightly different from any other two parts, but through their association with each other.

Saussure names these two parts of the sign the "signifier" and the "signified." "Signifier" refers to a meaningful form, while "signified" designates the concept which that form evokes. Within the linguistic system the signifier would be what Saussure calls a "sound-image," that is, the image of one of those sounds which we shape within our minds when we think, whereas the signified would be the meaning which that sound-image generates. (For Saussure, speech represents the realization or manifestation of the linguistic signifier, not the linguistic signifier itself. Writing, in turn, represents the transcription of speech.)

Course in General Linguistics stresses the "arbitrary" nature of the linguistic sign, the fact that the connection between its two parts is "unmotivated":

> The bond between the signifier and the signified is arbitrary. Since I mean by sign the whole that results from the associating of the signifier with the signified, I can simply say: *the linguistic sign is arbitrary.*
> The idea of "sister" is not linked by any inner relationship to the succession of sounds *s-ö-r* which serves as its signifier in French; that it could be represented equally by just any other sequence is proved by differences among languages and by the very existence of different languages: the signified "ox" has as its signifier *b-ö-f* on one side of the border and *o-k-s* (*Ochs*) on the other. [67–68]

The point upon which Saussure here insists is that no natural bond links a given signifier to its signified; their relationship is entirely conventional, and will only obtain within a certain linguistic system. The signifier "sister" produces a more or less equivalent concept in the minds of all English speakers, but not in the minds of German or French speakers.

The notion of "more or less equivalent" is vital to our understanding of both the signifier and the signified. No two English speakers will pronounce the same word identically on all occasions, and there is likely to be even more variety at the conceptual level. What permits us to recognize a word when it is spoken by a person from a dialectal region other than our own is the fact that the word in question more closely resembles our own version of it than it does any other word. Similarly, what enables us to communicate conceptually are certain shared features at the level of the signified. Even though one English speaker's notion of a sister may differ dramatically from another's, there will always be more points in common between the two notions of sister than there are between either's notion of a sister and that of a brother, father, or mother. In short, the identity of a given signifier or a given signified is established through the ways in which it differs from all other signifiers or signifieds within the same system. Saussure illustrates this point through a chess analogy: "a state of the set of chessmen corresponds closely to a state of language. The respective value of the pieces depends on their position on the chessboard just as each linguistic term derives its value from its opposition to all the other terms" (88). Elsewhere in *Course in General Linguistics* he notes that whereas the substitution of ivory for wooden chessmen would in no way affect the game, a decrease or an increase in the number of chessmen would not only transform the entire game but the value of each element within it (23).

Saussure isolates two sorts of signs which would seem to violate the principle that the connection between a signifier and its signified is always arbitrary: onomatopoeic words, and symbols. The first of these is easily disposed of: Saussure points out that signifiers like "whisper" or "murmur," which are ostensibly duplicative or imitative of their signifieds, vary substantially from one language to another, never more than partially approximate their signifieds, and ultimately become as conventional in their usage as any other signifier. The second category proves rather more problematic, both because the association of signifier and signified would indeed seem to be "motivated"

("One characteristic of the symbol is that it is never wholly arbitrary; it is not empty, for there is the rudiment of a natural
bond between the signifier and the signified. The symbol of
justice, a pair of scales, could not be replaced by just any other
symbol, such as a chariot" (68)), and because certain signifying
systems, like those of gesture, would seem to consist almost entirely of symbols. However, Saussure stresses that the significant semiotic fact here is the conventionalization of the relation
between the two terms, not their similarity. Because the second
of these relations tends to obscure the first, Saussure finds that
non-symbolic signifying systems make a more appropriate object of semiotic investigation than do symbolic ones:

> Signs that are wholly arbitrary realize better than the others
> the ideal of the semiological process; that is why language, the
> most complex and universal of all systems of expression, is also
> the most characteristic; in this sense linguistics can become the
> master-pattern for all branches of semiology although lan-
> guage is only one particular semiological system. [68]

This passage reveals the privileged status enjoyed by linguistics within the Saussurean scheme. It also suggests some of
the problems implicit in that valorization. By positing the linguistic model as the most semiotically "ideal," Saussure establishes a value system within which any language which relies
upon motivated signs would be automatically inferior. That
language would consequently be a less appropriate object of
study, and it would be seen as requiring a linguistic "supplement"—a verbal or written gloss or explanation. The Saussurean argument here functions to exclude many of the areas—
psycholanalysis, literary and cinematic investigation, anthropology, ideological analysis—which have otherwise benefited most
from it. Semiotics has become the interdisciplinary theory anticipated by Saussure only by ignoring his strictures about unmotivated signs, and by giving an equal place to languages in
which the signifier and signified are more intimately affiliated.

As Jonathan Culler observes in his monograph on Saussure,
the arbitrariness of the linguistic sign extends beyond the relation of signifier to signified. Each of the two parts of the lin-

guistic sign is itself arbitrary, which is another way of saying that neither part has any prior or autonomous existence:

> A language does not simply assign arbitrary names to a set of independently existing concepts. It sets up an arbitrary relation between signifiers of its own choosing on the one hand, and signifieds of its own choosing on the other. Not only does each language produce a different set of signifiers, articulating and dividing the continuum of sound in a distinctive way, but each language produces a different set of signifieds; it has a distinctive and thus "arbitrary" way of organizing the world into concepts or categories.[3]

The fact that the experiences of thinking and speaking differ from language to language—that both linguistic signifiers and linguistic signifieds are arbitrary—can be demonstrated through a simple exercise. Two French words are listed in most dictionaries as translations of the English noun "wish"—*voeu* and *désir*. These words clearly differ from each other at the level of the linguistic signifier—they are, in short, materially distinct. They also differ at the level of the linguistic signified. The signified of *voeu* overlaps with that of "wish" only in the very specialized sense of verbal wishes, as in "Best wishes!" Moreover, it occupies the same semantic space as a quite different English word, "vow." And *désir,* the alternative translation of "wish," represents the French equivalent of yet another English word—"desire." Not surprisingly, it does not correspond exactly to either English word; rather, it means something like "a continuous and forceful condition of wishing." Like forms, concepts enjoy no extra-systemic identity. Meaning emerges only through the play of difference within a closed system:

> . . . in language there are only differences. . . . a difference generally implies positive terms between which the difference is set up; but in language there are only differences *without positive terms.* Whether we take the signified or the signifier, language has neither ideas or sounds that existed before the linguistic system but only conceptual and phonic differences that have issued from the system. The idea or phonic substance that a sign contains is of less importance than the other signs that surround it. Proof of this is that the value of a term

may be modified without either its meaning or its sound being affected, solely because a neighboring term has been modified.[4]

As his insistence upon the arbitrary nature of the sign would indicate, Saussure's model does not take into account anything beyond the domain of signification. *Course in General Linguistics* has nothing whatever to say about any actual sister who might be in question when the word "sister" is spoken, written, or thought—about the connection, that is, between sign and referent. It is concerned exclusively with three sorts of systemic relationships: that between a signifier and its signified; those between a sign and all of the other elements of its system; and those between a sign and the elements which surround it within a concrete signifying instance. We have already dealt with the first of these, but the other two warrant further consideration.

Although Saussure describes as "associative" the relationships which one sign enjoys with all of the other signs in the same system, they have become more generally known as "paradigmatic." Paradigmatic relationships can be predicated on a similarity between two signs at the level of the signifier, the signified, or both. Linguistic examples of similarity at the level of the signifier would include words with the same prefix or suffix, words that rhyme, or homonyms. Synonyms and antonyms provide linguistic examples of similarity at the level of the signified (two words can only exist in an antonymic relationship if there is a point in common between them). Linguistic instances of similarity at the level both of the signifier and the signified are more difficult to find; Saussure cites the French words *éducation* and *instruction,* which share the same suffix and which both mean "schooling." Saussure emphasizes that paradigmatic relationships find their support in the human memory system, not in discourse: "Their seat is in the brain; they are part of the inner storehouse that makes up the language of each speaker" (123).

Saussure refers to the relations which a sign entertains with the other signs that surround it within a concrete signifying instance as "syntagmatic." These relationships can only be realized in discourse, and they always involve a formal proximity.

The various words within a sentence enjoy a syntagmatic relationship with each other, as do the shots in a film or garments of clothing worn together. *Course in General Linguistics* uses the image of a chain to illustrate the relationship which the elements of a "syntagm" or syntagmatic cluster enter into with each other.

A sign's value is determined both by its paradigmatic and its syntagmatic associations. Its value depends in part on those features that distinguish it from the other signs within its system, particularly those it most resembles, and in part on those features that distinguish it from the other signs adjacent to it in discourse ("In the syntagm a term acquires its value only because it stands in opposition to everything that precedes or follows it, or to both" (123)).

Another closely related distinction central to Saussure's semiotics is that between *langue* and *parole,* or "language" and "speech." By means of these categories Saussure distinguishes between the abstract linguistic system which pre-exists any individual use of it, and the manipulation of that system to produce concrete utterances. Like a paradigmatic cluster, language finds its locus only in memory—not so much in any single memory as in the memory of a culture. As Saussure points out, "language is not complete in any speaker; it exists perfectly only within a collectivity" (14). Speech, on the other hand, has an individual and localized existence. It is characterized by certain "accidental" features, like personal intonation or style, which have no place within the more stable and normative language system.

The opposition between *langue* and *parole* collapses at various points. Language is after all nothing more than the sum of all available speech instances. Similarly, every speaker is obliged to draw upon the existing linguistic resources. Nevertheless, Saussure not only maintains the distinction between the two categories, but privileges the former over the latter. Within the model advanced by *Course in General Linguistics,* only language constitutes a proper object of study for the simple reason that it alone facilitates investigation along "synchronic" rather than "diachronic" lines.

Synchrony and diachrony represent the last of the impor-

tant oppositional sets in Saussure's scheme. He articulates the
distinction between them in the course of a general discussion
of linguistics, and in an attempt to assess the relative importance of the values of simultaneity and the systematic over those
of successivity and evolution:

> *Synchronic linguistics* will be concerned with the logical and
> psychological relations that bind together coexisting terms and
> form a system in the collective mind of speakers.
> *Diachronic linguistics,* on the contrary, will study relations
> that bind together successive terms not perceived by the col-
> lective mind but substituted for each other without forming a
> system. [99–100]

Saussure here employs the categories of the synchronic and the
diachronic to distinguish between his own linguistics and that
which was current during his lifetime—to distinguish, that is,
between a linguistics predicated on relational terms and one
predicated on historical terms. Saussure struggled to turn linguistics away from comparative studies of words from different
historical moments, like Old English and Modern English, toward an analysis of words in the context of their language system. There is thus, as I suggested above, a certain symmetry
between the concepts "synchrony" and "language"; we can only
arrive at the second of these concepts through the first, since
the language system consists precisely of synchronous elements.
"Diachrony" and "speech" lend themselves to a similar linkage,
both because speech unfolds in time, syntagmatically, and because changes are introduced into language through speech:

> . . . everything diachronic in language is diachronic only by
> virtue of speaking. It is in speaking that the germ of all change
> is found. Each change is launched by a certain number of in-
> dividuals before it is accepted for general use. [98]

The central place given to the concept of synchrony in
Saussure's model has proven to be one of its most controversial
features. Saussure's critics argue that his linguistics leaves no
room for history—that it is static and incapable of accounting
for change. This criticism is to some degree warranted: Saus-

sure does deal almost exclusively with closed, systemic relationships. At the same time, he provides us with categories—diachrony and speech—by means of which it is possible to negotiate at least a partial peace with historical theories like Marxism.[5]

It falls beyond the scope of this book to attempt such a negotiation. However, one possible way of conceptualizing diachrony within the Saussurean scheme would be to see it as a series of successive synchronies, with speech functioning both as the agency of change from one synchrony to another, and as a relay between language and pressures external to it. This four-way relationship—the relationship, that is, between one synchrony and those which precede and follow it, speech, and an external diachrony or history—finds a very clear metaphoric articulation in Marcel Proust's *Within a Budding Grove*. The passage in question describes the effect which certain political or economic events had upon the closed system of nineteenth-century salons:

> . . . like a kaleidoscope which is every now and then given a turn, society arranges successively in different orders elements which one would have supposed to be immovable, and composes a fresh pattern. Before I had made my first Communion, ladies on the "right side" in politics had had the stupefaction of meeting, while paying calls, a smart Jewess. These new arrangements of the kaleidescope are produced by what a philosopher would call a "change of criterion." The Dreyfus case brought about another, at a period rather later than that in which I began to go to Mme. Swann's, and the kaleidoscope scattered once again its little scraps of color. Everything Jewish, even the smart lady herself, fell out of the pattern, and various obscure nationalities appeared in its place.[6]

The pattern that is formed with each shake of the drawing-room kaleidescope corresponds to what Saussure would call a synchrony or language system, while the innovations introduced into that pattern by daring hostesses, and which result in a new shake of the kaleidescope, provide the equivalent of what Saussure would call speech. Those innovations are themselves a response to economic, political, and social pressures, such as the Dreyfus case; in short, they are motivated by a diachrony external to the language system of the nineteenth-century French salon.

Saussure's definition of the sign has exercised an enormous influence over the development of semiotics, particularly in its relational emphasis. At the same time it must be noted that the definition has undergone so many subsequent transformations that it is by now scarcely recognizable. Some of those transformations were the result of philosophical disagreements with the values of Saussure's semiotic model. Others were brought about by the difficulties of extending that model to so-called "second-order" signifying systems, or motivated signs. Still others were induced by a dramatic shift of emphasis. Peirce's model, although it was elaborated even earlier than Saussure's, and at considerably greater length, can be seen as a helpful supplement to it, especially in its accommodation of non-arbitrary signs.

B) CHARLES SANDERS PEIRCE

The ideas of the American philosopher Charles Sanders Peirce are set forth in the eight volumes of his *Collected Papers* as well as in a considerable body of unpublished material. The semiotic scheme which emerges from the published writings differs from Saussure's scheme perhaps most markedly in its attentiveness to the referent, and in its reliance upon two interlocking triads.

The first of these triads consists of what Peirce calls the "sign," the "interpretant," and the "object." Signification is understood as involving all three in a complex interaction:

> A sign . . . is something which stands to somebody for something in some respect or capacity. It addresses somebody, that is, creates in the mind of that person an equivalent sign, or perhaps a more developed sign. That sign which it creates I call the *interpretant* of the first sign. The sign stands for something, its *object*. It stands for that object, not in all respects, but in reference to a sort of idea, which I have sometimes called the *ground*. . . .[7]

The sign which initiates the play of meaning within this model corresponds fairly closely to Saussure's signifier in at least one respect: it is a form capable of eliciting a concept. In another respect—its representational qualities—it would seem quite different. Unlike Saussure's signifier, Peirce's sign often either resembles or adjoins the object.

The interpretant is the "mental effect" or "thought" generated by the relation between the other two terms (I.303). It is thus virtually synonymous with the signified. Peirce attributes to the interpretant a quality which would be very alien to Saussure, but which many more recent semioticians have also attributed to the signified: the quality of endless commutability. In other words, the interpretant can become a sign which produces a new interpretant, and the same operation can occur with each subsequent interpretant:

> The meaning of a representation can be nothing but a representation. In fact, it is nothing but the representation itself conceived as stripped of irrelevant clothing. But this clothing never can be completely stripped off; it is only changed for something more diaphanous. So there is an infinite regression here. Finally, the interpretant is nothing but another representation to which the torch of truth is handed along; and as representation, it has its interpretant again. Lo, another infinite series. [I.171]

The "infinite series" to which any given interpretant belongs suggests a closed semiotics, what Eco in *A Theory of Semiotics* calls an "unlimited semiosis"; the endless commutability of the interpretant seems to preclude any reference to or dependence upon the object. Signs and interpretants (signifiers and signifieds) would appear to be locked in self-containment. Peirce reinforces this sense of semiotic closure when he adds that "The object of representation can be nothing but a representation of which the first representation is the interpretant" (I.171). At the same time the basis of Peirce's signifying triad would seem to be its insistence on the existential relation of sign and object, or signifier and referent—on the connection, that is, between signification and reality.

We can only arrive at a clear understanding of the third term of that triad—i.e. the object—through a discussion of those passages within *The Collected Papers* which are given over to the

topic of reality, since for Peirce the two categories are virtually
synonymous. These passages are fraught with contradictions.
On the one hand Peirce argues that "the real is that which insists on forcing its way to recognition as something *other* than
the mind's creation" (I.163), and on the other, he proposes that
"a reality which has no representation is one which has no relation and quality" (V.187). Yet the manner in which Peirce
combines these two statements on another occasion suggests that
he does not find them incompatible:

> . . . we have *direct experience of things in themselves.* Nothing can
> be more completely false than that we can experience only our
> own ideas. . . . Our knowledge of things in themselves is en-
> tirely *relative,* it is true; but all experience and all knowledge
> is knowledge of that which is, independently of being rep-
> resented. . . . At the same time, no proposition can relate, or
> even thoroughly pretend to relate, to any object otherwise than
> as that object is represented. [VI.73]

This passage provides a sampling of the way in which Peirce
manages to counter pragmatism with idealism; to acknowledge
materiality while at the same time rigidly divorcing it from idea.
The crucial distinction which is here maintained is that between
experience and thought. Peirce argues that we have *direct experience,* but *indirect knowledge* of reality. The former teaches us
that there is a world of things, but gives us no intellectual access
to them, while the latter supplies the only means of knowing
those things, but no way of verifying our knowledge. Reality
bumps up against us, impinges upon us, yet until we have found
a way of representing that reality, it remains impervious to
thought. At times Peirce pushes the argument even further,
insisting that only those portions of reality which are capable of
being represented can affect us:

> "But what," some listener . . . may say, "are we not to occupy
> ourselves at all with earthquakes, droughts and pestilence?"
> To which I reply, if those earthquakes, droughts, and pesti-
> lences are subject to *laws,* those laws being of the nature of
> signs, then, no doubt being signs of those laws they are thereby
> made worthy of human attention; but if they be mere arbitrary

brute interruptions of our course of life, let us wrap our cloaks
about us, and endure them as we may; for they cannot injure
us, though they may strike us down. [VI.235]

If representations provide us with our only access to reality,
then the authenticity of those representations becomes an issue
of pressing importance. Peirce never abandons his belief that
reality can be truly represented. However, he does admit that
the means for determining the truth of a representation lie beyond the reach of the individual. Although Peirce evolves three
criteria by which the truth of a representation can be known
(its insistence, its recognition by others, and induction), ultimately this cognitive process is diachronic—i.e. it unfolds over
an extended period of time—and collective:

The real . . . is that which, sooner or later, information and
reasoning would finally result in, and which is therefore independent of the vagaries of me and you. Thus, the very origin
of the conception of reality shows that this conception essentially involves the notion of a COMMUNITY, without definite
limits, and capable of a definite increase of knowledge. And so
those two series of cognition—the real and the unreal—consist
of those which, at a time sufficiently future, the community
will always continue to reaffirm; and of those which, under the
same conditions, will ever after be denied. [V. 186–87]

In view of the provisional nature of this reality, and the fact
that it can be known only via signs, it seems evident that the
object or referent is as fully excluded from Peirce's semiotic
scheme as it is from Saussure's. It is present within signification
only as a concept which may or may not be representative of it.
We can best understand the signifying transaction described by
Peirce in the following terms: the sign or signifier represents in
some capacity or other the object or referent, which is itself
available only as an interpretant or signified, and in so doing
elicits within the mind of an individual another interpretant or
signified. That interpretant or signified will in all likelihood
generate additional ones, in a kind of relay of signification.

Peirce tells us that reality is accessible to man because *man
himself is a sign*. This is one of Peirce's most radical assertions,

and it is also one of his most important. Man (and by "man" Peirce means that which is constitutive of the human subject) does not only know the world through language; he is himself the product of language:

> . . . the word or sign which man uses *is* the man himself. . . . the fact that every thought is a sign, taken in conjunction with the fact that life is a train of thought, proves that man is a sign. . . . the man and the . . . sign are identical. . . . Thus my language is the sum total of myself; for the man is the thought. [V.189]

The point upon which Peirce here insists is that our access to and knowledge of ourselves is subject to the same semiotic restrictions as our access to and knowledge of the external world. In other words, we are cognitively available to ourselves and others only in the guise of signifiers, such as proper names and first-person pronouns, or visual images, and consequently are for all intents and purposes synonymous with those signifiers.

This passage from Peirce anticipates more recent developments in semiotics, in particular those conducted by Emile Benveniste and Jacques Lacan, in which the categories of language and subjectivity are closely linked. For these theoreticians too the subject is a sign or signifier. Indeed, Lacan makes that point in terms which are more than a little reminiscent of Peirce's triadic formulations: "A signifier is that which represents a subject for another signifier."

Of course Peirce pays scant attention to the unconscious, and tends to assume that signification is an exclusively conscious phenomenon, whereas one of Lacan's more famous pronouncements ("The unconscious is structured like a language") stresses processes of signification of which the subject is unaware. Nevertheless, by bringing to the fore the notion that the subject is determined by signifiers rather than being a transcendental producer of them, Peirce laid the groundwork for those investigations. Moreover, no treatment of the relationship between subject and signifier would be complete without the Peircean scheme, which offers a more satisfactory explanation of the role of the cognitive subject in the signifying process than does that of Freud, Lacan, or Benveniste. Peirce reminds us that the connections which are productive of meaning can only be made in the mind of the subject—that a sign not only "addresses somebody," but that it "creates in the mind of that person an equivalent sign, or perhaps a more developed sign."

Peirce's second triad accounts for the different kinds of signs which human consciousness can interpret and accommodate. That triad consists of "icons," "indices," and "symbols." The iconic sign resembles its conceptual object in certain ways. It may share certain of the properties which that object possesses, or it may duplicate the principles according to which that object is organized:

> Those which partake of simple qualities . . . are *images;* those which represent the relations, mainly dyadic, or so regarded, of the parts of one thing by analogous relations in their own parts, are *diagrams*. . . .[II.157]

The most obvious icons are photographs, paintings, sculptures, and cinematic images, but algebraic equations and graphs are also iconic.

The indexical sign is defined by Peirce as "a real thing or fact which is a sign of its object by virtue of being connected with it as a matter of fact and by also forcibly intruding upon the mind, quite regardless of its being interpreted as a sign" (IV.359). Some of the examples Peirce cites are a weathervane, a pointing hand, and a symptom. Because of the emphasis Peirce places on the existential bond between the indexical sign and its object, some additional clarification would seem appropriate.

The signifying value of the weathervane resides not in its physical relationship to the wind, but in the concepts "wind" and "direction" which it permits the observer to link up. Similarly, the pointing finger functions as a sign not because of its adjacency to a given site, like Boston, but because it generates in the mind of the walker or the driver the conceptual terms "Boston" and "turn right." Finally, the signifying capacity of the symptom inheres not in its physical residence within the patient's body, but in its ability to assist the physician in making a diagnosis. Because the indexical sign is understood to be connected to the real object, it is capable of making that object conceptually present.

Peirce's final category, the symbol, designates a sign whose relation to its conceptual object is entirely arbitrary:

> A *Symbol* is a sign which refers to the Object that it denotes by virtue of a law, usually an association of general ideas, which operates to cause the Symbol to be interpreted as referring to that Object. . . . Not only is it general itself, but the Object to which it refers is of a general nature. Now that which is general has its being in the instances which it will determine. There must, therefore, be existent instances of what the Symbol denotes, although we must here understand by "existent," existent in the possibly imaginary universe to which the Symbol refers. [11.143–44]

Natural languages and notational systems of all sorts are preeminently symbolic, in Peirce's sense of that word. The signs which make up those systems are what Saussure would call "arbitrary"—their relation to their conceptual objects is purely conventional, unmotivated by any other association. (It should be noted that Peirce and Saussure use the term "symbol" in diametrically opposed ways; whereas Peirce means by it a relationship between two dissimilar elements, Saussure employs it to designate the union of elements which have some point in common.) Occasionally one of these signs will in some way resemble its conceptual object, but that resemblance will be incidental to its status as a symbol. The symbol represents a general class of things, rather than a single, discrete object—thus the sign "sister" refers to the general idea of a sister, though it may in addition evoke the image of a specific sister.

Peirce's division of signs shows not only greater flexibility than Saussure's, but a keener sense of the overlapping functions served by a single signifying entity. For instance, Peirce insists on the vital role played in all communication by the icon:

> The only way of directly communicating an idea is by means of an icon; and every indirect method of communicating an idea must depend for its establishment upon the use of an

icon. Hence, every assertion must contain an icon or set of icons, or else must contain signs whose meaning is only explicable by icons. [11.158]

What Peirce is saying here is that a picture of a tree can directly communicate the idea of a tree even to a person who speaks an entirely different language, whereas the word "tree," addressed by one English speaker to another, will convey no meaning unless it evokes the mental image (icon) of a tree.

Peirce's icon bears many affinities with what Freud calls the "thing-presentation," the mental image of an object which joins with the "word-presentation" to form a signifying unit, and without which there could be no linguistic meaning. The icon also anticipates Lacan's notion of the "imaginary," a spectrum of visual images which precedes the acquisition of language in the experience of the child, and which continues to coexist with it afterwards.

Peirce stresses that linguistic syntagms are dependent not only on iconic, but indexical support. Indexical elements help to transform general assertions into specific statements, to locate a discourse in relation to time and space. For example, a proper name elicits the mental image of a living person, or one specific to a particular historical period, a work of literature, or a legal fiction. Thus instead of referring to a whole class of things, the way the word "tree" does, a proper name makes a direct and individual reference, functioning like a pointing hand. Expressions that direct our attention, such as "that," "this," "which," "here," "now," and "yonder," also provide indexical assistance. Personal pronouns operate very much like proper names, requiring an understanding on the part of the listener or reader of the specific persons who at the moment of enunciation constitute the grammatical subject and the grammatical object. Speech is often accompanied by extra-linguistic indices, such as gestures or facial expressions. (As we will see later in this chapter, certain indexical elements, most notably personal pronouns, also enjoy a very central place within Benveniste's semiotic model.)

The icon and index supplement each other as fully as they

do the symbolic or conventional signifier. A photographic image, for instance, enjoys a relation both of similarity and adjacency to its object:

> Photographs . . . are in certain respects exactly like the objects they represent. But this resemblance is due to the photographs having been produced under such circumstances that they were physically forced to correspond point by point to nature. In that respect, then, they belong to the second class of signs, those by physical connection. [11.159]

In much the same way a portrait both resembles and indicates its object, at least for the spectator who enjoys what Peirce would call "collateral acquaintance" with that object (i.e. for the spectator who, as a consequence of some prior experience with the object, has conceptual access to it). For Peirce the richest signs or signifiers are always those which in this way combine iconic, indexical, and symbolic elements [IV.359–61].

The advantages offered by this classification of signifiers over that offered by Saussure become perhaps most evident in cinematic analysis. Saussure's scheme provides no way of distinguishing between linguistic signifiers, photographic signifiers, or signifiers generated by the codes of editing, camera movement, lighting, and sound. Peirce's scheme, on the other hand, enables us to make a number of valuable distinctions. By means of it we are able to note that whereas the relation of linguistic signifiers to their signifieds is primarily conventional, with elements of iconicity and indexicality, the signifiers of photography, editing, camera movement, lighting, and sound are characterized by a preponderance of indexical or iconic properties.

Every cinematic image is iconic. Indeed, the photographic signifier often enjoys so intimate a relationship to its signified that it may seem almost superfluous to distinguish between them. It may seem like an exercise in hairsplitting to say, for instance, that the photographic image of a horse functions as a signifier for the mental image of a horse. At the same time the iconicity of a cinematic image is often quite complex, since it tends to show us more than one representation, and those representations may form various groupings (a family, a corporation, a class of students). The cinematic image is also (indirectly) indexical, since it is produced by exposing film stock to light which organizes objects in space.

Camera movement supplies mostly indexical signifiers, drawing our attention first to one thing, then another. When it simulates movement which is depicted within the narrative of the film, like a car chase or a fall, it is also iconic.

The signifiers created by lighting similarly control the viewer's gaze, inducing him or her to concentrate on particular features of the image rather than others. Consequently, these signifiers belong to the indexical category. But because lighting often participates in the representation of day and night, and sometimes emanates from lamps and light fixtures which provide part of the setting, it can also generate iconic signifiers.

Editing gives rise to signifiers which are again emphatically indexical—cross-cutting from one event to another directs and coerces the viewer's attention, as do the fade-in, fade-out, and dissolve.* When the code of editing is keyed to the gaze of certain characters within the narrative of the film it becomes iconic as well, depicting what is seen by a particular pair of eyes.

The sound-track, exclusive of music, is primarily iconic, simulating the noises of speech, sirens, horns, screams, doors opening and closing, birds, barking dogs, etc. However, because these sounds often alert us to unsuspected or as yet unseen occurrences and objects, they also participate in indexicality.

It should of course be emphasized that signifiers of all sorts, even the most purely iconic or indexical, can either become conventionalized, and so provide a base for the accretion of additional meaning, or depend on convention from the outset. For example, a particular system of lighting characterizes Hollywood films of the 1930s and 1940s, where illumination is used to accentuate the female face. The standardization of this effect permits it to signify more than "look here," to suggest such values as "star," "studio system," and "ideal female beauty."

Similarly, in many silent films the iris-in and the iris-out

*A *dissolve* combines two cinematic images on screen momentarily, while one fades and the other takes its place.

constitute standard transitional devices from one shot to another.* The indexical value of these devices pales beside their
connotative enrichment in recent films. When the iris-in and
iris-out are used in a film like *Tom Jones,* they signify "story
from the past," "quaintness," "old-fashioned charm."

Convention also plays a central role in iconic signification.
The history of perspective, Impressionist painting, Oriental
lithographs, narrative norms, not to mention the examples always cited by Peirce—graphs and algebraic equations—show that
we need to be schooled in systems of representation before certain signifiers will reveal their iconicity to us. This is true also
of road-signs, which indicate to the initiated that he or she will
find a stop-sign, a curve, or a downgrade ahead, but which remain meaningless to the uninitiated. It is not only a matter of
collateral acquaintance with the object, but with the signifier as
well.

Peter Wollen's widely read *Signs and Meaning in the Cinema*
stresses the relevance of the Peircean scheme to the study of
film and makes some very suggestive remarks about particular
examples of iconicity and indexicality, but the topic has not been
widely pursued by other film theoreticians.[8] This is surprising
since the emphasis in Peirce's semiotics on the mediating role
of the icon would seem to have special pertinence to the analysis of cinematic signification. It would also seem to supplement
the recent amalgamation of film study with Lacanian theory, in
which the category of the "imaginary" figures so centrally. One
of the most important of recent books on the cinema, Christian
Metz's *Le Significant imaginaire,* attempts to account for the film
image as an imaginary signifier (a signifier which stands in visually for an absent object), an argument which finds a logical
pragmatic extension in Peirce's notion of iconicity.[9] We will return to this work in a later chapter.

The semiotician who has evinced the most long-lasting in-
terest in Peirce is not a film theoretician but a linguist. Roman
Jakobson not only repeatedly emphasizes the importance of
Peirce's signifying model, but expands upon his remarks about

---

*An *iris-in* involves the expansion of a small image to fill the entire frame,
while an *iris-out* involves the conflation of a full-size image to a small portion of
the frame.

the iconic and indexical properties of language. In a widely read essay, "Shifters, Verbal Categories and the Russian Verb," Jakobson comments at length upon those words, like pronouns, that are "distinguished from all other constituents of the linguistic code solely by their compulsory reference to the given message" i.e., words whose application always depends upon a specific context.[10] Elsewhere he elaborates upon the iconic perimeters of language, noting that not only does the sequence of words in a sentence often indicate a conceptual sequence (e.g., "The child arose, made her bed, dressed, and ate breakfast"), but that in many languages the plural form of a word has an additional morpheme, whereas the singular form never does. Jakobson also observes that "in various Indo-European languages, the positive, comparative, and superlative degrees of adjectives show a gradual increase in the number of phonemes, e.g. *high-higher-highest, altus, altior, altissimus.*"[11]

Those features of Peirce's semiotic system which seem of most lasting value, and which indeed anticipate or facilitate later theoretical developments, include the connections the system establishes between signification and subjectivity; the account it provides of motivated signifiers; and the emphasis it places upon the endless commutability of the signified, upon the capacity of the signified to generate a chain of additional meanings. Two important theoreticians—Roland Barthes and Jacques Derrida—share the last of these concerns, one from a rhetorical and the other from a philosophical point of view. Barthes's attempts to deal with the commutability of the signified also involve him in an examination of motivated signifiers. Both of these projects are part of his larger treatment of connotation.

C) ROLAND BARTHES

The breadth of Roland Barthes's theoretical achievement can be no more than hinted at in these introductory pages, although a subsequent chapter will comment in greater detail on *S/Z*. The topics addressed by his numerous articles and books include style, pleasure, semiotics, literature, photography, fashion, and popular culture. Because of the liveliness of his prose, and the sophistication of his textual interpretations, Barthes has

probably done more than any other single theoretician to introduce recent semiotics to American readers.

Barthes has repeatedly returned to the issue of connotation.
It constitutes a central theme in such diverse works as *Elements
of Semiology, Writing Degree Zero,* "The Rhetoric of the Image,"
"The Photographic Image," *S/Z,* and perhaps most importantly
Mythologies, a collection of essays devoted to aspects of French
popular culture. The topic re-emerges with such insistence because Barthes invariably directs his attention to what are known
as "second-order" signifying systems—systems which build on
already existing ones. Literature is a prime example of a second-
order signifying system since it builds upon language. Barthes
describes these systems as "connotative," and in *Mythologies* he
sharply distinguishes them from "denotative" or "first-order"
signifying systems.

Barthes was not the first theoretician to propose the category of connotation as an indispensable one for semiotic analysis. The Danish linguist Louis Hjelmslev not only isolated the
category much earlier, but in *Prolegomena to a Theory of Language* formulated the model with which Barthes works in *Mythologies:*

> . . . it seems appropriate to view the connotators as content
> for which the denotative semiotics are expression, and to des-
> ignate this content and this expression as a *semiotic,* namely a
> *connotative semiotic.* In other words, after the analysis of the
> denotative semiotic is completed, the connotative semiotic must
> be subjected to an analysis according to just the same proce-
> dure. . . .
>
> Thus a connotative semiotic is a semiotic that is not a lan-
> guage, and one whose expression plane is provided by the
> content plane and expression plane of a denotative semiotic.
> Thus it is a semiotic one plane of which (namely the expres-
> sion plane) is a semiotic.[12]

Hjelmslev here elaborates a signifying model within which the
denotative signifier and the denotative signified join together
to form the connotative signifier. In other words, the denotative sign, which in the case of language would be the unit
formed by the sound image and the concept it evokes, or in the

case of photography the unit formed by the photograph and the concept it elicits, becomes in its entirety the starting point for the connotative process. Barthes illustrates this definition with a chart (slightly adjusted here for clarity):

1. Denotative Signifier	2. Denotative Signified	
3. Denotative Sign I CONNOTATIVE SIGNIFIER		II CONNOTATIVE SIGNIFIED
III CONNOTATIVE SIGN		

The connotative sign consists of both parts of the denotative sign as well as the additional meaning or meanings which they have helped to generate.[13]

Barthes appropriates Hjelmslev's model, but he also complicates it. He identifies connotation with the operation of ideology (also called "myth"). For Barthes ideology or myth consists of the deployment of signifiers for the purpose of expressing and surreptitiously justifying the dominant values of a given historical period. He cites as an example the full-page photographs of ornamental cookery in the French journal *Elle*. These photographs offer a falsification of food—poultry and fish which have been painstakingly glazed and coated, and either made to look like something else altogether, or reconstituted in imitation of their original condition. They evoke not merely the concept of "food," but those of "wealth," "art," and "inaccessibility." These photographs unabashedly affirm that expensive cuts of meat can never be anything but a dream for the majority of the people who read *Elle*. At the same time they

articulate that dream for the working class, promoting desire
for bourgeois products.

Similarly, the *Guide bleu,* most middle-class of French travel
guides, perpetuates nineteenth-century values through its cele-
bration of mountainous terrain (invariably characterized as
"picturesque"), the tone of moral exaltation it adopts when
speaking of certain kinds of art, and its presentation of native
populaces in terms of types ("the Basque is an adventurous
sailor, the Levantine a light-hearted gardener, the Catalan a
clever tradesman and the Catabrian a sentimental highlander"
(75)). The reader of the *Guide bleu* comes away with a good deal
more than an assortment of historical, geographical, artistic,
and sociological facts; he or she imbibes with those facts (indeed *through* those facts) a host of ideological assumptions about
history, geography, art, and sociology.

Perhaps the most illuminating of Barthes' various examples
is a little allegory he tells about the imbrication of French jour-
nalism and French colonialism:

> I am at the barber's and a copy of *Paris-Match* is offered to
> me. On the cover, a young Negro in a French uniform is sa-
> luting, with his eyes uplifted, probably fixed on a fold of the
> tricolor. All this is the *meaning* of the picture. But, whether
> naïvely or not, I see very well what it signifies to me: that France
> is a great Empire, that all her sons, without any color discrim-
> ination, faithfully serve under her flag, and that there is no
> better answer to the detractors of an alleged colonialism than
> the zeal shown by this Negro in serving his so-called oppres-
> sors. I am therefore faced with a greater semiological system:
> there is a signifier, itself already formed with a previous sys-
> tem (*a black soldier is giving the French salute*); there is a signified
> (it is here a purposeful mixture of Frenchness and militari-
> ness); finally, there is the presence of the signified through the
> signifier. [116]

Within this formulation the photographic image of the black
soldier saluting a French flag functions as the denotative signifier, while the concept of a black soldier saluting a French flag
provides the denotative signified. The photographic image and
its corresponding concept are then seen as conjoining to form

the denotative sign. That sign becomes a signifier in a second signifying transaction, that of connotation. Thus the sign of the black soldier saluting a French flag constitutes in its entirety a signifier for such ideological signifieds as "nationalism" and "militarism."

Barthes's scheme represents an improvement over Saussure's not only in that it accommodates connotation as well as denotation, but in that it accounts for motivated as well as unmotivated signifying relationships. The relationship between glossy photographs of ornately prepared food and the concepts "wealth," "art," and "inaccessibility" is not arbitrary in the way that the relationship between the word "food" and the concept which it evokes is understood to be. There are points of similarity between each of the connotative signifieds and the connotative signifer (e.g. the cuts of meat which are shown are in fact very costly; they have been artificially fabricated; and they are photographed from a low angle, as if to emphasize their remoteness). An analogous argument could be made for the connotative operations of the *Guide bleu:* the first level of motivation in each of the racial stereotypes cited by Barthes is one of synecdoche—of taking the part for the whole. The *Guide bleu* assumes from certain instances of Levantine gardeners that all Levantines are gardeners. The attribution of lightheartedness to this group of gardeners suggests a number of closely related connotative signifieds, among which would be "contentedness with one's state in life," "lack of emotional complexity," and— by implication—"primitivism" and "cultural inferiority." Finally, the connotations "nationalism" and "militarism" are respectively motivated by the depiction within the *Paris-Match* photograph of a tricolor and a soldier. (It must of course be noted that in the instances of the *Elle* and *Paris-Match* photographs even the denotative sign is motivated; the denotative signifier enjoys what Peirce would call both an iconic and an indexical relationship with its denotative signified.)

Barthes's model also suggests that the relationship between a connotative signifier and a connotative signified can only be explained through reference to a larger social field, a social field which is structured in terms of class interests and values. Saussure does not exclude the category of culture from his argument, but it figures there merely as a collectivity which maintains a series of neutral and arbitrary linguistic conventions— conventions of syntax, grammar, and meaning. Barthes's very different notion of culture is not genuinely collective, but riven with contradictions. These contradictions are covered over and smoothed out by ideology or myth, which creates the world in the image of the dominant class. One of the major devices for transforming actual heterogeneity into apparent homogeneity is here seen to be connotation, which reduces all textual materials, all cultural artifacts, all signifying formations to a circumscribed group of privileged signifieds. Since ideology motivates the relationship between those materials, artifacts, and formations on the one hand, and a circumscribed group of privileged signifieds on the other, that relationship can no longer be perceived as either neutral or arbitrary.

There are of course certain problems with this model, some of which Barthes himself attempts to resolve in *S/Z* and elsewhere. One such problem is the assumption that whereas connotation necessarily involves an ideological coercion of the reader or viewer, denotation engages that reader or viewer at an ideologically innocent level. A careful reading of certain other theoreticians, like Louis Althusser, suggests that during the child's linguistic initiation, when he or she is ostensibly learning denotation rather than connotation, he or she is already positioned within ideology. Through the first words which the child learns, which generally include "want," "no," "mother," and "father," he or she enters the realm of negation, desire, and the family. From that point forward it becomes preposterous to posit any act of listening or speaking which would be free of ideology.

Another problem with this early formulation is its conflation of the terms "myth" and "ideology." Barthes suggests in *Mythologies* that ideology is a condition of false consciousness promoted through fictions sponsored by the dominant class, fictions which it is presumably possible to penetrate by means of a deconstructive analysis. This definition implies that there is a reality outside of ideology to which we would have direct access were it not for the myths of the ruling class. However, as Althusser observes in "Marxism and Humanism," we cannot step outside of ideology since it is only inside of it that we find our subjectivity and our social reality.[14] As long as there is culture there will continue to be ideology. At the same time it is important to keep in mind that there is always a heterogeneity of conflicting ideologies concealed behind the dominant one. While it may not be possible to step outside of ideology altogether, it *is* possible to effect a rupture with one, and a rapprochement with another.

A third difficulty with the model advanced in *Mythologies* is that it associates connotation with a signifying operation which necessarily results in an impoverishment of meaning. The denotative signifier can be as small as the curl worn on the forehead of an American film actor to indicate "Romanness," or as extensive as a novel by Jules Verne. It is apparent that if a gesture or a photograph can open onto the same amount of meaning as an entire film, or a 500-page novel, connotation leads to a serious attrition. We are led to assume that each paragraph of the novel, or each image in the film, repeats essentially the same ideological message.

In *S/Z* Barthes also equates connotation with cultural inscription, but he formulates the equation quite differently. Culture is seen as imposing itself upon the text as insistently as before, but not so monolithically. *S/Z* suggests that ideological imperatives express themselves through a multiplicity of codes which "invade" the text in the form of key signifiers. Each of these signifiers represents a digression outside of the text to an established body of knowledge which it connotes; each one functions as an abbreviated version of the entire system (code) of which it is a part.

Barthes registers considerable ambivalence about these codes, and by implication about connotation. On the one hand, they concoct a "nauseating mixture of common opinions, a smothering layer of received ideas," but on the other hand, they provide access to whatever plurality of meaning the classic text affords. And within the context of *S/Z*, plurality carries the highest value.

S/Z also rethinks the relationship between connotation and denotation. Denotation is associated with closure and singularity. It becomes the enemy of free play, opposing even the limited plurality made possible by connotation. The very authenticity of denotation is called into question—it is charged with being an imposter, a metaphysical fiction which passes itself off as the "hearth, center, guardian, refuge, light of truth":

> . . . denotation is not the first meaning, but pretends to be so; under this illusion, it is ultimately no more than the *last* of the connotations (the one which seems both to establish and to close the reading), the superior myth by which the text pretends to return to the nature of language. . . .[15]

We will have occasion in a later chapter to examine in greater detail Barthes's notion of the ideal text, and the terms under which that text can be produced. However, I would like to note here that such a text would be irreducible to the sorts of meanings Barthes discovers in *Elle* or the *Guide bleu*. It would consist of a "triumphant plural" of signifiers which would "float" above the signified, refusing to be in any way anchored down or constrained. This aesthetic closely approximates that of the French philosopher, Jacques Derrida.

D) JACQUES DERRIDA

Jacques Derrida is the author of a number of enormously influential books, of which *Writing and Difference* and *Of Grammatology* are perhaps the most widely known in America. Those features of Derrida's argument which are most relevant to the present discussion are his critique of the sign, and the interpretive practice which that critique encourages.

In the penultimate chapter of *Writing and Difference*, "Structure, Sign and Play," Derrida argues that Western metaphysics has always organized itself around a central transcendental signified, but that this signified changes constantly—thus the Monad, center of Neo-Platonism, yields to God, center of Christianity, which in turn gives way to consciousness, center of Romanticism, etc.[16] What he means by a central transcendental signified is a term which is essential to the articulation of a given signifying system, but which is itself understood as existing independently of that system. By drawing our attention to the possibility of replacing one such term by another, Derrida helps us to understand that in fact none of them exists apart from the system it helps to determine. Each of these privileged signifieds derives its value and meaning from its place within a larger structure, a structure which moreover antedates it. Derrida's writing emphasizes the principle of "structurality" against that of "essence," and in so doing he effects a break with classical philosophy:

> The substitute does not substitute itself for anything which has somehow existed before it. Henceforth, it was necessary to begin thinking that there was no center, that the center could not be thought in the form of a present being, that it was not a fixed locus but a function, a sort of non-locus in which an infinite number of sign-substitutions came into play. This was the moment when language invaded the universal problematic, the moment when, in the absence of a center or origin, everything became discourse . . . that is to say, a system in which the central signified, the original or transcendental signified, is never absolutely present outside a system of differences. The absence of the transcendental signified extends the domain and play of signification infinitely. [280]

This passage is more than a little reminiscent of Saussure, particularly in the stress it places upon the concepts "system" and "play of differences." Derrida also insists that there are no positive terms, only those established relationally. Derrida, however, finds in Saussure's definition of the sign some remnants of the idealism which he ostensibly renounces. *Of Grammatology* criticizes *Course in General Linguistics* for the sharp distinction which it maintains between the signifier and the signified, a distinction which is congruent with the traditional opposition of matter and spirit, or substance and thought. That opposition has always been elaborated in ways which privilege the second of these categories over the first—which posit spirit or thought as something that precedes matter or substance. Derrida points out that "There has to be a transcendental signified for the difference between signifier and signified to be somewhere absolute and irreducible."[17] In other words, the distinction between signifier and signified can only be rigorously maintained if one term within the realm of signification is believed to be final, incapable of referring beyond itself to any other term. If there is no such term, then every signified functions in turn as a signifier, in an endless play of signification.

Derrida isolates Saussure's remarks about writing as especially indicative of the sort of idealism which he is at pains to eradicate. In those remarks Saussure privileges speech over writing by defining the latter as representative of the former:

> Language and writing are two distinct systems of signs; the second exists for the sole purpose of representing the first. The linguistic object is not both the written and spoken forms of words; the spoken forms alone constitute the object. [23–24]

The written notation is here understood as a signifier of the spoken word. As it turns out, the spoken word is itself a signifier of the "real" signifier, the sound image (Saussure notes that "the linguistic signifier is not phonic but incorporeal").[18] The last of these terms is a "psychological" entity, which within the Saussurean scheme qualifies it to be the most primary of the three signifiers. This hierarchy makes explicit the privileged position of the ideational register within the Saussurean semiotics, the impulse of that semiotics always to subordinate the more material term to the less.

Course in General Linguistics associates the quality of "secondariness" exclusively with the signifier, and that term is always understood to be to some degree "sensory." Derrida, on the other hand, insists that all signifying terms—signifieds as well as signifiers—are secondary. No absolute distinction can be maintained between the former and the latter, since both carry the "traces" of all of the other signifying elements with which they interconnect.

The system of writing is exemplary for Derrida not only because it literally consists of traces, thereby drawing attention to the nature of language, but because it makes manifest the principle of deferral upon which all forms of signification rely. Its syntagms dramatize the fact that signification occurs along a chain in which one term displaces another before being itself displaced:

> . . . the signified always already functions as a signifier. The
> secondarity that it seemed possible to ascribe to writing alone
> affects all signifieds in general, affects them always already,
> the moment they *enter the game*. There is not a single signified
> that escapes . . . the play of signifying references that consti-
> tute language.[19]

These signifying references may occur within the confines of
one system or code, or they may take place between numerous
systems or codes.

Although Derrida concentrates both in *Writing and Difference* and *Of Grammatology* on philosophical rather than literary
texts, a passage from Chapter 2 of Charles Dickens's *Bleak House*
will help to demonstrate how the "game" of signification is
played:

> How Alexander wept when he had no more worlds to con-
> quer, everybody knows—or has some reason to know by this
> time, the matter having been rather frequently mentioned. My
> Lady Dedlock, having conquered *her* world, fell, not into the
> melting, but rather the freezing mood. An exhausted compo-
> sure, a worn-out placidity, an equanimity of fatigue not to be
> ruffled by interest or satisfaction, are the trophies of her vic-
> tory. She is perfectly well-bred. If she could be translated to
> heaven tomorrow she might be expected to ascend without
> rapture.[20]

The present discussion will be limited to the phrase "perfectly
well-bred," although that phrase is inevitably imbricated not only
within the rest of the paragraph which surrounds it, but the
novel as a whole. The three words in question have been used
together so frequently as to constitute a monolithic sign. They
will consequently be treated as a single unit.

The first commutations necessitated by the activity of reading are those involved in the shift from the graphic notation to
the sound image, and the sound image to the corresponding
concept. Both commutations would be described by Barthes as
"denotative." The denotative complex yields immediately to a
series of connotative transactions, transactions which are mediated by what Barthes would call "cultural codes." (We will

return to the topic of cultural codes later in this book. Suffice it to say at this point that a cultural code is a conceptual system which is organized around key oppositions and equations, in which a term like "woman" is defined in opposition to a term like "man," and in which each term is aligned with a cluster of symbolic attributes. In the case of "woman" those symbolic attributes might be "emotional," "pliant," and "weak," whereas those associated with "man" would be more likely to be "rational," "firm," and "strong." Cultural codes provide the basis for connotation.)

The textual context helps to determine which cultural codes will be operative at any given juncture. Two are particularly conspicuous not only in Chapter 2 of *Bleak House*, but in other passages devoted to Lady Dedlock as well: the code of animal training, and the code of nineteenth-century manners. These codes by no means circumscribe the play of signification, since the reader may easily commute the signifieds they yield into signifiers for further connotative transactions, transactions which will this time be mediated by the cultural codes which he or she brings to the text.

The code of animal training operates quite overtly in *Bleak House*. For instance, in the next paragraph Bob Stables (whose name is itself a signifier in the code) avers that Lady Dedlock is "the best groomed woman in the whole stud." And in a much later passage, Bucket describes the death of Tulkinghorn, the master trainer who attempts to subdue Lady Dedlock, as the occasion of an equine revolt ("Mr. Tulkinghorn, deceased, he held all these horses in his hand, and could have drove 'em his own way, I haven't a doubt; but he was fetched off the box head foremost, and now they have got their legs over the traces, and are all dragging and pulling their own ways" (736)).

Read according to this code, "perfectly well-bred" connotes impeccable behavior based on impeccable blood-lines, which in turn signifies "thoroughbred horse." (This example demonstrates that even within a single cultural code there is considerable instability at the level of the signified, what Barthes on one occasion calls "skidding.")

The code of nineteenth-century manners, which predominates in all of the scenes at Chesney Wold, establishes a connection between "perfectly well-bred" and the concepts of "haughtiness," "coldness," and "elegance." These concepts connote "aristocracy." All four terms form a constellation around Lady Dedlock's name. In fact her character is chiefly defined, at least initially, through the code of nineteenth-century manners.

Thus a curious exchange takes place beneath the demure signifier "perfectly well-bred": the concept of "haughtiness" competes with the concept of "to be ridden," and "coldness" with "prize possession." These oppositions become increasingly manifest in Lady Dedlock's behavior as the novel progresses.

Yet another commutation can be effected when the concept "perfectly well-bred" is absorbed into a code which is not part of the textual apparatus of *Bleak House*, but which the twentieth-century reader inevitably brings with him or her to the book: the code of psychoanalysis. Here the little phrase provides a signifier for "repression"—a signified which it is possible to derive as well from the concepts "to be ridden," "prize possession," "haughty," "cold," and "elegant." And of course a great deal is repressed in Lady Dedlock's dealings with the fashionable world, including the information that she is neither aristocratic nor cold. These last details are also withheld from the reader (i.e., repressed by the text) for some considerable time.

Compensating for these strange vacillations at the level of the signified is an extraordinary redundancy at the level of the text's signifiers. "Freezing mood," "exhausted composure," "worn-out placidity," "equanimity of fatigue," "without rapture" all tell the same story—a story of boredom which conceals from our eyes, as well as the eyes of the aristocratic world, something which will never be completely revealed. The paragraph contains a repressed account of repression.

While "repression" may be the last signified we have been able to isolate, it too functions as a signifier, pointing beyond itself to "truths" which can only be partially exhumed. In its totality, this passage provides a classic example of what Derrida calls "supplementarity": the compensation through proliferation on the part of the signifier for a signified which can never be made fully present. It demonstrates that meaning is never

anything but a slippage or displacement from one term to another:

> . . . there have never been anything but supplements, substi-
> tutive significations which could only come forth in a chain of
> differential references, the "real" supervening, and being added
> only while taking on meaning from a trace and from an invo-
> cation of the supplement. . . .[21]

For Peirce, Barthes, and Derrida, the signified is endlessly
commutable; through the intervention of what Peirce calls the
"interpretant," what Barthes describes as "connotation," or what
Derrida refers to as "free play," one signified always gives way
to another, functions in its turn as a signifier. We have just
tested that assumption against a passage from *Bleak House,* discovering in the process that a complex network of signification
underlies even the smallest and least ostentatious of textual
units.

It is important to stress at this juncture, however, that the
classic text usually functions to cover over the heterogeneity of
its signifying operations, to harmonize its differences and contradictions. Within the firmly maintained boundaries of that text
the play of meaning is carefully circumscribed; there are certain "authorized" signifieds which must sooner or later emerge
as dominant, which in fact enjoy a transcendental status. All
other textual elements remain subordinate. The dominance of
one signifying term over another is determined by the triumph
of one cultural code over another, as many a poem by Andrew
Marvell dramatizes.

"Clorinda and Damon," for example, stages a witty conflict
between two powerful and seemingly irreconcilable cultural
codes—Christianity and Ovidianism—only to resolve that conflict through admittedly artificial means at the conclusion. In
the process that poem lays bare the economy of the classic text—
the signifying plurality which always threatens it, and which it
must at all costs hold in check:

C. *Damon* come drive thy flocks this way.
D. No: 'tis too late they went astray.
C. I have a grassy Scutcheon spy'd,

> Where *Flora* blazons all her pride.
> The Grass I aim to feast thy Sheep:
> The Flow'rs I for thy Temple keep.
> D. Grass withers; and the Flow'rs too fade.
> C. Seize the short Joyes, then, ere they vade.
> Seest thou that unfrequented Cave?
> D. That den? C. Loves Shrine. D. But Virtue's Grave.
> C. In whose cool bosome we may lye
> Safe from the Sun. D. not Heaven's Eye.
> C. Near this, a Fountaines liquid Bell
> Tinkles within the concave Shell.
> D. Might a Soul bath there and be clean,
> Or slake its Drought? C. What is't you mean?
> D. These once had been enticing things,
> *Clorinda*, Pastures, Caves, and Springs.
> C. And what late change? D. The other day
> *Pan* met me. C. What did great *Pan* say?
> D. Words that transcend poor Shepherds skill,
> But He ere since my Songs does fill:
> And his Name swells my slender Oate.
> C. Sweet must *Pan* sound in *Damons* Note.
> D. *Clorinda's* voice might make it sweet.
> C. Who would not in *Pan's* Praises meet?

Chorus

> *Of* Pan *the flowry Pastures sing,*
> *Caves eccho, and the Fountains ring.*
> *Sing then while he doth us inspire;*
> *For all the World is our* Pan's *Quire.*

Clorinda reads all of the details of the landscape according to the code of Ovidianism, which celebrates erotic experience at the expense of spiritual values, while Damon counters with Christianity, which casts a cold eye on physical pleasure. She introduces the first signifier—"this way"—which he immediately associates, through the parable of the lost lamb, with the broad road which leads to hell. Clorinda elaborately redefines the landscape as a *locus amoenus,* a place where all the senses can be gratified. In quick succession, "this way" becomes a *memento mori,* evoking the rigors of the spiritual life, and a signifier for the sweetness and shortness of earthly things, licensing a *carpe diem* argument.

Having extracted all of the Ovidian and Christian meaning they can from the first of their signifiers, the participants move on to another. Once again, Clorinda supplies the theme, this time choosing "that unfrequented Cave." Damon momentarily falters, unable to remember the appropriate signified for "cave" within this code, but his companion unhesitatingly identifies it as one of those amorous retreats recommended by Ovidianism. Recalling that within Christianity this signifier points to the bondage of the flesh, Damon retorts that the cave is rather "Virtue's Grave."

The game gains momentum. As Clorinda begins to expatiate upon the advantages of her amorous retreat, Damon takes advantage of the standard sun/son pun to introduce Christianity's most powerful signified. Clorinda attempts to salvage the signifier of the cave by incorporating it within her description of yet another signifier ("Near this, a Fountaines liquid Bell/Tinkles within the *concave* Shell"), but Damon brings the competition to a close by connecting up the fountain with two Christian signifieds: baptismal waters and communion wine.

However, the game is not yet over. The Chorus still has its part to perform, and it does so with a vengeance. It effectively closes off all significatory play through the assertion of transcendental meaning. The Chorus reduces the multiplicity of pastoral signifiers to a single "pantheistic" signified; even the limited plurality of signifieds generated by the codes of Ovidianism and Christianity gives way before the monolithic organization of "Pan's Quire." ("Pan" is of course the pastoral name for Christ.)

Within the classic text, one cultural code generally asserts itself as "truer" than the others and ultimately pulls rank, just as the Chorus does in "Clorinda and Damon." Marvell's poem is unusual, though, in the skepticism with which it records Clorinda's defeat. It pokes fun at the facility with which the Chorus manages to transform the landscape which she has so lovingly detailed first into mere "Pastures," "Caves" and "Fountaines," and then into a single, collective entity. The Chorus's final equation (world = signifier, Pan = signified), so confidently and so easily made, effects a comic reduction.

It should be noted that Damon shares to a large degree the Chorus's impatience with the varieties and intricacies of earthly beauty, and consequently with the realm of signifiers. It is Clorinda, after all, who provides the raw materials for the game. Damon feels more comfortable naming the signifieds. This is not surprising since his discourse is governed by the code of Christianity, which not only privileges signified over signifier, but subordinates all of its signifying components to one central signified. Some cultural codes, like Ovidianism, permit casual matings to occur between the elements that create meaning, and give as much scope to "foreplay" as they do to significatory consummation. Others, like Christianity, make meaning a moral issue. The latter tend to outweigh the former in concrete textual situations.

It would seem helpful to point out at this juncture that the terms "myth" and "ideology" used in *Mythologies* correspond closely to what Barthes calls "cultural codes" in *S/Z*. Both are associated with a paradoxical operation whereby signifying formations are opened up to connotative meaning, but the scope of that meaning is tightly controlled. In both works Barthes describes connotation as the means whereby a text can be made to express the dominant values of a given historical period. In *S/Z*, however, Barthes is not content merely to establish connotation's repressive potential; he articulates as well an interpretive strategy whereby the classic text's limited plurality can be maximized, a strategy which bears very specifically upon connotation. *S/Z* proposes a model of reading in which all of the contradictory meanings of each "lexeme" or textual element are activated by the reader before he or she proceeds to the next one, and in which no attempt is ever made to harmonize those contradictions.

This model of reading (which can be extended as well to cinematic viewing) is predicated upon the endless commutability of the signified, upon the assumption that the play of meaning has no necessary closure, no transcendental justification. It is ideally suited to the project of uncovering the cultural matrix

within which every classic text is situated, of clarifying for us a
point which semiotics has increasingly emphasized—that the individual literary or cinematic work is only one component in a
larger discursive network. In *The Archaeology of Knowledge,* Michel
Foucault indicates the degree to which recent history challenges the formalist tenet that "the text itself will tell you everything you need to know about it," and insists instead on the
relational status of every signifying instance:

> The frontiers of a book are never clear-cut: beyond the title,
> the first lines, and the last full stop, beyond its internal config-
> uration and its autonomous form, it is caught up in a system
> of references to other books, other texts, other sentences: it is
> a node within a network. . . . The book is not simply the ob-
> ject that one holds in one's hands; and it cannot remain within
> the little parallelepiped that contains it: its unity is variable and
> relative. As soon as one questions that unity, it loses its self-
> evidence; it indicates itself, constructs itself, only on the basis
> of a complex field of discourse.[22]

We have followed the shifting fortunes of the sign from
Saussure and Peirce to Barthes and Derrida, charting the theoretical movement away from denotation to connotation, away
from a signified which always maintains its specificity vis-à-vis
the signifier to one which refers in turn beyond itself. We have
discovered a variety of ways in which a signifier can be motivated by its signified, ranging from what Peirce would call "indexical" and "iconic" relationships to what Barthes would call
"ideological" or "mythic" ones. The Barthesian model, to which
we will return in Chapter 6, focuses attention on the interactions between individual signs and texts, and cultural codes.
These codes help to reveal some of the relational principles
that determine the larger discursive field, otherwise known as
the symbolic order.

The alignment of signification with the symbolic order has
been one of the most important achievements in the history of
semiotics. However, it has only been made possible by the inclusion of a third category—that of subjectivity. The theoreticians who have most exhaustively treated this last category are
of course Sigmund Freud and Jacques Lacan, and they have

done so in ways which are enormously relevant to our understanding of the sign. Indeed Lacan quite self-consciously utilizes the vocabulary and assumptions of semiotics. Prior to addressing those arguments, however, it would seem important to demonstrate that as soon as theoretical attention is directed away from *langue* to *parole* the category of the subject proves as indispensable to linguistics as it does to psychoanalytic semiotics. That demonstration can best be made through the collected essays of Emile Benveniste, a linguist in the Saussurean tradition who nonetheless insists upon the subjective bases of language.

E) EMILE BENVENISTE

The most important essays of the contemporary French linguist Emile Benveniste have been collected in the volume entitled *Problems in General Linguistics*. Those essays return repeatedly to three terms which are shown to be theoretically inseparable: language, discourse, and subjectivity. The first two terms correspond quite closely to the Saussurean set *langue* and *parole,* while the third designates both a grammatical entity and a speaker.

Benveniste establishes the impossibility of isolating language from discourse, or discourse from subjectivity, through an analysis of linguistic elements that have an indexical status, in particular pronouns and verb tenses. In "Subjectivity in Language" he describes the pronouns "I" and "you" as signifiers which are only capable of signifying in concrete discursive situations—as signifiers without conventional signifieds. The unstable value of the first of these especially interests him:

> There is no concept "I" that incorporates all the *I*'s that are uttered at every moment in the mouths of all speakers, in the sense that there is a concept "tree" to which all the individual uses of *tree* refer. The "I," then, does not denominate any lexical entity. . . . We are in the presence of a class of words, the "personal pronouns," that escape the status of all the other signs of language. Then, what does *I* refer to? To something very peculiar which is exclusively linguistic: *I* refers to the act of individual discourse in which it is pronounced, and by this it

> designates the speaker. It is a term that cannot be identified
> except in what we have called elsewhere an instance of dis-
> course and that has only a momentary reference. The reality
> to which it refers is the reality of the discourse. . . . And so it
> is literally true that the basis of subjectivity is in the exercise of
> language.[23]

One of the points which Benveniste makes here is that the signifier "I" always implies a speaker, to whom it refers. Similarly,
the signifier "you" always implies a listener, to whom the speaker
talks. These roles are endlessly reversible, as are the signifiers
which depend upon them; the person who functions as a
speaker for one moment functions as a listener for the next.
They are also only intermittently activated, as a consequence of
which the signifiers "I" and "you" have only a periodic meaning. In the interval between two discursive instances, these pronouns lose all their value. They lack the standardized and continuous significance of other linguistic terms.

Benveniste notes that language contains other elements
whose status is equally dependent upon discourse, and equally
marked by subjectivity—words, that is, which only take on
meaning in relation to a speaker. "Here" and "there," which
are among the examples cited by Benveniste, evoke a concept
of distance which is relative to the place occupied by the person
who utters them. Verb forms imply a similar conceptualization
of time, one keyed to the moment in which the discourse occurs (Benveniste writes in "The Nature of Pronouns" that "the
'verb form' is an inextricable part of the individual instance of
discourse: it is always and necessarily actualized by the act of
discourse and in dependence on that act" (220)).

Pronouns and verbs are not incidental linguistic components; on the contrary, language is inconceivable without them.
By demonstrating that they become active as signs only with
discourse, Benveniste shows the impossibility of separating
langue from *parole,* even for purposes of analysis. He deflects
attention away from the abstract signifying system emphasized
by Saussure to those concrete situations in which signification
occurs, and the subject which figures so centrally there. Benveniste underscores the impossibility of treating signification in
isolation from the last of these terms when he observes that

"language is marked so deeply by the expression of subjectivity that one might ask if it could still function and be called language if it were constructed otherwise" (225).

Language and subjectivity are shown in *Problems in General Linguistics* to be equally interdependent; the former is as determinative for the latter as the latter is for the former. Indeed, without language there would be no subjectivity. Benveniste insists that the individual finds his or her cultural identity only within discourse, by means of the pronouns "I" and "you." He or she identifies with the first of these, and is defined in opposition to the second:

> Language is . . . the possibility of subjectivity because it always contains the linguistic forms appropriate to the expression of subjectivity, and discourse provokes the emergence of subjectivity because it consists of discrete instances. In some way language puts forth "empty" forms which each speaker, in the exercise of discourse, appropriates to himself and which he relates to his "person," at the same time defining himself as *I* and a partner as *you*. The instance of discourse is thus constitutive of all the coordinates that define the subject and of which we have briefly pointed out only the most obvious [i.e. pronouns, verb forms, etc.]. [227]

Subjectivity is here grasped in the relational terms earlier used by Saussure to explain the operations of language. Like the linguistic sign, the subject relies upon another term within the same paradigm—here the personal pronoun "you"—for its meaning and value. And that paradigm can only be activated through discourse. In the space between two discursive events, subjectivity, like the pronouns which sustain it, falls into abeyance. Benveniste emphasizes the radical discontinuity which characterizes the condition of subjectivity, its constant stops and starts.

"The Nature of Pronouns" distinguishes between two sorts of subject which are involved in any discursive event: the speaking subject, or the "referent," and the subject of speech, or the "referee." The first of these subjects is the individual who participates in discourse, which in the case of language would be the speaker or writer. The second consists of the dis-

cursive element with which that discoursing individual identifies, and in so doing finds his or her subjectivity. In the case of
language that discursive element would be the pronoun "I":

> What then is the reality to which *I* or *you* refers? It is solely
> a "reality of discourse," and this is a very strange thing. *I* can-
> not be defined except in terms of "locution," not in terms of
> objects as a nominal sign is. *I* signifies "the person who is ut-
> tering the present instance of the discourse containing *I*." This
> instance is unique by definition and has validity only in its
> uniqueness. . . . *I* can only be identified by the instance of
> discourse that contains it and by that alone. It has no value
> except . . . in the act of speaking in which it is uttered.
> There is thus a combined double instance in this process: the
> instance of *I* as referent and the instance of discourse con-
> taining *I* as the referee. The definition can now be stated pre-
> cisely as: *I* is "the individual who utters the present instance of
> discourse containing the linguistic instance *I*." [218]

Although these two subjects can only be apprehended in relation to each other, they can never be collapsed into one unit.
They remain forever irreducible to each other, separated by
the barrier between reality and signification, or what Lacan
would call "being" and "meaning." The speaking subject enjoys
the status of the referent, whereas the subject of speech functions instead as a signifier.

Benveniste extends the rubric of discourse to "every utterance assuming a speaker and a hearer, and in the speaker, the
intention of influencing the other in some way," whether that
utterance is verbal or written (208–9). Since the publication of
Problems in General Linguistics that rubric has been extended to
a variety of other signifying formations, including cinema. Some
film theoreticians, notably those associated with the English
journal *Screen,* have also appropriated Benveniste's distinction
between the speaking subject and the subject of speech, and
have used it as a means of accounting for two different cinematic levels: the level of enunciation and the level of fiction.[24]

The level of enunciation is in effect that of production—of
camera movement, editing, composition, sound-recording,
sound-mix, script, etc. The level of fiction designates the nar-

rative within which the spectator of the finished film is encouraged to "find" him or herself, and the characters with whom he or she is encouraged to identify. The speaking subject of the cinematic text is that agency responsible for the text's enunciation. The subject of speech, on the other hand, can best be understood as that character or group of characters most central to the fiction—that figure or cluster of figures who occupy a position within the narrative equivalent to that occupied by the first-person pronoun in a sentence.

The cinematic elaboration of Benveniste's model both enriches and complicates that model. It enriches what it appropriates by establishing a homology between the pronouns which confer subjectivity on the speaker of a sentence, and the character representations which confer subjectivity on the viewer of a film. (With certain minor adjustments, a similar homology can be established between the pronoun "I" and the character representations within a novel or a poem.) However, the cinematic elaboration of Benveniste's model also suggests that one more category is needed in order to make that model sufficiently flexible to accommodate all of the subjective transactions which occur within discourse: the category of the spoken subject, i.e. the subject who is constituted through identification with the subject of the speech, novel, or film. It encourages us to distinguish between the speaking subject (i.e. the agency of the discourse); the subject of speech (i.e. the discursive element); and the spoken subject (i.e. the subject produced through discourse). The first and third subjects may or may not coincide.

The linguistic example tends to obscure the last of these categories since it projects a protagonist who functions simultaneously as speaking and spoken subjects. (In fact, as we shall see, the autonomy of that speaker is quite limited.) However, within the cinematic instance those subjects are quite sharply differentiated. There can be no possible confusion of the speaking subject of the filmic text (i.e. the complex of apparatuses responsible for that text's enunciation) with its spoken subject (i.e. the viewer). They remain on opposite sides of the screen.

A much likelier confusion would be that of the speaking subject with the subject of the film's discourse, since many cin-

ematic texts attribute to a fictional character faculties which actually belong to the apparatuses of enunciation, such as coercive vision or hearing, or control of the story. Mark Rutland,
for example, seems to be the prime mover in Hitchcock's *Marnie*. His gaze is shown to exceed that of any of the other characters in the film; he looks even when no one else does, and
always sees more. Moreover, by inducing Marnie to say things
she doesn't want to say, either by engaging her in a game of
"free association" or by reactivating traumatic memories, he
seems to be equally in charge of the film's sounds. While watching *Marnie* we tend to forget that the real source of its images
is the camera, and that its sounds proceed from a recording
apparatus. The chapter of this book devoted to the theory of
suture will explore these issues in greater depth.

To say that the likeliest confusion of all would be that of the
viewer or spoken subject with the subject of speech would be
slightly to misstate the case. Within this semiotic model the
viewer does not have a stable and continuous subjectivity, but
one which is activated intermittently, within discourse. The cinematic text constitutes the viewer's subjectivity for him or her;
it engages the viewer in a discursive exchange during which he
or she is spoken as subject. To the degree that a given film
conforms to dominant cultural values, it speaks the viewer's
subjectivity in familiar ways, and so creates the illusion of stability and continuity. (As I suggested above, this scheme would
apply as fully to literary texts as it does to cinematic ones.)

Benveniste describes discourse as a signifying transaction
between two persons, one of whom addresses the other, and in
the process defines him or herself. The French Marxist philosopher Louis Althusser helps us to understand that discourse
may also consist of an exchange between a person and a cultural agent, i.e. a person or a textual construct which relays
ideological information. (Althusser isolates priests and educa-
tors as particularly important cultural agents, but the description which he offers would apply as well to a television pro-
gram, a photograph, a novel, or a film.) The agent addresses
the person, and in the process defines not so much its own as
the other's identity. In "Ideology and Ideological State Apparatuses," Althusser refers to the address as "hailing," and its

successful outcome as "interpellation." Interpellation occurs when the person to whom the agent speaks recognizes him or herself in that speech, and takes up subjective residence there:

> . . . ideology "acts" or "functions" in such a way that it "recruits" subjects among the individuals (it recruits them all) or "transforms" the individuals into subjects (it transforms them all) by that very precise operation which I have called *interpellation* or hailing, and which can be imagined along the lines of the most commonplace police (or other) hailing: " 'Hey, you there!' "
>
> Assuming that the theoretical scene I have imagined takes place in the street, the hailed individual will turn round. By this mere one-hundred-and-eighty-degree physical conversion, he becomes a *subject*. Why? Because he has recognized that the hail was "really" addressed to him, and that "it was *really him* who was hailed" (and not someone else).[25]

Within the situation outlined by Althusser, the speaking subject would always be sharply differentiated from the spoken subject. However, since the spoken subject would be constituted only through the subject of speech, those two categories would be closely linked.

Frank Capra's film *It's a Wonderful Life* provides a particularly lucid example of a textual hailing which results in the smooth interpellation of the viewer. The opening shot of that film discloses a town-limit sign which reads: "You are now in Bedford Falls." As Benveniste points out, the pronoun "you," like the pronoun "I," lacks any conventionalized meaning. It only assumes significance within a discursive situation. Here there is no fictional character who stands in for the viewer, as is usually the case, to whom the "you" might be understood to refer. Instead, the appeal is direct: the pronoun "you" only means something to the degree that the viewer identifies with it, recognizes him or herself in the subject of speech. The rest of the sentence then organizes itself around the viewer, locating him or her in the narrative space soon to be inhabited by George Bailey, who will function thereafter as the chief signifier of his or her subjectivity. By identifying with the second-person pronoun in the statement "You are now in Bedford

Falls," the viewer permits his or her subjectivity to be established by the figure of George Bailey, and circumscribed by the limits of small-town America.

Benveniste himself notes that even with a linguistic event of the sort described by him the speaking subject is not really in control of his or her own subjectivity. To begin with, the subject's discourse is constrained by the rules of language; it can only speak by means of a pre-existing linguistic system. Moreover, "language" must here be understood in the broadest possible sense, as encompassing not only the operations of denotation, but those of connotation. In other words, every utterance must be conceived as having various levels of signification, and issuing from multiple voices. It is spoken not only by the palpable voice of a concrete speaker, writer, or cluster of mechanical apparatuses, but the anonymous voices of cultural codes which invade it in the form of connotation. As Barthes remarks in *S/Z*, "Alongside each utterance, one might say that off-stage voices can be heard: they are the codes: in their interweaving, these voices (whose origin is 'lost' in the vast perspective of the *already-written*) de-originate the utterance. . . ." (21) These "off-stage" voices belong to earlier discourses; they repeat what has already been said, written, or filmed, and to a very large degree determine what can now be said, written, or filmed.

The autonomy of the speaking subject is further qualified by the inclusion of the unconscious within the semiotic argument. In "Language and Freudian Theory," Benveniste suggests that a discourse unfolds simultaneously along more than one axis, and that it has its origins in a split subject; he proposes, that is, that a discourse contains a latent as well as a manifest level, and that it issues from an unconscious as well as a conscious speaking subject. The latent discourse can only be discovered through the manifest one, just as the unconscious subject can only be reached through the conscious one. Both projects require a student who has been schooled in psychoanalytic interpretation, and who is as attentive to the gaps in the discourse as to its manifest content:

> If the content informs him about the image which the subject
> has of the situation and about the position in it that he attri-

butes to himself, he searches through this content for a new content: that of the unconscious motivation that proceeds from the buried complex. Beyond the innate symbolism of language, he will perceive a specific symbolism which will be formed, without the subject being aware of it, as much from what is omitted as from what is stated. And within the history in which the subject places himself, the analyst will provoke the emergence of another history, which will explain the motivation. He will thus take the discourse as the translation of another "language," which has its own rules, symbols and "syntax," and which goes back to the deep structures of the psyche. [67–68]

Benveniste suggests in this passage that those moments of seeming silence within and around discursive events—those moments when language would appear to cease, and with it subjectivity—are not really silent at all. They are filled with the inaudible sounds of a second discourse, a discourse of which the subject remains oblivious. The subject inhabits one psychic space consciously, but another unconsciously. The division between those spaces permits the subject to enter into two discourses alternately or even at the same time, discourses which are often in startling opposition to each other. Not only is the *content* of each likely to contrast markedly with the other, but the *form* as well. Benveniste emphasizes that the unconscious discourse uses a very different language from that employed by the conscious discourse—a language with its own "rules, symbols and syntax. . . ."

The concept of a split subject derives of course from Freud, as does the argument that each part acquires its specificity from a distinct signifying system. Benveniste's introduction of the subject into linguistic semiotics comes in the wake of Freud's much earlier and more daringly innovative alignment of the terms "language" and "subjectivity," an alignment which can be said to have immediately *semioticized* psychoanalysis. At one point *The Interpretation of Dreams* encourages us to think of the subject in terms of its interior divisions, one of which houses that system associated with conscious discourse, and another of which accommodates the raw materials of unconscious discourse. At another juncture, it proposes that we conceptualize the subject in more dynamic terms, as a complex of signifying processes. However, whatever the illustrative metaphor it employs, *The Interpretation of Dreams* consistently approaches subjectivity as a staging-ground for two kinds of signification. Freud elaborates these two kinds of signification in ways which are so complex, and which have so many ramifications not only for our understanding of subjectivity but literature and film as well, that the next two chapters will be given over to a lengthy treatment of them.

Benveniste also enriches linguistic semiotics with the contributions of Lacan. He utilizes the notion of a split subject to underscore one of the most important of the latter's points—that the subject is never autonomous because it is always constrained by what is said in "another scene." Since the discourse which defines the conscious subject must be understood at least in part as a response to that which defines the unconscious subject, and *vice versa,* neither can be conceived exclusively in terms of its capacity to speak; both are simultaneously spoken, are motivated to engage in discourse by an agency beyond themselves.

Another Lacanian tenet which informs *Problems in General Linguistics* is that subjectivity is entirely relational; it only comes into play through the principle of difference, by the opposition of the "other" or the "you" to the "I." In other words, subjectivity is not an essence but a set of relationships. Moreover, it can only be induced by discourse, by the activation of a signifying system which pre-exists the individual, and which determines his or her cultural identity. Lacan stresses that language even coerces seemingly extra-linguistic subjective events, such as the Oedipal crisis. It does this through the primacy which it gives to the "Name-of-the-Father," i.e. the paternal signifier. Benveniste's assertion that "language is . . . the possibility of subjectivity" thus has firm grounding in Lacan's writings.

A final feature of Benveniste's argument which has its origin in those writings is its insistence that the discourse of the unconscious subject can only be apprehended *through the conscious discourse.* Like Lacan he encourages us to listen with new ears to the conscious discourse, to learn to read it as the translation of another discourse which without that effort will remain forever submerged. We will deal with the relationship of discourse and subjectivity in much greater detail in the chapters that follow.

Benveniste's writings suggest that even from the most "orthodox" of semiotic perspectives—the linguistic—the sign cannot be detached from discourse, discourse from the subject, or the subject from the symbolic order. Language can only be studied through the concrete signifying formations within which it manifests itself, formations which implicate the subject as signifier, as product of the discourse. Moreover, language, discourse, and subject must all be understood as determined by the particular symbolic order within which they emerge.

We turn now to a discussion of those signifying processes responsible for the construction of the two very different discourses isolated by Benveniste—the conscious and the unconscious.

2

Primary and Secondary Processes

It has been often remarked that Sigmund Freud "discovered" the unconscious, but only recently have his readers begun to observe that his discovery has as many implications for semiotics, or the study of signification, as it does for psychoanalysis, or the study of the subject. Indeed, by means of it Freud shows the two disciplines to be virtually synonymous. Not just the unconscious, but *both* of the "territories" that comprise the geography of subjectivity are seen to derive their identity from the signifying systems which are most frequently employed there— an affective and sensory system in the case of the unconscious, and a relational and linguistic one in the case of what is called the "preconscious." Freud encourages us, in short, to view the subject as a signifying complex.

The centrality of the subject to discourse is also compellingly demonstrated by the early writings of Freud. Not only do those writings equate the subject with the signifying systems which define the unconscious on the one hand, and the preconscious on the other, but they establish that all discourse proceeds from the interactions between these two systems. Discourse must thus be understood as the product of a psychic "assembly-line."

This chapter will examine the landscape and languages of subjectivity as described by one of Freud's earliest psychic models, that provided by *The Interpretation of Dreams*. We will progress from the initial topographical elaboration of that model to its reconceptualization in more dynamic and specifically semiotic terms, concluding with a brief discussion of the role played by desire in signification.

A) THE EARLY TOPOGRAPHY

The Interpretation of Dreams provides one of the most important of Freud's topographies, and certainly the most semiotically suggestive. It divides the mind into three areas—memory, the unconscious, and the preconscious. This topography indicates as well two temporary conditions connected with the operations of the psyche: perception and motor response. Freud illustrates these psychic divisions with the following spatial metaphor, which is here modified slightly for purposes of clarification: [1]

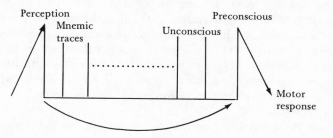

The mnemic traces (i.e. memory traces) represent the imprints left upon the most recessed area of the mind by the flow of perception. These traces assume a sensory form (visual, acoustic, olfactory, tactile, gustatory), and they possess a strong affective value (i.e. they are emotionally charged). They supply the unconscious with its raw signifying material. A useful metaphor might be that of a slide capable of projecting upon a psychic screen not only images, but sounds, smells, tastes, and tactile sensations. New mnemic traces are constantly being added.

The unconscious is a part of the mind not accessible to consciousness except in disguised form. It contains repressed materials—forbidden impulses, taboo recollections, etc. The unconscious comes into existence simultaneously with the subject's first assimilation of cultural prohibition. It has unlimited recourse to the mnemic traces, but its communications with the preconscious are carefully monitored.

The preconscious is the repository of cultural norms and prohibitions. It contains data which are capable of becoming conscious—memories which can be voluntarily recalled. Therefore, movement from the preconscious to the conscious is essentially fluid, although the conscious can accommodate only a finite amount of information at any given moment. Within this topography the conscious is no more than a kind of adjunct to the preconscious, a receiving room for internal and external—i.e. psychic and perceptual—stimuli.

Perception initiates activity within the various regions of the mental apparatus, leaving memory traces at one end, and prompting motor response at the other. Since for Freud the only motivating force behind the operations of either unconscious or preconscious is want, and since the idea of want assumes a deficiency, those perceptions would seem to be of a primarily negative sort—i.e. stimuli leading to an awareness of some insufficiency. Freud illustrates this awareness with the example of a hungry infant, but the example is a crude one, whose usefulness is almost entirely limited to the subject's pre-symbolic existence.

Lacan distinguishes between need (i.e. undifferentiated physical appetite) and desire (i.e. that permanent condition of alienation from a mythically "good" object which results from self-recognition and access to language). We will examine these categories in considerable detail in Chapter 4. Suffice it to say here that even Freud's own writings militate against the notion that the psychic economy revolves on the wheels of appetite. The wishes that seek fulfillment in dreams, parapraxes, daydreams, neuroses, and hysterical symptoms are the product of *repression,* not biological need.

B) THE PLEASURE PRINCIPLE

According to Freud, the perception of deficiency triggers mental activity because of the psychic dominance of the "unpleasure principle" (later termed the "pleasure principle"). What this means is that the impulse to avoid unpleasure—i.e. to avoid an increase in tension—governs all psychic activity. When confronted with experiences that inspire excitation (i.e. tension), the mind attempts to substitute for them experiences that diminish that excitation. The consequent mental exertion is prompted by the wish for pleasure, and the condition of quiescence that follows in the event of success corresponds precisely to Freud's notion of pleasure. For Freud, pleasure represents the absence of unpleasure; it is a state of relaxation much more intimately connected with death than with life. Indeed, *Beyond the Pleasure Principle* (1920) at one point refers to the pleasure principle as a "Nirvana principle" (XVIII.56).

This notion of pleasure as a zero degree of tension finds an exemplary literary expression in Thomas Mann's story, *Death in Venice*. The central figure in that text, Aschenbach, has devoted his life to "hard, nerve-taxing work, work which has not ceased to exact his uttermost in the way of sustained concentration, conscientiousness, and tact"—i.e. to what Freud would designate as "unpleasure." The temptation to leave Munich for Venice is experienced by Aschenbach as a "craving for freedom, release, forgetfulness," and characters and objects who embody that temptation are consistently associated with death. For instance, the stranger who first inspires in Aschenbach the inclination to travel is standing in a mortuary chapel, and the gondola which transports the latter to the Venetian landing combines the values of voluptuousness and loss-of-being:

> That singular conveyance, come down unchanged from ballad times, black as nothing else on earth except a coffin—what pictures it calls up of lawless, silent adventures in the plashing night; or even more, what visions of death itself, the bier and solemn rites and last soundless voyage! And has anyone ever remarked that the seat in such a bark, the arm-chair lacquered in coffin-black and dully black-upholstered, is the softest, most luxurious, most relaxing seat in the world? . . . It was warm here in the harbour. The lukewarm air of the sirocco breathed upon him, he leaned back among his cushions and gave himself to the yielding element, closing his eyes for very pleasure

in an indolence as unaccustomed as sweet. "The trip will be short," he thought, and wished it might last for ever.[2]

For Aschenbach pleasure means precisely the elimination of all tension, the surrender to what Freud calls "Nirvana."

It is also in keeping with Freud's scheme that Aschenbach's initial response to the promptings of pleasure is hallucination ("what he felt was no more than a longing to travel; yet coming upon him with such suddenness and passion as to resemble a seizure, almost a hallucination. Desire projected itself visually. . . ."(5)), since that is the most "rudimentary" solution to a felt lack, the one most characteristic of the unconscious. Freud stresses that the unconscious and the preconscious react very differently to perceptions which create unpleasure—that they resort to contrary *"processes of excitation or modes of its discharge."* The unconscious marshals a response that is primarily dependent upon the sensory and affective data of the mnemic traces, whereas the preconscious attempts to chart cognitive relationships between those traces.

When confronted with unpleasure, the unconscious strives to establish a "perceptual identity" with a previous gratification. In other words, it seeks an hallucinatory satisfaction:

> A hungry baby screams or kicks helplessly. But the situation remains unaltered, for the excitation arising from an internal need is not due to a force producing *momentary* impact but to one which is in continuous operation. A change can only come about if . . . an "experience of satisfaction" can be achieved which puts an end to the internal stimulus. An essential component of this experience of satisfaction is a particular perception (that of nourishment, in our example), the mnemic image of which remains associated thenceforward with the memory trace of the excitation produced by the need. As a result . . . next time this need arises a psychical impulse will at once emerge which will seek to re-cathect the mnemic image of the perception and to re-evoke the perception itself, that is to say, to re-establish the situation of the original satisfaction. [V. 565–66]

It is characteristic of unconscious thought to rely in this way on sensory (in particular visual and auditory) projections as a means of achieving gratification. The unconscious also shows itself to be quite inflexible in its strategies for effecting change: once it has discovered a solution to the experience of unpleasure, it will attempt to reinstitute that solution every time the same unpleasure is felt.

The preconscious is "born" of disillusionment with the solutions provided by the unconscious. Its emergence is closely connected with the child's recognition of an external register which hallucination is powerless to affect. The preconscious is that agency by means of which imaginary gratification is abandoned, and some more substantial gratification substituted for it (i.e. the hungry child discards the memory of a bottle of milk for a bottle which is more palpably present, or Aschenbach breaks off his reveries about Venice and takes a boat there).

In order to gain access to a more authentic gratification, the preconscious must also make use of memories, but in a very different way from the unconscious. Whereas the latter strives to recover the full sensory and affective value of the desired mnemic trace, the former tries to exclude sensory and affective values in favor of the connections between that mnemic trace and those adjacent to it; it attempts to recover the relationships between one memory and those related to it logically or chronologically. Instead of establishing a *perceptual* identity with the past, the preconscious works to establish a *thought* identity with it:

> All thinking is no more than a circuitous path from the memory of a satisfaction . . . to an identical cathexis of the same memory which it is hoped to attain once more through an intermediate stage of motor experiences. Thinking must concern itself with the connecting paths between ideas, without being led astray by the *intensities* of those ideas. [V. 602]

Thus, to return once more to the primitive example of the hungry child, the preconscious would undertake to chart the relationships between the memory of the bottle of milk and the memories of those other objects in its environment whose manipulation might secure an actual bottle of milk.

The primary operation of the pleasure principle poses an

obstacle to preconscious thought. The connecting paths which
the latter is determined to trace inevitably lead to distressing
memories as well as to gratifying ones, something intolerable to
the dominant psychic mechanism. Equally intolerable to that
mechanism is the renunciation of immediate pleasure for one
ultimately more substantial.

From the very outset, then (we must of course understand
the chronology of this model as a convenient myth), there is a
strong opposition between instinctual pleasure and the preconscious. The preconscious seeks to diminish the force of this
opposition by stripping the memories upon which it relies of
their affect and sensory appeal—to view them, in other words,
relationally rather than phenomenologically. It substitutes
thought for sensory apprehension; gives priority to relationships between memories rather than to discrete recollections;
and attempts to detach affect from idea. According to Freud,
preconscious memories "exhibit no sensory quality or a very
slight one in comparison with perceptions" (V. 540).

C) REPRESSION AND DISGUISE

It is to be assumed that initially the unconscious and the preconscious are not so much sharply differentiated psychic compartments as divergent ways of responding to a wish acknowledged by both. Later, howevever, the preconscious acquires the
status of a censor, blocking the entrance of those wishes it deems
unacceptable, as well as the memories associated with those
wishes. The preconscious comes to exercise a repressive authority, determining not only which unconscious materials may
gain access to the conscious, but the shape which those materials must take.

The pleasure principle operates unchecked in the unconscious, exerting a particularly strong pressure through the first
wishes which were refused access to the conscious—infantile
impulses, generally of an Oedipal nature. These impulses, Freud
argues, constitute the motivating force of dreams (as well as
parapraxes, jokes, day-dreams, and neuroses), which are by nature wish-fulfilling. However, both wish and fulfillment must
be thoroughly disguised or they will be rejected by the pre-

conscious. Condensation and displacement provide the necessary means for this disguise. They do the "dream-work"—i.e. they create acceptable representations for unacceptable wishes. Freud stresses the difference between this mental activity and that which characterizes conscious thought:

> The dream-work is not simply more careless, more irrational, more forgetful and more incomplete than waking thought; it is completely different from it qualitatively and for that reason not immediately comparable with it. It does not think, calculate, or judge in any way at all; it restricts itself to giving things a new form . . . the dream has above all to evade censorship, and with that end in view the dream-work makes use of a *displacement of psychical intensities* to the point of a transvaluation of all psychical values. The thoughts have to be reproduced exclusively or predominantly in the material of visual and acoustic memory traces, and this necessity imposes upon the dream-work *considerations of representability*. . . . Little attention is paid to the logical relations between the thoughts. . . . [V. 507]

The unconscious ignores the relationships which are such an important component of preconscious thought. As Freud points out, it lacks any capacity to say "if," "just as," "either/or," "because," or "although." Furthermore, the unconscious provides no rationale for the selections and combinations it makes, and distributes emphasis in a way generally quite baffling to waking thought; things which the preconscious would deem of small importance may be invested with extraordinary value in unconscious constructions, while those whose significance the preconscious would strenuously emphasize may be relegated to obscure corners. Finally, the unconscious works with materials very different from those utilized by the preconscious, i.e. with sensory impressions, most notably sounds and images, but also tastes, smells, and tactile sensations. Even the body itself can function as an unconscious signifying network, as the example of hysteria would suggest.

These signifying conventions are not to be understood as failings on the part of the unconscious. On the contrary, whereas the preconscious seeks to establish logic and facilitate cognition, the unconscious works to disintegrate logic and thwart cognition. Dreams, perhaps the most "classic" variety of unconscious signification, and the model on which Freud bases most of his conclusions, are successful to the degree that they are able to transform "dream-thoughts" (i.e. thoughts from the preceding day, themselves quite rational) into an argument which is indecipherable to the unconscious.

The dream-thoughts are thoughts which did not succeed in gaining consciousness, either because they were interrupted, involved an unacceptable wish, or were connected in some way with taboo interests. These thoughts have had attention withdrawn from them, have been as it were left adrift. Because no strong ties as yet exist between them and any more permanent elements of the psychic economy, they provide an admirable "cover" for the forbidden impulses which preoccupy the unconscious, and which motivate the construction of dreams. All that is necessary for this construction to take place is that some connection, no matter how remote, be established between the dream-thoughts and the dream wish or wishes (Freud insists that every dream is inspired by multiple wishes). The intensity which properly belongs to the repressed materials is then *displaced* onto unacknowledged thoughts from the recent past and elements from each source are combined through *condensation* to supply the dream with its characters, its narrative, and its *mise-en-scène*.

Condensation and displacement are two of the most important features of the dream-work, i.e. of the operation whereby the dream-thoughts are transformed into a dream capable of fulfilling on a symbolic level various wishes which themselves remained hidden and repressed. Condensation involves the compression into a single feature of qualities belonging to two or more. Although that compression can take many forms, it always requires that there be points of affinity between the elements it conjoins. Displacement is subject to the same restriction. However, instead of combining two or more things, displacement involves the transfer of psychic intensity from one to another; it invests an innocent and often unimportant object with the affect which properly belongs to one which is taboo. Condensation and displacement are agencies of distortion and disguise. They formulate the repressed wish or wishes in such a way that they are acceptable to the psychic censor, i.e. to that part of the mind which reflects cultural norms and prohibitions.

We will have occasion to discuss the operations of condensation and displacement in considerably more detail in Chapter 3, and we will at that time exploit the full illustrative value of Freud's dream of the botanical monograph. However, I would like to refer to it here briefly in order to render more concrete the notions of "dream-thoughts" and "dream-work." Freud gives us this transcript of the dream:

> I had written a monograph of a certain plant. The book lay before me and I was at the moment turning over a folded coloured plate. Bound up in each copy there was a dried specimen of the plant, as though it had been taken from a herbarium. [IV. 169]

The dream is a wish-fulfillment many times over. It speaks to the dreamer's feeling that he should have been mentioned in print as one of the discoverers of cocaine; to his sense that he ought to bring his wife flowers more often, and to the related hope that he might love her more; to the wish that the volume in which the dream is recorded were already completed and in print; and, most rudimentarily, to a masturbatory impulse, itself disguised by a "screen memory"* from the dreamer's childhood in which he and his sister "blissfully" tore apart a book of colored plates given to them by their father.

All of these wishes (and doubtless others) have been condensed into a simple scenario in which the dreamer examines an illustrated book containing a dried specimen of a plant. Freud notes that the point of greatest intensity in the dream is the colored plate, which is to say that the affect which technically belongs to the objects of the various wishes behind the dream has been displaced onto it. In other words, the dream-work has substituted the colored plate for various taboo objects, and has transferred to it their psychic value.

The dream-thoughts which provided this dream with its sig-

---

*An intense but seemingly insignificant childhood memory, often itself a composite, which conceals another, repressed memory.

nifying materials are elaborately reconstructed by Freud. They include a host of horticultural references (a conversation with a Professor Gartner about a patient named Flora, during the course of which Freud congratulated the Professor's wife on her "blooming" appearance; a train of thought about a dissertation Freud had written years ago on the coca-plant; the recollection that artichokes have always been his "favorite flower"; and a joke about wives and floral gifts). The allusions to books in the dream-thoughts are almost as dense.

The dream-work appropriated this extensive signifying network as a vehicle for satisfying a whole series of wishes, ranging from the infantile to the commonplace. The simplicity of the dream belies the extraordinary effort which must have gone into it—the effort involved in discovering a single image capable of supporting not only all of the horticultural references in the dream-thoughts, but those to books as well, and of transferring to the focal point of that image the intensity which has been generated by at least five wishes.

The dream-work is not limited to the operations of displacement and condensation. It also entails the conversion of the dream-thoughts into another language, more suitable for dream-representation—a language whose registers are sensory and affective. Freud depicts this conversion as a backward movement:

> . . . dreaming is on the whole an example of regression to the dreamer's earliest condition, a revival of his childhood, of the instinctual impulses which dominated it and the methods of expression which were then available to him.[V. 548]

Once again we are reminded that the signifying strategies adopted by the unconscious differ markedly from those which predominate in waking life. In unconscious discourse, sensory and affective values pre-empt relational thinking, and the past has priority over the present.

The madeleine episode from *Swann's Way* may help to clarify these additional differences between unconscious and preconscious signification. In it the present gives way to the past through the intervention of a sensory experience (the taste of the cake dipped in tea) to which a powerful affect is connected (the happiness of Marcel's childhood in Combray). The memories recalled by the taste of tea-soaked cake are described by Proust as "involuntary"; they cannot, in other words, be summoned up at will in the way that preconscious memories can. These memories emerge into the cognitive space of Marcel's consciousness only with great difficulty, and in the absence of all of the normal preoccupations of waking life:

> Undoubtedly what is thus palpitating in the depths of my being must be the image, the visual memory which, being linked to that taste, has tried to follow it into my conscious mind. But its struggles are too far off, too much confused; scarcely can I perceive the colorless reflection in which are blended the uncapturable whirling medley of radiant hues, and I cannot distinguish its form, cannot invite it, as the one possible interpreter, to translate to me the evidence of its contemporary, its inseparable paramour, the taste of cake soaked in tea; cannot ask it to inform me what special circumstance is in question, of what period in my past life.
>
> Will it ultimately reach the clear surface of my consciousness, this memory, this old, dead moment which the magnetism of an identical moment has travelled so far to importune, to disturb, to raise up out of the very depths of my being? I cannot tell. Now that I feel nothing, it has stopped, has perhaps gone down again into its darkness, from which who can say whether it will ever rise? Ten times over I must essay the task, must lean down over the abyss. And each time the natural laziness which deters us from every difficult enterprise, every work of importance, has urged me to leave the thing alone, to drink my cup of tea and to think merely of the worries of to-day and my hopes for to-morrow, which let themselves be pondered over without effort or distress of mind.[3]

This episode reads almost like a gloss on Freud's early topography, insisting as firmly as the latter on two psychic territories which are sharply differentiated from each other, both in terms of the memories and mental activities which are proper to each, and the barrier which separates them. The account Proust provides of those memories and those mental activities also conforms to a remarkable degree with that offered by

Freud. For instance, the childhood memories for which Marcel searches in the "abyss" of his unconscious are characterized by an extraordinary sensory and affective intensity; they invoke in him an "all-powerful joy," and invade his senses with an "exquisite pleasure." They are dislodged by an experience which duplicates one of them at the sensory level, and in the process revitalizes the affect connected to the whole group. Although taste here plays a much more central role than it does in the formation of dreams, it functions primarily as the conscious signifier for a cluster of unconscious visual images of Combray, images which finally spring to life in Marcel's conscious mind like Japanese "crumbs of paper" in a bowl of water.

This passage also confirms Freud's notion that the preconscious/conscious system attempts to reduce the sensory and affective intensity of the original memories so as to facilitate a more flexible and less emotionally disruptive intellectual operation; Marcel's strongest conscious impulse is to limit his thoughts to those things which habitually concern him—to ideas with a low quota of affect, which consequently "let themselves be pondered over without any effort or distress of mind." Indeed, the "Overture" section of *Swann's Way* is in large part a meditation on custom, "that skillful but unhurrying manager" who contrives to make "any room [or any memory] seem habitable." All of the contents of the preconscious are regulated by "custom"; not only have they been reduced through constant repetition to a condition of familiarity, so that they no longer arouse any very intense emotional response, but they have been organized as well in accordance with larger cultural norms and prohibitions.

D) PRIMARY AND SECONDARY PROCESSES

Toward the conclusion of *The Interpretation of Dreams,* Freud stresses the purely pedagogic uses of his topographic diagram, and suggests that the unconscious and preconscious do not represent so much a psychic geography as different "processes of excitation or modes of its discharge" (V. 610). He associates the unconscious with what he calls the "primary process," and the preconscious with what he calls the "secondary process." The former strives for an immediate evacuation of tension, whereas the former attempts to block that evacuation, and to store up the energy for other purposes, i.e. those of thought:

> All that I insist upon is the idea that the activity of the *first* . . . system is directed toward securing the *free discharge* of the quantities of excitation, while the *second* system, by means of the cathexes emanating from it, succeeds in *inhibiting* this discharge and in transforming the cathexis into a quiescent one, no doubt with a simultaneous raising of its level. I presume, therefore, that under the dominion of the second system the discharge of excitation is governed by quite different mechanical conditions from those in force under the dominion of the first system. When once the second system has concluded its exploratory thought-activity, it releases the inhibition and damming-up of the excitations and allows them to discharge themselves in movement. [V. 599–600]

Stated in other terms, the primary and secondary processes represent two very different ways of responding to the pleasure principle. The primary process seeks immediate gratification through hallucination, but the end result is always disillusionment and unpleasure. The secondary process traces a more circuitous route to gratification, which necessitates the temporary toleration of unpleasure, but promises a more satisfying conclusion. Any further explanation of these processes requires the introduction of two additional terms, "drive" and "cathexis."

Freud defines "drive" (incorrectly translated as "instinct" in the *Standard Edition*) as the mental representative of a somatic impulse. A drive provides a psychic mediation and expression of a physiological phenomenon.[4] It is a semiotic category, constituting as it does an entity which "stands in" or "speaks" for something else. This representation generally takes the form of a wish, and as I indicated above, it provides the motivating force behind all psychic activity, from dreams to rational thought. A drive strives to discharge the quantity of excitation which it carries. It presses toward release because of the domination of the pleasure principle, which views the accumulation of such excitation as unpleasurable.

Within the primary system, this excitation remains "freely mobile"—i.e. capable of infinite displacement in its search for discharge. What this means is that if a drive is blocked in its movement toward one object, it will redirect its energies toward another. It is perhaps even more important to note that under the supervision of the primary process a drive is concerned less with objects than with the affect which has become attached to the memories of those objects during the history of the subject. Since the exclusive goal of the primary process is a regeneration of pleasurable affect, it will resort with equal alacrity either to an object whose capacity to gratify has already been demonstrated, or, in the absence of any such object, to the mnemic trace which represents that object. The primary process makes no distinction between internal and external registers (e.g. between the image of a breast and an actual breast).

This indifference to distinctions is reflected in all of the activities of the primary process. If a particular memory has been in some way censored by the preconscious, the primary process will not hesitate to negotiate the transference of its pleasurable affect to a more acceptable memory (e.g. from the visual image of the subject's father to that of a teacher). The only "rules" governing such displacements are those of contiguity and similarity. I will comment further on this last point below.

Because the primary process engineers endless displacements, its discursive formations are characterized by what J. Laplanche and J. B. Pontalis call a constant "sliding of meaning."[5] However, despite the fluidity of its constructions, the primary process is characterized by a remarkable single-mindedness. It resorts again and again to the same strategies for obtaining pleasure, even though the result is inevitably unpleasurable. The primary process is incapable of "learning" from experience.

The secondary process functions in an altogether different manner, one which finds perhaps its clearest articulation in *Beyond the Pleasure Principle*. It checks the impulsive displacements of the primary system by "binding" the excitation behind every wish. In other words, it inhibits the dissipation of that energy until a genuine solution to the wish which represents it has been found. At that time the secondary process permits the release of some of the excitation, but not all of it; it maintains the rest as a constant cathexis (i.e. investment) within the preconscious. It does this because subsequent excitation can be more easily bound if there is a hypercathexis (i.e. surplus investment) within the system (XVIII. 30). Because the discharge permitted by the secondary process is so much smaller than that encouraged by the primary process, the pleasures—but also, of course, the un-pleasures—of the former are much less intense than those of the latter:

> . . . there seems to be no doubt whatever that the unbound
> or primary processes give rise to far more intense feelings in
> both directions than the bound or secondary ones. . . . at the
> beginning of mental life the struggle for pleasure was far more
> intense than later but not so unrestricted; it had to submit to
> frequent interruptions. In later times the dominance of the
> pleasure principle is very much more secure, but it itself has
> no more escaped the process of taming than the other instincts
> in general. [XVIII. 63]

So far this discussion of "bound" and "unbound" energy has remained extremely abstract. How precisely, we might ask, does the secondary process succeed in "binding" the excitations which press for discharge, and what role does affect play in this operation? Freud provides a number of cryptic but consistent explanations, all of them having to do with the introduction of a linguistic structure into the psychic economy.

The preconscious can only seek out more reliable paths of gratification if it has at its disposal those memories which con-stitute the subject's culturally admissable history, and if it has the resources for manipulating those memories in voluntary and relational ways. However, as long as the mnemic traces retain their full affective and sensory intensity, such a manipulation is impossible; certain memories are automatically privileged be-cause of their pleasurable affect, and others as automatically avoided because of the unpleasure which they evoke. More-over, the sensory vividness of the original memories blurs the distinction between the internal and external registers. For these reasons it is imperative that the secondary process diminish both the affective and sensory values of the mnemic traces, and Freud suggests that this conversion is effected through language:

> . . . in order to make more delicately adjusted performances possible, it later became necessary to make the course of ideas less dependent upon the presence or absence of unpleasure. For this purpose the *Pcs.* system needed to have qualities of its own which could attract consciousness; and it seems highly probable that it obtained them by linking the preconscious processes with the mnemic system of indications of speech, a system not without quality. By means of the qualities of that system, consciousness, which had hitherto been a sense organ for perceptions alone, also became a sense organ for a portion of our thought-processes. Now, therefore, there are, as it were, *two* sensory surfaces, one directed towards perception and the other towards the preconscious thought-processes. [V. 574]

The operation here described connects up the mnemic traces with an already existing linguistic structure, which imposes upon them a whole series of paradigmatic and syntagmatic relationships, and enables them to be voluntarily recalled.

This linguistic structuration would also seem to provide the agency for "binding" the excitation which would otherwise push for an immediate discharge. Freud notes in *The Interpretation of Dreams* that "verbal memories" (i.e. signifiers in Saussure's sense of the term) "endow the process of thinking with a new mobile cathexis"; in other words, they maintain within the psychic economy a constant state of quiescent energy which makes possible the activity of thought. The psychic organism's libidinal resources are thus redistributed across the whole surface of the preconscious network. Instead of a supersaturation at one point, which results in an intolerable tension and the need for release, all of the preconscious memories—verbal and otherwise—now contain a very small emotional charge. That emotional charge keeps them accessible to cognition.

Finally, the linguistic organization of the mnemic traces functions to diminish their affective intensity. Freud repeatedly opposes language to affect, which is the chief obstacle in the path of the secondary process. The famous story about his grandson, recounted both in *The Interpretation of Dreams* and

Beyond the Pleasure Principle, offers a concrete illustration of the way in which language strips memories of their affective value: At the age of one and a half, this child, who was extremely attached to his mother and consequently experienced her departures as unpleasurable, created a game by means of which he "mastered" or "bound" that unpleasure. This game involved throwing away a small wooden toy attached to a string and then pulling it back again, to the verbal accompaniment of *"fort!"* (gone) and *"da!"* (back). It was so effective that when the child's mother died shortly thereafter, he suffered only minimal distress.[6] As Freud tells us in *Project for a Scientific Psychology,* (1895), language permits "the highest, securest form of cognitive thought process" (I. 374)—highest and most secure because the farthest removed from affect.

This scheme attributes the condition of being organized like a language not to the unconscious, as Lacan would argue, but to the preconscious. Not only is the second of these psychic areas the storehouse or repository of words and the rules governing their use, but it comes into existence simultaneously with that linguistic organization. Thus just as the unconscious is largely synonymous with the sensory and affective memories which it embraces, so the preconscious is virtually indistinguishable from the verbal memories which it accommodates. (The term "preconscious" is one which Freud abandons later as he reconceives the topography of the mind, but it proves singularly helpful in accounting for the distinction between the primary and secondary systems, and in describing that part of the psychic economy which is never entirely conscious, but which is always accessible to consciousness. Freud alternatively refers to this region as the "unconscious ego.")

In the important essay, "The Unconscious" (1915), Freud explains the very different sorts of signifying strategies employed by the primary and secondary processes, and emphasizes once again the linguistic organization of the preconscious/conscious "area":

> . . . the conscious presentation comprises the presentation of the thing plus the word belonging to it, while the unconscious presentation is the presentation of the thing alone. The system

> *Ucs.* contains the thing-cathexes of the objects, the first and true object-cathexes; the system *Pcs.* comes about by this thing-presentation being hypercathected through being linked with the word-presentations corresponding to it. It is these hyper-cathexes . . . that bring about a higher psychical organization and make it possible for the primary process to be succeeded by the secondary process which is dominant in the *Pcs.* Now, too, we are in a position to state precisely what it is that repression denies to the rejected presentation in the transference neuroses: what it denies to the presentation is translation into words which shall remain attached to the object. A presentation which is not put into words, or a psychical act which is not hypercathected, remains thereafter in the *Ucs.* in a state of repression. [XIV. 201–2]

The unconscious is obliged to express itself exclusively through "thing-presentations"—i.e. the mnemic traces left behind by perceptual flow. Freud suggests that these memories are pre-dominantly visual and auditory. The preconscious, on the other hand, has at its disposal a double signifying register, consisting of "thing-presentations" and "word-presentations." These two categories coincide with what Saussure calls "signifieds" and "signifiers"; the thing-presentation, like the linguistic signified, designates a concept, while the word-presentation or linguistic signifier refers to a sound image. Once again we are reminded of the profound interconnections between linguistic semiotics and psychoanalysis, interconnections which result both from the fact that language can only be activated through discourse, within which the subject figures centrally, and from the fact that subjectivity is itself a product of two signifying activities, one unconscious and the other preconscious or conscious.

This formulation of the preconscious demystifies repression, showing the latter to be an event which is played out at the level of signification. It makes clear the degree to which language defines the limits of what the human subject can know, both about the world and itself, since phenomenal and psychic experiences which have been denied linguistic expression remain quite simply unknowable. For Freud these "unspeakable" materials constitute the focal point of subjectivity. He writes in *The Interpretation of Dreams* that "the core of our being, consisting of unconscious wishful impulses, remains inaccessible to the understanding . . . of the preconscious" (V. 603). He thus gives priority, as least in his early writing, to the unconscious discourse—i.e. to those signifying formations motivated by the unconscious, such as dreams, parapraxes, daydreams, neuroses—rather than to preconscious constructs.

We would want to stress even more than Freud the *social* nature of both the preconscious and the unconscious—the degree to which both parts of the inner economy are structured by an outer one. The preconscious is shaped by forces which are external to it; its prohibitions and its imperatives, as well as the principles which govern its dispositions, reflect the culture whose language it speaks. Moreover, since the unconscious is constituted in opposition to the preconscious, it is as fully defined as is the latter by culture. The desires it cherishes have not only been silenced, but produced by the censoring mechanism. In other words, they are mediated through those prohibitions which serve to structure society.

As Claude Lévi-Strauss has demonstrated, the most recurring cultural prohibition is the incest taboo. That taboo does not always operate in the same way; sometimes it outlaws the sexual alliance between one set of family members, and sometimes another set.[7] However, it would seem always to appear in one guise or another, and to have a quite specific effect upon the unconscious. Since in Western societies the forbidden alliances are those between father and daughter, and mother and son, unconscious desire most frequently takes an Oedipal form.

It is important to stress that although some version of the incest taboo would seem to exist in all known cultures, it is not "natural" or "spontaneous." It always serves a precise ideological function, constructing subjects who fit smoothly into the existing social order. The Oedipus complex, for instance, through mechanisms which we will discuss in detail in Chapter 4, produces subjects who are sexually differentiated in predictable ways, and whose desires are congruent with patriarchy. Gilles Deleuze and Felix Guattari suggest that those desires are also compatible with capitalism.[8] Thus we cannot attribute to the unconscious a prelapsarian or "archaic" status; preconscious and unconscious develop through mutual tension, a tension which

is introduced through language and which reflects the larger
cultural order.

Liliana Cavani's notorious film *The Night Porter* illustrates
vividly the antagonistic relationship between primary and secondary activities, those signifying activities which are most
characteristic of the unconscious and preconscious, respectively. It dramatizes the reliance of the former of these upon
affective and sensory data, and the latter upon language. Cavani's film also renders transparent the inevitable collaboration
between the preconscious and a larger cultural regime.

The Night Porter is ostensibly the story of a postwar encounter between a female concentration camp inmate and the Nazi
officer who tortured and photographed her while masquerad-
ing as a camp doctor. Max, the Nazi officer, has chosen an in-
conspicuous job as a hotel clerk after the war. Lucia, one of the
few survivors from her camp, has married a conductor, and
while on tour with him meets Max again. She voluntarily resumes her sado-masochistic relationship with him. Much of the
film is devoted to an exploration of this relationship.

However, *The Night Porter* gives equal time to Max's interactions with a group of ex-Nazis who frequent the hotel where
he works, and who effectively provide him with his cultural
context. While these men clearly defy the larger social order of
postwar Vienna, where the story takes place, they have so organized themselves as to duplicate the structures of that order
and to function as their own microcosm. One of the group is a
psychiatrist, another assumes the role of prosecuting attorney,
and the values of art and aristocracy are respectively represented by a male dancer, and a large blonde woman called "the
Countess." These figures all violently oppose what they perceive as the "private" experience of Max and Lucia—private
because it now lacks institutional basis and because it is predicated on affect. Their own energies are devoted to the collective disposal of all traces of the guilty past.

The means by which they propose to do this warrant close
attention. Each member of the group is assigned a trial date,
and on that occasion he or she is summoned before the others
to face an exhaustive inquiry into his or her war crimes. The
prosecuting attorney levels severe charges, and the defendant

is obliged to respond at length to each one. The group then "talks through" the crimes, and at the conclusion of the trial the prosecuting attorney burns all of the extant documents that could serve to incriminate the defendant. Known survivors of the concentration camp are similarly eliminated.

These trials closely resemble the strategies mapped out by Freud in *Beyond the Pleasure Principle* for dealing with traumatic neuroses, i.e. with neuroses which issue from painful and un-resolved memories:

> The patient . . . is obliged to *repeat* the repressed material as a contemporary experience. . . . The physician cannot as a rule spare his patient this phase of the treatment. He must get him to re-experience some portion of his forgotten life, but must see to it, on the other hand, that the patient retains some degree of aloofness, which will enable him, in spite of every-thing, to recognize that what appears to be reality is in fact only a reflection of a forgotten past. If this can be successfully achieved, the patient's sense of conviction is won, together with the therapeutic success that is dependent on it. [XVIII. 18–19]

In both situations, the subject is compelled to re-experience a distressing past, but in such a way as to increase the distance between it and the present. What this really means is that the sensory and affective intensity of the memories in question is drastically reduced by submitting them to a linguistic organi-zation. After that organization—i.e. after the subordination of the past to language—the unwanted memories no longer have the capacity to project themselves with hallucinatory emphasis onto the screen of the present. (The fact that painful memories could ever force their way to such prominence may seem at odds with the dictates of the pleasure principle, but Freud ob-serves in *Beyond the Pleasure Principle* that certain materials have to be "worked through" or "bound" before gratification can even be sought. The capacity to defer pleasure is a secondary devel-opment.)

The Night Porter utilizes flashbacks to establish the point that Max and Lucia, on the other hand, cherish a fascination with the past. Various episodes from the concentration camp, in which Max injures Lucia, or photographs her in positions of vulnerability or fear, are recalled with extraordinary sensory and affective intensity by each of them, in an attempt to bring past and present into an ever greater alignment. They stage a number of transactions calculated to revive the feelings of the war years, in which a pink dress, similar to one worn by Lucia in the concentration camp, and Max's old Nazi uniform enjoy a privileged status. These items function much like the morsel of cake soaked in tea in *Swann's Way*—i.e. they duplicate the sensory qualities of certain memories and in the process revitalize the affect attached to them.

(It must be noted that for a complex of reasons Max and Lucia derive the liveliest gratification from physical pain. In their case, unlike that of the other characters, the pleasure principle still operates at the behest of the primary process, giving preeminence to sensory detail and affect. However, it is clear that there has been a definitive interference on the part of the secondary process at some point in the past. In other words, because of certain prohibitions against direct erotic exchanges between camp officers and camp inmates, Max and Lucia have made a libidinal investment in pain, which they now experience as pleasure.)

Further consolidating the connections between these two characters and the primary process is the fact that there is virtually no verbal communication between them. They avoid it not only as a distraction, but a threat to their hallucinatory experiments. Max refuses to go through with the trial which his group has scheduled for him, and he and Lucia hole up in a small apartment with limited supplies and submerge themselves in affect.

Max's circle responds to his "regression" with outrage and vindictiveness. They cut off his access to food and slowly starve the couple to death. These characters function in every respect as a sort of preconscious: not only do they place the same emphasis on linguistic structuration and cultural norms, but they keep the unruly impulses represented by Max and Lucia under a constant surveillance. The latter succumb to the inevitable consequence of a complete absorption in primary pleasures—death.

E) DESIRE AND SIGNIFICATION

Earlier I stated that the signifying strategies of the primary process reveal a remarkable inflexibility; its choices are always predicated on affect and always made in response to a naïve interpretation of the pleasure principle. Confronted with need, it will invariably project an hallucinatory gratification. The secondary process displays considerably more ingenuity in the solutions it supplies to those same needs; it is more experimental and innovative in its utilization of the mnemic traces.

Although the primary process represents the signifying operation most characteristic of the unconscious, and the secondary process that which is most indicative of the preconscious, Freud encourages us to make certain distinctions between the two sets. One of the more important of these distinctions is chronological: The primary and secondary processes would seem to predate the unconscious and preconscious division, a division which is induced by repression. In other words, the unconscious is established simultaneously with the desires it houses—desires which are on the one hand culturally promoted, and on the other linguistically blocked. The desires which most classically inaugurate the Western unconscious are of course those that comprise the Oedipus complex.

Because these originary desires are permanently blocked, they are not capable of any real gratification; instead, they initiate a series of displacements which continue throughout the entire existence of the subject and structure that subject's psychic reality. All consciously held desires derive, through a long chain of displacements, from those that organize the unconscious.

We recall that displacement designates the operation whereby affect is transferred from an unacceptable object to an acceptable one. (Freud writes in *The Interpretation of Dreams* that "in this way, ideas which originally had only a *weak* charge of intensity take over the charge from ideas which were originally *intensely* cathected" (IV. 177)). This operation, by means of which the primary process responds to repression, would seem at first glance to contradict the assertion that this process is characterized by a strategic monotony. However, it is important to understand that displacement and strategic monotony are not contradictory—that the slippage of affect from one term to another is not at all incompatible with the compulsively repetitive nature of the solutions the primary process adopts. That process makes no distinctions among various objects or thing-presentations (i.e. the memories of those objects). Its sole concern is with the affect attached to those objects or thing-presentations. Despite its capacity for endless displacements, the primary process always undertakes the same search—the search for pleasurable affect. If that affect remains inaccessible so long as it is connected to one object or thing-presentation, the primary process will shift it to another.

Having done this, the unconscious will behave as if the substitution were in fact the original. It will insist upon an absolute identification of the objects or memories between which there has been an affective exchange. The impulse to conflate those things that exist in a representational or substitutive relationship to each other can be seen in all of the signifying formations in which the primary process plays a dominant role, as I will attempt to demonstrate through the complex example of the hysterical symptom.

Freud writes in "Hysterical Phantasies and Their Relation to Bisexuality" (1908) that the hysterical symptom is the product of multiple repression. What is initially repressed is the subject's desire to engage in some sort of forbidden activity, generally of a quite specifically sexual nature. The repressed desire continues to express itself afterwards, but now in the guise of a fantasy which may be accompanied by a complementary motor response, such as a cough or a twitch. Finally, the fantasy is also repressed, and a physical symptom, lacking any physiological basis, remains as the sole witness of the original impulse. This symptom emerges on a bodily site which is altogether removed from that connected with the repressed desire, and which is usually sexually "innocent" (i.e. which does not have major erotic connotations), such as a leg, the eyes, the mouth. However, it assumes all of the value and intensity of the fantasy it replaces, just as the fantasy earlier took over all of the psychic intensity of the forbidden action (IX. 154–66).

François Truffaut's film *The Story of Adele H.* elegantly

dramatizes these successive displacements. The title character, who is an hysteric, compulsively and quite literally writes herself into a death narrative. Her most important symptom is precisely this activity of writing and both its "form" and its "content" warrant the closest attention. The physical activity or form of writing is terribly important to Adele—she consumes vast quantities of paper and ink, and while engaged with those items she invariably falls into a trance-like state. Eventually the pathological nature of this activity is confirmed by the emergence of an additional symptom: the radical impairment of Adele's vision. The constant theme or content of this scribbling is the passion which unites her to her fictive lover Pinson, in whom she seeks to submerge herself. Adele's romantic reveries about Pinson, and the letters she compulsively writes to him, represent a displacement away from an earlier fantasy, which still occasionally surfaces in her dreams. In that fantasy Adele sees herself drowning, an event which satisfies two closely related wishes. By means of it she takes the place of her sister Leopoldine, "everybody's favorite," who drowned with her husband during their honeymoon, and so fulfills a masochistic desire for self-immolation. Her identification with Leopoldine also permits Adele to achieve a longed-for intimacy with her famous father, Victor Hugo, who idolized Leopoldine. Thus through a series of displacements, Adele's compulsive writing and eventual hysterical blindness come to gratify not only certain Oedipal desires, but the wish for self-punishment (i.e. death) which those desires generate. The activity of moving a pen across paper becomes informed with the affect which properly belongs to the memory of Victor Hugo, and at one point in the film Adele clutches her manuscript to her as passionately as if it were indeed her father. Similarly, her eyes are punished with blindness as if they were that part of her body which had yearned for a "sinful" proximity with him, in a very literal duplication of the Oedipus legend.

In its tendency to insist upon the absolute identity of two things or ideas, the primary process diverges most dramatically from the secondary process. Whereas the former maintains no distinction between the original object of a desire and the object which replaces it, the latter insists at all points on *difference*, upon those features or qualities that separate one signifying element from another.

Since Freud associates the secondary process so consistently with language, the principle of difference which is so central to that process can perhaps best be grasped through a linguistic example. We recall Saussure's assertion that

> . . . in language there are only differences *without positive terms*. Whether we take the signified or the signifier, language has neither ideas nor sounds that existed before the linguistic system, but only conceptual and phonic differences that have issued from the system. The idea or phonic substance that a sign contains is of less importance than the other signs that surround it.[9]

This passage from *Course in General Linguistics* draws attention to the fact that every linguistic sign depends for its status upon its relation to all of the other elements within the same system, upon the ways in which it differs even from those it most resembles.

For instance, within the closed system of the English language, "cabin" and "hovel" function as synonyms of "hut." What this means is not that they are identical terms, but that they help to establish, through their microscopic conceptual differences from it, the value of the word "hut." Each overlaps with the others to a large degree, but not entirely ("hut" refers to a primitive dwelling, "cabin" to a rustic one, and "hovel" to one in disrepair). Each of the words always implies the others, in that it is defined by the points at which it conceptually diverges from them. (Similarly, each word is defined by the points at which it formally diverges from phonetically adjacent words, such as those with the same prefix or suffix.) Since the status of each term depends on its slight difference from certain others, to collapse those differences would be to jeopardize the signifying value of the entire cluster.

We have been speaking here about *paradigmatic* relationships—i.e. the connections between the members of a paradigm—but the same principle obtains with syntagmatic chains. Here too it is imperative that distance be maintained between the various elements which comprise the whole, whether it is a sentence or a musical bar, and that there be enough variety among those elements so that the reader or listener can distinguish them from each other. (It has often been noted that too much alliteration or assonance within a given linguistic syntagm tends to interfere with the operations of logical meaning.)

The issue of logic is more than a little pertinent to the present discussion, since the secondary process subjects the original mnemic traces to a radical transformation and reorganization precisely so as to facilitate *thought*. As we noted above, the affective intensity of those memories hinders the search for logical relationships between them, since only those conducive to pleasure could push their way to consciousness. The secondary process links up the mnemic traces or thing-presentations to word-presentations as a means both of drastically reducing their sensory and affective intensity and of systematizing them. After their linguistic organization, those memories facilitate rather than thwart thought. They have been converted into a sophisticated cross-reference system, in which each term connects up with many others in a variety of ways.

We have discussed in some detail the two signifying processes responsible for the production not only of meaning but of subjectivity—the "languages" of the unconscious and the preconscious. For purposes of clarification, we have maintained a fairly firm division between them. However, Freud stresses that neither the primary nor the secondary process is alone capable of signification; it is only through their collaboration that discourse occurs, and that the subject is constituted.

Thus the mnemic traces to which the unconscious has such vivid access only become signifiers of various desires as a consequence of repression (i.e. of preconscious interference). In fact, the unconscious only resorts to discourse—to dreams, parapraxes, neuroses, fantasies—because its raw materials are excluded from consciousness. The dream-work—what one might call the "production-line" behind the dream—clearly illustrates the transition from censorship to signification:

> The unconscious wish links itself up with the day's residues and effects a transference on to them. . . . A wish now arises

which has been transferred on to the recent material; or a recent wish, having been suppressed, gains fresh life by being reinforced from the unconscious. This wish seeks to force its way along the normal path taken by thought-processes, through the *Pcs* . . . to consciousness. But it comes up against the censorship, which is still functioning and to the influence of which it now submits. At this point it takes on the distortion for which the way has already been paved by the transference of the wish on to the recent material . . . Its further advance is halted, however, by the sleeping state of the preconscious . . . The dream-process consequently enters onto a regressive path, which lies open to it precisely owing to the peculiar nature of the state of sleep, and it is led along that path by the attraction exercised on it by groups of memories; some of these memories themselves exist only in the form of visual cathexes and not as translations into the terminology of the later systems. In the course of its regressive path the dream-process acquires the attribute of representability . . . when the content of the dream has become perceptual [it has] . . . found a way of evading the obstacle put in its way by the censorship. . . . [V. 573–74]

The dream-work proceeds by finding elements acceptable to the censorship which can consequently be put in the place of ones that are unacceptable. In other words, the pressure of preconscious surveillance obliges the unconscious to resort to circuitous representation, to find signifiers capable of concealing or disguising their signifieds, while at the same time speaking for them. Thus, although the dream is an unconscious discourse, it is the product of interactions between both the primary and secondary systems; it is what Freud calls a "compromise," fulfilling to some extent the wishes of both.

It is also important to stress once again that certain infantile wishes become the pivot of unconscious signification (i.e. are transformed into desires) only because of the intervention of the preconscious, an intervention which takes the form both of differentiation and prohibition. The secondary process, not the primary one, defines the subject's mother as distinct from all other women, and isolates the subject's father from the available group of male adults. In short, the privileged status enjoyed by certain mnemic traces over all others is the result of a secondary interference in the sensory and affective register of the unconscious. As a consequence of that interference, the affect which attaches itself to certain memories can never be entirely evacuated or displaced, and those memories play a critical role in the subject's history.

And while the secondary process brings into existence a more sophisticated and flexible signifying network, with a double register of acoustic images and concepts, its discursive activities are similarly coerced by the primary process. We have observed several times already that for the secondary process there are "no positive terms," only an endless play of differences within a closed system. Mathematics would seem to provide the closest approximation to a purely secondary discourse, but it contrasts dramatically with most of the other discourses which would also seem to belong to the preconscious. Language, for instance, serves constantly as a vehicle for expressing the privileged status of one term over all others, as a means of attributing to an object, a memory, or a word a transcendental, extra-systemic value. These moments of fixation within linguistic discourse, in which there would seem after all to be certain positive terms, are created by the eruptions of desire into the relational logic of the secondary process. They are critical moments in the production of not only meaning but subjectivity.

An example from *Swann's Way* may help to make this discussion less abstract. It is taken from a section of the novel largely devoted to Marcel's youthful preoccupation with certain foreign or distant cities:

> . . . the production of these dreams of the Atlantic and of Italy ceased to depend entirely upon the changes of the seasons and of the weather. I need only, to make them reappear, pronounce the names: Balbec, Venice, Florence, within whose syllables had gradually accumulated all the longing inspired in me by the places for which they stood. Even in spring, to come upon the name of Balbec sufficed to awaken in me the desire for storms at sea and for the Norman gothic; even on a stormy day the name of Florence or of Venice would awaken the desire for sunshine, for lilies, for the Palace of the Doges and for Santa Maria del Fiore. [296]

Marcel has dreamed for a long time of visiting Balbec, Venice, and Florence. Those desires have been mediated through a variety of cultural artifacts ranging from travel and art books to novels and paintings. However, they also hook up with an extended series of prior desires for unobtainable objects, desires which would seem to have commenced with Marcel's mother, and the kisses of which she is so chary. The travel dreams are thus the product of a quite intricate collaboration between the primary and the secondary processes.

In the first stage of that collaboration, years before he dreamt of visiting distant places, Marcel differentiated his mother from all other women, and assimilated certain cultural prohibitions surrounding her. The birth of his repressed desire for her must be understood as having occurred simultaneously with these two preconscious activities, and as having resulted in the formation of his unconscious. Marcel's subsequent desires have all been displacements away from that original one, and have been to some degree organized by it. However, those desires have also been structured by secondary mediations of all sorts, including novels, music, and art, mediations which have aligned his desires with dominant cultural values.

The displacement of desire away from the memories of various images of Balbec, Venice, and Florence onto the words themselves dramatizes what is probably the most interesting of all the primary and secondary interactions, since it brings the latter process under the domination of the former, and reverses the usual order of psychic events. Normally the word-presentation or linguistic signifier would function to dampen down the affective and sensory appeal of the thing-presentation or signified, achieving a victory of the secondary process over the primary. Here, however, the primary process triumphs: the word-presentation is itself informed with all of the affective and sensory intensity of an important thing-presentation. Three linguistic signifiers thus become the agency of the very qualities which they are intended to circumvent. Freud observes that it is characteristic of the primary process to treat words as if they were things, with all the same affective and sensory properties.[10]

We can safely assert the dominance of the primary process

over the discourses of the unconscious, and the secondary process over those of the preconscious, but it would be incorrect to attribute to either process a monopoly in their respective discursive domains. Parapraxes can only be understood as primary invasions into the linguistic order of the secondary system, while dreams rely upon the elaborations of the preconscious for their occasion and thematic premise. Essays, poems, novels, and plays, which depend upon the linguistic order for their articulation, dramatize the way in which desire constantly disrupts that order, resulting on the one hand in clusters of highly privileged and emotionally resonant signifiers, and on the other hand in the tug of a narrative which promises eventual closure. Film accommodates the primary process in ever more complex ways; because one of the registers of its inscription is that used by the unconscious in the production of dreams, it has the capacity not only to depict the displacements of waking desire but to do so in a language familiar to the sleeping subject. The totality of image and sound tracks permits it to engage simultaneously in the discourses of the unconscious and the preconscious.

The Freudian scheme not only clarifies the precise nature of what we have called, after Benveniste, the unconscious and preconscious discourses, but demonstrates that semiotics and psychoanalysis cannot be separated. Since the preconscious subject is entirely organized through language, and since language functions as an agency for repressing and hence for structuring the unconscious, subjectivity can only be understood through the operations of signification. Moreover, since all signifying formations are produced through the collaboration of the primary and secondary processes, signification is equally inconceivable apart from subjectivity.

The next chapter will further address the imbrication of signification and subjectivity, this time by isolating three sets which are fundamental to discursive practice: condensation and displacement, metaphor and metonymy, and paradigm and syntagm. We will follow Christian Metz in imagining a sort of continuum stretching from the extreme of the primary process to the extreme of the secondary one, along which different signifying strategies can be plotted—signifying strategies which are all characterized by the way in which they respond to similarity and contiguity. Chapter 3 will attempt to show that condensation and displacement represent the habitual response of the primary process to similarity and contiguity, while paradigm and syntagm constitute the normal response of the secondary process. Metaphor and metonymy will be seen as occupying a mediate position between the other two sets, as strategies for responding to similarity and contiguity which are the result of an almost perfect equilibrium between the unconscious and the preconscious.

3

Similarity and Contiguity

The sets condensation and displacement, metaphor and metonymy, and paradigm and syntagm are central to any investigation of discourse since they orchestrate the interactions of signifiers and signifieds. These sets are so closely related as to have been frequently conflated; the connections between them have been remarked by Roman Jakobson in "The Metaphoric and Metonymic Poles," by Jacques Lacan in "Agency of the letter in the unconscious," and most recently by Christian Metz in *Le Signifiant imaginaire*. However, as Metz points out, the differences between the various pairs are as profound as their affinities, and discursive analysis has much to gain from a careful discrimination between them.

The basis for the frequent association of the terms "condensation," "metaphor," and "paradigm" would seem to be that all three derive from the perception of similarity. In much the same way, displacement, metonymy, and syntagm are all seen as involving the principle of contiguity. The differences are less easy to isolate, but Metz proposes that the desired clarification is to be found in the pages of *The Interpretation of Dreams*. In other words, he suggests that we should look for an explanation of metaphor and metonymy, and paradigm and syntagm in the same theoretical model which so brilliantly defines condensation and displacement. *Le Signifiant imaginaire* stresses that the three sets can only be distinguished from each other, and the discursive status of each one established, through an argument which takes into account the role of the subject in signification, and the opposition of the primary and secondary processes.

This chapter will follow the path indicated by Metz and approach the three pairs as the products of very different accommodations between the primary and secondary processes. We will deal first with those categories which Freud himself links up most fully with the primary process—condensation and displacement—and then with those which would seem to be most symptomatic of secondary logic—paradigm and syntagm. We will move on next to metaphor and metonymy, which enjoy an intermediate status, and conclude with a discussion of the imbrications of all three sets in discourse.

The discussion which follows does not conform at all points with Metz's elaboration of the sets condensation and displacement, paradigm and syntagm, and metaphor and metonymy. Like much recent film theory, it found its initial inspiration but not its final realization in the alliances forged by *Le Signifiant imaginaire* between psychoanalysis and a more classic semiotics.[1]

The major points of coincidence and divergence can be quickly sketched: Like Metz we will resist both the Lacanian conflation of the unconscious with the preconscious,[2] and the contrary tendency (represented by the French art theoretician Jean-François Lyotard) to pit the unconscious against the preconscious in ways which admit of no communication between them.[3] In other words, we will maintain the semiotic integrity of those two psychic regimes while at the same time indicating their constant interaction. This chapter will propose, with *Le Signifiant imaginaire,* that the primary process cannot be studied in isolation from the secondary process, and that as a pure state it does not even exist.[4] However, it will insist more firmly than *Le Signifiant imaginaire* upon the differences between the sets condensation and displacement, paradigm and syntagm, and metaphor and metonymy, leaving to one side the mixed categories suggested by that book.[5] Finally, the Freudian model will enjoy an ever more central place in the discussion which follows than it does in *Le Signifiant imaginaire.*

A) CONDENSATION AND DISPLACEMENT

As we noted in Chapter 2, the primary process responds both to similarity and contiguity through the assertion of complete identity; it denies, that is, that any differences separate similar elements, or that any distance divides contiguous ones. Freud tells us that condensation and displacement provide the agencies whereby the primary process habitually reacts to the perception of either affinities or adjacencies when an unconscious impulse has been blocked. Displacement involves the transfer of psychic intensity from an unacceptable element to an acceptable one, while condensation effects the formation of a new signifier from a cluster of previous signifying materials (thus a dream image combines the face of one person, the dress of another, the name of a third, and the voice of a fourth). In other words, the first of these agencies neutralizes the differences between two similar or contiguous things by asserting their emotional equivalence, while the second achieves the same thing by insisting on their absolute coincidence.

Parapraxes or slips of the tongue, neuroses, hysterical symptoms, and even jokes are all products of condensation and displacement. For instance, the *bon mot* repeated by Freud in *Wit and Its Relation to the Unconscious* (1905)—"He treated me most famillionairely"—is the result of a condensation of the words "familarly" and "millionaire."[6] Similarly, the bathing rituals of a neurotic derive their affective value from a displacement, and must be read as the symptom of an unconscious desire. However, because dreams are Freud's own preferred discursive formation, and because they are the products of a very rich and intricate series of condensations and displacements, responding to an equally rich and intricate network of similarities and contiguities, they will constitute our chief example. We will begin by distinguishing between their two levels.

Freud divides dreams into their manifest and latent content. The former of these consists of everything that can be remembered about a dream after waking, and the latter, the dream-thoughts which were the occasion for the dream as well as the infantile wishes which were its motivating force. A dream thus implies two sets of analogical and contiguous relationships: those between the manifest level and the dream-thoughts, and those between the dream-thoughts—including the suppressed or neglected wishes they often contain—and the much more recessed desires of the unconscious. Consequently the representational value of each manifest element—i.e., its relationships of similarity and contiguity to repressed materials and to the dream-thoughts—must be established with the greatest care. A given detail may signify an infantile desire, a recent suppressed wish, or both, and it may find its inspiration from some part of the dream-thoughts which is seemingly unrelated to either.

The acceptable materials which comprise the content of the dream thus have multiple points of contact (i.e. relationships of similarity and contiguity) with the dream-thoughts; every manifest detail connects up with a number of latent ones, and every latent element which finds expression in the dream does so several times over. In other words, the relationship between the manifest and latent content is *overdetermined*. Freud comments on this phenomenon in connection with the dream of the botanical monograph, to which we have already had occasion to refer:

> . . . the elements "botanical" and "monograph" found their way into the content of the dream because they possessed copious contacts with the majority of the dream-thoughts, because, that is to say, they constituted "nodal points" upon which a great number of the dream-thoughts converged, and because they had several meanings in connection with the interpretation of the dream. [SE IV. 283]

Each manifest signifier refers to a group of latent signifieds; indeed, like the botanical monograph, the manifest signifier may itself be a composite of features drawn from various signifieds. And no latent signified is obliged to rely exclusively on one manifest signifier—rather, its message is dispersed among the group of signifiers which make up the manifest content, and as a result *it will get through:*

> . . . a dream is not constructed by each individual dream-thought, or group of dream-thoughts, finding (in abbreviated

form) separate representation in the content of the dream—in the kind of way in which an electorate chooses parliamentary representatives; a dream is constructed, rather, by the whole mass of dream-thoughts being submitted to a sort of manipulative process in which those elements which have the most numerous and strongest supports acquire the right of entry into the dream content—in a manner analogous to election by *scrutin de liste*. [IV. 284]

The transfer of elements from the dream-thoughts to the manifest content of the dream is achieved through the activities of condensation and displacement. The first of these activities is the agency of extraordinary economies; under its influence the part stands for the whole, a single figure represents a diverse group, and geographically remote locations converge in a composite image. Condensation joins together in an abbreviated and highly compressed form selected elements from the dream-thoughts, and more remote memories with which they have some feature in common. It treats affinity as the basis for an absolute identification.

The accompanying process of displacement makes possible the fulfillment of a repressed desire through a series of surrogate images, since it transfers to the latter the affect which properly belongs to the former. In other words, it obliges elements from the dream-thoughts to stand in for an unconscious wish, investing them with an importance which far exceeds them. Because displacement always involves elements from the dream-thoughts which are regarded as being of little consequence by the preconscious, it is responsible for the fact that the dream is "differently centered" than is the signifying network from which it derives.

Freud's dream about Irma offers striking examples of both condensation and displacement, dramatizing the obliviousness of the dream-work to the differences upon which the preconscious insists:

A large hall—numerous guests, whom we were receiving.— Among them was Irma. I at once took her on one side, as though to answer her letter and to reproach her for not having accepted my "solution" yet. I said to her: "If you still get pains, it's really only your fault." She replied: "If you only knew what pains I've got now in my throat and stomach and abdomen—it's choking me"—I was alarmed and looked at her. She looked pale and puffy. I thought to myself that after all I must be missing some organic trouble. I took her to the window and looked down her throat, and she showed signs of recalcitrance, like women with artificial dentures. I thought to myself that there was really no need for her to do that.—She then opened her mouth properly and on the right I found a big white patch; at another place I saw extensive whitish grey scabs upon some remarkable curly structures which were evidently modelled on the turbinal bones of the nose.—I at once called in Dr. M., and he repeated the examination and confirmed it. . . . Dr. M. looked quite different from usual; he was very pale, he walked with a limp and his chin was clean-shaven. . . . My friend Otto was now standing beside her as well, and my friend Leopold was percussing her through her bodice and saying: "She has a dull area low down on the left." He also indicated that a portion of the skin on the left shoulder was infiltrated. (I noticed this, just as he did, in spite of her dress.) . . . M. said: "There's no doubt it's an infection, but no matter; dysentery will supervene and the toxin will be eliminated." . . . We were directly aware, too, of the origin of the infection. Not long before, when she was feeling unwell, my friend Otto had given her an injection of a preparation of propyl, propyls . . . propionic acid . . . trimethylamin (and I saw before me the formula for this printed in heavy type). . . . Injections of that sort ought not to be made so thought-lessly. . . . And probably the syringe had not been clean." [IV. 107]

The night before this dream, Freud had written out the case history of Irma, a patient whom he was treating for hysteria, but in whom certain somatic symptoms persisted. Earlier that day he had visited a colleague and old friend, with whom he had discussed Irma. That friend, Otto, had seemed to disapprove of his treatment. Freud planned to send the case history to Dr. M., whom he believed would support the diagnosis of hysteria.

In Freud's analysis of the dream we learn that the figure who there carries the name of Irma is in fact the product of a complex condensation. She has the bad teeth of an otherwise attractive governess Freud had recently examined; the recalcitrance of a woman Freud wanted to treat for hysteria, but who had declined to put herself into his hands; and the puffiness of yet another potential patient, more intelligent and therefore more desirable than Irma. The white patch on the throat of the dream patient links her with Freud's eldest daughter, Mathilde, who had suffered from a serious illness several years before the dream, as well as a patient of the same name who died as a consequence of his misdiagnosis. The fantasmatic Irma even incorporates features of Freud himself—the scabs on her throat resemble the nasal swellings from which he was suffering at the time, and the skin infection on her shoulder recalls the rheumatism which afflicted him at night. Finally, her name connects her with the actual Irma. Condensation here provides the means whereby at least seven figures are fused into a single representation, and Freud suggests that others may well be included in the composite sketch.

The word "trimethylamin" is the site of the most important displacement in the dream of Irma's injection. Although it appears there in bold letters, it occupies an obscure corner of the dream-thoughts—so obscure that Freud was able to uncover it only through the dream's etymological hesitancy ("a preparation of propyl, propyls, propionic acid . . . trimethylamin"). The evening before the dream, Freud's wife had opened a bottle of liqueur given to them by Otto, which emitted a disagreeable odor of fusel oil (amyl), and which apparently triggered a chain of chemical associations in which trimethylamin somehow figured. Years before Fleiss had suggested that this chemical was one of the products of sexual metabolism, making it an ideal shorthand inscription not only of all of Freud's major discoveries, including those involving hysteria, but of the unconscious desires behind those discoveries. The dream-work consequently invested it with the cumulative affect of those discoveries and desires, making it the pivotal point in the dream.

Condensation and displacement proceed along the paths of similarity and contiguity which link the dream-thoughts to each other and to certain repressed materials. Some of these relationships are sensory, others are linguistic, temporal, and logical (i.e. have been established by the preconscious). The primary process exploits all of them indiscriminately. I will attempt to demonstrate this part of the dream-work by charting the network of similarities and contiguities in the thoughts behind the dream of the botanical monograph.

Several days prior to this dream, Freud came across a *Festschrift* in which Koller was named as one of the discoverers of the anesthetic properties of cocaine. The volume contained no reference to Freud, who had years earlier introduced Koller to cocaine through his dissertation on the coca-plant. Shortly after Freud wrote the dissertation, he and Koller had assisted Konigstein when the latter operated on Freud's father for glaucoma, one of the diseases whose cure was facilitated by cocaine. During the operation, Koller commented on the fact that it had brought together the three people responsible for the discovery of cocaine. The day before the dream, Freud fantasized that if he were ever to suffer from glaucoma himself, he would travel to Berlin and stay with Fleiss while undergoing the necessary operation at the hands of an unknown doctor. When that doctor remarked on the virtues of cocaine, Freud would think, but not say, that he himself was partly responsible for its discovery.

The day preceding the dream Freud also encountered Professor Gartner, one of the other contributors to the *Festschrift*. He complimented Gartner's wife on her "blooming" appearance, and eventually the conversation turned to the topic of Flora, one of Freud's patients. The same day, Freud received a letter from Fleiss which contained these sentences: "I am very much occupied with your dreambook. I see it lying finished before me and I see myself turning over its pages." He had also passed a bookstore with a monograph titled *The Genus Cyclamen* in the window, and remembered that cyclamens were his wife's favorite flower. It occurred to him that he should give her flowers more often. Finally, Freud had a conversation with Konigstein in which the latter reprimanded him for spending so much time and money on his hobbies, which included the acquisition of monographs.

The analysis of the dream produced a series of associated memories which should be inserted here: 1) As a high school student, Freud had helped his friends clean bookworms out of a herbarium. 2) He had never been a good botany student. 3) As a medical student he had become obsessed with collecting monographs, attracted to them because of their colored plates.

He ran up a large debt, for which his father rebuked him. 4) As small children, Freud and his sister enthusiastically tore apart a book of colored plates given to them by their father (this was his most vivid childhood memory, and it would seem to have provided a screen for a repressed masturbatory impulse).

As the following diagram will show, the dream-thoughts are linked to each other and to the memories which they evoked by an astonishing number of interconnections. (I have listed the elements in the manifest content of the dream on the left-hand side; recent events and dream-thoughts in the middle column; and related unrepressed memories on the right-hand side.)

Manifest Content	Recent Events and Dream-Thoughts	Related Unrepressed Memories
monograph	*Festschrift* letter from Fleiss	dissertation on coca-plant
	conversation with Konigstein	medical school debts
	book in window	
certain plant	Gartner	father's operation
	"blooming"	
	Flora	dissertation on coca-plant
	glaucoma day-dream	poorly-learned botany lessons
	The Genus Cyclamen	
folded colored plate		book with colored plates
lay before me	letter from Fleiss	
dried specimen from herbarium	Gartner	poorly learned botany lessons
	"blooming"	
	Flora	inspection of herbarium
	glaucoma day-dream	
	The Genus Cyclamen	dissertation on coca-plant

One additional detail which does not lend itself to this sche-
matization remains to be mentioned. The thought that cyclamens were his wife's favorite flower prompted Freud to recall
that artichokes were his own favorite, and that in order to eat
them it is necessary to pull them apart piece by piece (like the
book of colored plates). This train of thought mediates between
the screen memory which conceals the real inspiration for the
dream, and the botanical references in the events of the dream
day.

The points of greatest intensity in the dream-thoughts all
have to do with the lack of respect shown Freud by his col-
leagues—Konigstein's reprimand, the encounter with Gartner,
which reminds Freud of the *Festschrift,* and the glaucoma day-
dream all suggest that he has not received the recognition he
deserves. The dream-thoughts not only contain the suppressed
wish for professional acknowledgment, but the means whereby
that wish can be gratified: the letter from Fleiss arouses the
hope that once the book on dreams is published, Freud's col-
leagues will be obliged to recognize his scientific contribution.

The dream weaves the appropriate compensatory narrative,
a narrative in which Freud finds himself proudly looking
through a recently published and handsomely put together book
authored by himself. The topic of the book is no longer recognizable, having nothing to do either with cocaine or the
interpretation of dreams. Instead, it is devoted to a subject which
Freud never found particularly interesting—botany. The affect
which more properly attaches itself to professional recognition
has been displaced onto the study of flora and fauna. This shift
in emphasis away from those elements of the dream-thoughts
that are most central to those that are most peripheral (i.e. from
those in which there has been the most psychic investment to
those in which there has been the least) is one of the critical
projects of displacement. By means of this shift an indifferent
element in the dream-thoughts comes to replace one whose
presence in the signifying formation of the dream would be
much likelier to attract the attention of the censoring mechanism.

A second displacement necessarily takes place during the

dream-work: the transfer of psychic intensity from the repressed desire whose fulfillment constitutes the dream's most
rudimentary premise to the elements which represent it in the
manifest dream. Freud proves unusually reticent about the nature of that desire in the botanical monograph dream, but he
does indicate the memory which screens it. He thus makes it
possible for us to map the path of this displacement in much
the same way as that which transforms the psychic values of the
dream-thoughts.

In both cases displacement occurs along what Freud calls
"associative links." It would seem of particular importance to
the present discussion to determine whether those links are
predicated on contiguity or similarity, since the absolute symmetry of the terms "displacement," "metonymy," and "syntagm" can only be maintained in the event that all three always
observe the principle of contiguity.

Not only the dream of the botanical monograph but the
trimethylamin example would seem to call that symmetry into
question, since in each instance displacement occurs along lines
of similarity as well as contiguity. In the first case there is a
transfer of psychic value from one term to another along a signifying chain which consists of words which are closely related
to each other formally or semantically; here displacement takes
place among elements which are both similar and contiguous.
In the second instance displacement is facilitated by a dense
network of similarities (verbal, sensory, etc.), both between the
dream-thoughts and the memories they evoke, and among the
dream-thoughts themselves. The items in the middle column
of the diagram may enjoy a relationship of temporal contiguity
to each other in that they all occurred or were thought during
a circumscribed period of time (approximately 14 hours), but
their relationship with the items in the right-hand column does
not have the same rationale. The relationships of similarity
among the elements of the two groups are much more striking,
and provide most of the bases for linking them together. A
point which Freud makes about the manifest content of dreams
further confuses the issue: he observes that within that context
contiguity often indicates relationships of similarity (V. 661).

The dream-work would seem much more preoccupied with relationships of similarity than with any other. Freud writes that

> One and one only of these logical relations is very highly favoured by the mechanism of dream-formation; namely, the relation of similarity, consonance or approximation—the relation of "just as." This relation, unlike any other, is capable of being represented in dreams in a variety of ways. Parallels or instances of "just as" inherent in the material of the dream-thoughts constitute the first foundations for the construction of a dream; and no inconsiderable part of the dream-work consists in creating fresh parallels where those which are already present cannot find their way into the dream owing to the censorship imposed by resistance. The representation of the relation of similarity is assisted by the tendency of the dream-work towards condensation. [IV. 320]

The dream-work is not interested in indicating or even maintaining relationships between different elements. It seeks to collapse distinctions—to achieve an absolute identification between repressed materials and those which substitute for them in the dream, as well as between the various dream-thoughts. A large number of signifying segments from the preceding day must be forged together, and this must be managed in a way that permits the additional imbrication of much earlier memories and desires. Displacement is consequently much likelier to follow lines of similarity than those of contiguity—to move from one signifying segment to another via points of coincidence (this procedure is neatly illustrated by the grouping: Gartner, blooming, Flora, coca-plant, cocaine, botany, cyclamen).

The principle of contiguity may play an important role initially, in that displacement is limited to materials which enjoy a certain proximity. However, the dream-work seems to be intent on taking things out of one context (i.e. out of the linguistic, relational, and temporal organization of the preconscious) and putting them into an altogether different one (i.e. a context in which the criterion of representability figures centrally, and in which difference—relational, temporal—no longer obtains). It breaks down syntagmatic clusters and chronological divisions. Displacement in dreams would thus seem to occur from one signifying chain to another, and not along individual chains in the majority of cases.

Freud describes the activity of the dream-work upon the dream-thoughts in terms which suggest the almost instantaneous loss of original context to which each train of thought is subjected:

> The dream-thoughts . . . reveal themselves as a psychical complex of the most intricate possible structure. Its portions stand in the most manifold logical relations to one another: they represent foreground and background, conditions, digressions and illustrations, chains of evidence and counter arguments. Each train of thought is almost invariably accompanied by its contradictory counterpart. This material lacks none of the characteristics that are familiar to us from our waking thought. If now all of this is to be turned into a dream, the psychical material will be submitted to a pressure which will condense it greatly, to an internal fragmentation and displacement which will, as it were, create new surfaces, and to a selective operation in favor of those portions of it which are the most appropriate for the construction of situations. . . . In the course of this transformation . . . the logical links which have hitherto held the psychical material together are lost. It is only, as it were, the substantive content of the dream-thoughts that the dream work takes over and manipulates. [V. 660]

The emphasis which this passage places on the "substantive content" of the dream-thoughts once again suggests that relationships of similarity are more likely to determine the path of displacements, at least in dreams, than are those of contiguity. Indeed, the latter are probably as completely disrupted during the compression and fragmentation to which the dream-thoughts are subjected as are the logical and causal links which bind those thoughts together.

Although it is most characteristic for condensation to proceed along lines of similarity, it is also possible for that operation to exploit relationships of contiguity. A parapraxis, for instance, often merges two words which the speaker intended to pronounce one after the other. Condensation is thus no more symmetrical with metaphor and paradigm than is displacement with metonymy and syntagm. Like displacement, condensation is an expression of the primary impulse to abolish difference and assert unity, and the distinction between similarity and contiguity would appear to be as frequently disregarded as any other. If both operations show a preference for relationships of similarity, that is presumably because similarity persists even after contiguity has been interrupted, and because it lends itself more to what Freud calls "considerations of representability."

(An extension of this lack of discrimination is that the dream-work does not care whether the similarities between two things are minimal or manifold; it will insist as readily upon the absolute identity of opposites, which generally have only one point of coincidence, as upon that of closely allied terms. Freud writes that

> The way in which dreams treat the category of contraries . . . is highly remarkable. It is simply disregarded. "No" seems not to exist so far as dreams are concerned. They show a particular preference for combining contraries into a unity or for representing them as one and the same thing. Dreams feel themselves at liberty, moreover, to represent any element by its wishful contrary. . . . [IV. 318]

Binary opposition constitutes an essential structuring device for the secondary process. Its elimination is one of the most important means available to the primary process for combating preconscious logic.)

Condensation can function in a variety of ways. It can portray a person, place, or thing, while giving it another's name; create a representation out of features drawn from a group of people, places, or objects; project a person, place, or object into a context which "belongs" to another; or fabricate a person, place, or object which bears a "family resemblance" to those it represents.

The botanical monograph in Freud's dream bears a family

resemblance to the *Festschrift*, the dissertation on the coca-plant, the book on which he was at the time working (*The Interpretation of Dreams*), the monograph in the window, and the book of colored plates. It incorporates features both from the study of the genus Cyclamen and from the book of colored plates. Moreover, the dream features it in a situation in which Freud would have liked to find *The Interpretation of Dreams*. However, the botanical monograph addresses a topic of so little interest to Freud, that despite its manifold similarities to all of the other volumes, it provides an admirable "cover" for them.

The manifest content of a dream, most exemplary of primary formations, connects up with its latent content on the basis of similarity and contiguity; its signifiers, that is, either resemble or in some way adjoin its signifieds. The signifying relations established by the operations of condensation and displacement are thus highly motivated, unlike those generated by the secondary process.

However, the dream strives to conceal this motivation, and to insist upon the autonomy and authenticity of its manifest content. It attempts to foster in the dreamer the belief that its sounds and images have a life of their own—to collapse the distinctions between signifiers and signifieds, as well as those between sleeping and waking life. Dreams project transparent narratives (narratives which efface all signs of their fictional status). Those self-conscious exceptions, which contain the observation that "this is only a dream," have failed to disguise their latent content sufficiently for the satisfaction of the preconscious, and can only pacify that agency by repudiating any claim to reality.

Dream analysis involves the restoration of the many differences abolished by the primary process, from those that separate similar and contiguous elments within the dream thoughts, to those that distinguish the manifest from the latent level. It progresses, in other words, by reasserting secondary logic—by opposing as fully as possible to the operations of condensation and displacement those of the paradigm and the syntagm. We will turn now to those very contrary strategies for articulating similarity and contiguity.

B) PARADIGM AND SYNTAGM

The secondary process differs radically from the primary; its aims, as well as its means, could not be more divergent. The primary process is entirely under the sway of the pleasure principle, and thus seeks the shortest route to gratification. It avoids all memories with painful affect attached to them and is thus incapable of tracing the connecting paths between memories. Indeed, relational logic is altogether alien to the primary process; it concerns itself exclusively with the affective value of certain highly privileged memories—a value which it will, however, quickly transfer to other similar or contiguous memories in the event of secondary interference. Since affect is ultimately the primary process's only real concern, it disregards those features that distinguish similar or contiguous memories from each other.

The secondary process, on the contrary, circumvents the pleasure principle by radically diminishing the affective value of the various memories at its disposal. It does not abandon the prospect of pleasure, but it is capable of deferring that prospect almost indefinitely while searching out the most reliable route to it. The secondary process concerns itself less with any individual memory trace than with the relationships which connect one with all of the others, and it at every point maintains the distinctions between even similar and contiguous traces. The secondary process manages all of these things through language.

Freud tells us that preconscious thought or secondary signification is made possible by binding word-presentations or linguistic signifiers to the original memories or thing-presentations. We recall his assertion that "in order to make more delicately adjusted performances possible, it . . . became necessary to make the course of ideas less dependent upon the presence or absence of unpleasure," and that this important task is effected "by linking the preconscious processes with the mnemic system of indications of speech" (V. 574). As a result of this linkage, the original memory traces undergo a radical transformation: they lose sensory and affective intensity, but they gain meaning.

It is important to stress that the memories or thing-presentations become linguistic signifieds only after the binding operation has been completed. The conceptual network does not pre-exist and determine the linguistic one, but comes into existence along with and in relation to it. The memory traces take on significance only after they have been organized.

Saussure indicates that the principle of linguistic organization, both at the level of the signifier and at that of the signified, is difference ("In language, as in any semiological system, whatever distinguishes one sign from the other constitutes it. Difference makes character just as it makes value and the unity in it.").[7]

A sign's value is determined in part by the ways in which it deviates from the other members of the abstract groups to which it belongs—i.e. by its place within the system. Its significance is not only mediated, but established, by that value. Thus the linguistic unit "black" derives value and consequently significance from those qualities which distinguish it from "white," "grey," "blue," "green," etc. It would assume a new value if some of the other units were eliminated, or if others were added; in the first instance its semantic field would be extended, and in the second it would be circumscribed. Outside of signifying systems like language or painting, the concept "black" does not exist. In the realm beyond signification we have what Peirce would call an "experience" of that color, but no knowledge.

Not only does the concept "black" not exist apart from the various signifying systems within which it figures, but it does not exist outside of discourse. There is no such thing as abstract signification, or signification in the abstract. Since signifying elements derive a large part of their value from those qualities that distinguish them from their neighbors, meaning emerges only through the activation of *langue* in *parole,* the system in discourse. As Saussure points out, "a term acquires its value only because it stands in opposition to everything that precedes or follows it, or to both" (123).

("Discourse" has here a very wide application, encompassing not only speech, writing, and artistic activities of all sorts, but any articulation, even one which takes the form of an ar-

chitectural structure or a road map. It does not imply any conscious intention, although it does require both a sender and a
receiver. The sender may be as unlocalized as culture, or as
specific as a poet. However, even in the latter instance it would
be a mistake to attribute too much autonomy to the speaker,
who, as we noted in Chapter 1, is always simultaneously spoken
elsewhere.)

Discourse involves the operations of selection and combination. Certain signifying elements must be chosen rather than
others, and they must be linked together in some manner. A
user of language, for instance, must first select a group of words
from the manifold resources of the system, and then cluster
them together to create a sentence. As Saussure was the first to
observe, each word which is selected enjoys a relationship of
similarity with numerous other words which are associated with
it in some way, and a relationship of contiguity with those which
surround it discursively. The first of these sets is generally called
a "paradigm," and is realized only at the level of the system;
while the second goes under the name of "syntagm," and is
realized only at the level of discourse. This is another way of
saying that paradigmatic relationships determine a signifying
element's systemic value, while syntagmatic relationships determine the same element's discursive value.

There are many bases for a paradigmatic relationship. Such
a relationship can be established between signifiers or signifieds, and it can be predicated on extreme or only slight resemblance. Saussure gives some idea of the range of possible paradigmatic relationships:

> . . . through its grasp of the nature of the relations that bind
> the terms together, the mind creates as many associative series
> as there are diverse relations. For instance, in *enseignement*
> "teaching," *enseigner* "teach," *enseignons* "(we) teach," etc., one
> element, the radical, is common to every term; the same word
> may occur in a different series formed around another com-
> mon element, the suffix . . . or the association may spring
> from the analogy of the concepts signified (*enseignement, in-
> struction, apprentissage, éducation,* etc.); or again, simply from the
> similarity of the sound-images (e.g. *enseignement* and *justement*
> . . . [125–26]

In short, words with the same prefix, words with the same suffix, and synonyms all constitute paradigmatically related sets. So does another category, which would seem to require additional clarification: antonyms.

Any term which helps to define the value of another within the same system is paradigmatically related to it. In order for one term to be of such assistance to another, it must have points of divergence as well as points of coincidence. Some paradigmatic sets are characterized by the fact that they overlap at more points than they differ, and others—whose relationship is generally described as binary opposition—by the fact that they differ at more points than they overlap. But in each instance there is an implied comparison, and an implied distinction. An antonym is a linguistic example of binary opposition. It connects up with the term which it helps to define only at one point, otherwise standing in marked contrast to it.

Syntagmatic relationships, unlike paradigmatic ones, are always based on the same principle: formal contiguity. A syntagmatic cluster consists of elements which are discursively adjacent, elements which as Saussure puts it are "chained together." A sentence offers the best linguistic example of such a cluster, and it helps us to understand that each part connects up not only with the other parts, but with the whole (*Course in General Linguistics* emphasizes that "The whole has value only through its parts, and the parts have value by virtue of their place in the whole" (128)). A word depends for its value, and hence its significance, both on its immediate neighbors and on its location within the linear organization of the sentence in which it appears. In the same way, the sentence can only be conceived in relation to its parts. To shift a verb or noun from one clause of a sentence to another would be to alter drastically not only the status of the verb or noun but the sentence itself.

Syntagmatic relationships do more than establish contiguity between two or more terms; they also maintain distance between the same terms. That distance is essential to the operations of meaning, because without it there would be no signifying chain. Instead, a mere jumble of sounds would emerge from a speaker's mouth, or a single indecipherable photographic image from the developing process of a strip of film.

Saussure's model applies to all predominantly secondary discourses; it accounts for relationships of similarity and contiguity in film, literature, music, painting, photography, and architecture as well as language. For instance, "shot" and "reverse shot" are paradigmatically connected in the system of cinematic photography; "dissolve," "lap dissolve," "fade," and "iris in" are all paradigmatically related in the system of cinematic editing; and abab bcbc cdcd ee, abba abba cdcd ee, and abba abba cde cde comprise a paradigm within the system of poetic rhyme. The first of these examples is based on binary opposition (in other words, a reverse shot purports to show the field occupied by the camera in the preceding shot, and is thus the cinematic equivalent of an antonym). The second groups together assorted ways of marking the end of a shot, while the third cites some of the rhyme schemes which help to organize the sonnet form. All three thus derive their coherence from a quite striking similarity.

The term "syntagmatic" also proves adaptable to other discourses beside the linguistic. The successive sounds and images in a cinematic sequence enjoy syntagmatic relationships with each other; the spatial disposition of objects in a painting or photograph establishes a syntagmatic connection between them; and the unfolding of events in a novel depends upon numerous syntagmatic clusters—sentences, paragraphs, chapters, etc.

Because the distances between secondary elements are so carefully preserved through the elaboration of paradigmatic and syntagmatic relationships, no element can ever be completely equated with any other. And since there are no privileged terms, only an infinite play of differences, no element can ever be said to represent (i.e. to be subservient to) another, either at the paradigmatic or syntagmatic level. The choice of one term does not imply the repression or censorship of those which are paradigmatically connected to it; on the contrary, since their association with the chosen term defines it, they are all present in their absence, which is to say present through their *differences*. And the syntagmatic operation requires so high a degree of differentiation that a device like alliteration or assonance, which establishes a relationship of similarity between contiguous terms, can disrupt the forward movement of a signifying chain.

The secondary process insists as emphatically on the differences between the signifier and the signified as it does between various signifiers, or various signifieds. Whereas the primary process blurs the distinction between the signifier and signified, treats the former as if it were the latter, the secondary system maintains a discontinuity between those two levels. Saussure il-illustrates that discontinuity with an algebraic line

$$\left(\frac{\text{signifier}}{\text{signified}}\right).$$

This line is not, as in the case of dreams, a bar of repression; it is simply the demarcation of greatest difference (material/conceptual) in a network of differences.

It would seem important to stress once again that all of the discourses with which this book is concerned are the result of "facilitations" between the primary and secondary processes, and not the exclusive domain of one or the other. We have already discussed this point in relation to the production of dreams, but a similar clarification should be made in relation to films and literature.

In an essay entitled "The Apparatus," Jean-Louis Baudry establishes numerous points of similarity not only between dreams and films but between the psychic topography outlined in *The Interpretation of Dreams* and the cinematic apparatus. He notes that films share with dreams a "capacity for figuration, translation of thoughts into images, reality extended to representations"—that both provide the subject with an experience that is "more than real."[8] In other words, Baudry attributes to films the same sensory and affective intensity which characterizes dreams, suggesting the profound influence of the primary process in their construction. He connects up the effect which films have upon the viewing subject—the effect of an experience which is "more than real"—with the fact that like dreams they stage a return to an earlier psychic state, before the reign of the secondary process. Baudry even sees the cinematic apparatus as the response to a wish which can be traced back as far as Plato: "the wish to construct a simulation machine capable of offering the subject perceptions which are really representations mistaken for perceptions" (121).

At the same time it is obvious that we would not have films, any more than dreams, without the intervention of the secondary process. The cinematic text relies upon a complex syntagmatic organization, an organization which is implicit not only in the relationship between successive shots or images, but within individual images, in the guise of composition, and at the level of the narrative. Paradigmatic relationships play as central a role in the production of cinematic meaning. An image of darkness, for instance, gains its value from its implied opposition to an image of brightness; a low-angle shot to a high-angle shot; and a medium shot to a close-up. Similarly, a tracking shot derives its identity from those qualities which distinguish it from a pan or a zoom, just as one editing strategy is defined by all the others. The secondary process makes its influence felt in scores of other ways, ranging from the linguistic domination of the sound track to the cultural norms and prohibitions which structure the narrative.

Whereas the signifiers which comprise the visual track of a cinematic text would seem at first glance to reflect the dominance of the primary process, those which constitute a literary text have more evident connections to the secondary process. Literature depends upon a medium which has been elaborated for the suppression of affect and the articulation of difference—i.e. language. In using that medium, a poem or novel is obliged to adhere at least to some degree to its paradigmatic and syntagmatic rules. Some literary texts deliberately break those rules (e.g. *Finnegans Wake,* the poetry of e e cummings), but that violation has the paradoxical effect of evoking the rules themselves. More often the rules are carefully observed. However, these syntagmatic and paradigmatic relationships provide the support for metonymic and metaphoric ones, and almost always the play of linguistic difference succumbs to the dynamic of desire; certain terms are privileged over others and signifying positions become "fixed." Besides, as we observed above, literature is a "second-order language," and in it the operations of connotation are as critical as those of denotation. As Barthes points out, connotation introduces into texts what might be called a "cultural unconscious," provides one of the chief vehicles for ideological meaning. Literary texts, like cinematic ones, are the products of diverse interactions between the primary and secondary processes and are consequently rich in metaphoric and metonymic configurations.

C) METAPHOR AND METONYMY

Whereas condensation and displacement treat similarity and contiguity as the basis for absolute identification, and paradigm and syntagm establish an irreducible difference among similar and contiguous elements, metaphor and metonymy respond to similarity and contiguity as the basis for the *temporary replacement* of one signifying element by another. In other words, metaphor and metonymy mediate between the extremes represented by the other two sets; they assert neither the complete identity nor the irreducible difference of similar and contiguous terms, but rather what Proust would call their "multiform unity." Within metaphor and metonymy the primary and secondary processes find a kind of equilibrium, one which permits profound affinities and adjacencies to be discovered without differences being lost.

The second volume of *Remembrance of Things Past*, which is virtually a treatise on metaphor and metonymy, uses the paintings of Elstir to dramatize the partial coalescence of diverse elements which each is capable of effecting:

> Sometimes in my window in the hotel at Balbec . . . I had been led by some effect of sunlight to mistake what was only a darker stretch of sea for a distant coastline, or to gaze at a belt of liquid azure without knowing whether it belonged to sea or sky. But presently my reason would re-establish between the elements that distinction which in my first impression I had overlooked. In the same way I used, in Paris, in my bedroom, to hear a dispute, almost a riot, in the street below, until I had referred back to its cause—a carriage for instance that was rattling towards me—this noise, from which I now eliminated the shrill and discordant vociferations which my ear had really heard but which my reason knew that wheels did not produce. But the rare moments in which we see nature as she is, with poetic vision, it was from those that Elstir's work was taken. One of his metaphors that occurred most commonly in the

seascapes which he had round him was precisely that which, comparing land with sea, suppressed every line of demarcation between them. It was this comparison, tacitly and untiringly repeated on a single canvas, which gave it that multiform and powerful unity, the cause . . . of the enthusiasm which Elstir's work aroused in certain collectors.[9]

This passage brilliantly evokes the conflicting impulses of the primary and secondary processes which metaphor and metonymy manage briefly to harmonize. The primary process manifests itself here in Marcel's confusion of land with sea, and sea with sky, as well as his mistake of the sound of carriage wheels for that of a street brawl. (It is of course on the basis of contiguity that the first two sets are conflated, and of similarity that the third one suffers an analogous fate.) The secondary process asserts itself in the form of "reason," insisting on the rearticulation of those features which distinguish similar and contiguous elements from each other. However, Elstir's paintings are organized around visual metaphors and metonymies which blur the boundaries between sea and land without reducing them to a single term. The sea makes the viewer think of the land, and the land the sea. In these metaphors and metonymies the primary and secondary processes reach an ideal accommodation. Metaphor and metonymy can thus be seen as signifying formations which facilitate a movement back and forth—a "transversality"—not only between the two elements which they conjoin, but between the primary and secondary processes, the unconscious and the preconscious.

Unlike condensation and displacement, or paradigm and syntagm, the categories of metaphor and metonymy have a long and illustrious heritage. They are of course most familiar as verbal tropes. Nevertheless, the definitions which are rehearsed and the examples which are cited from Aristotle through the eighteenth century indicate that language is not fundamental to either metaphor or metonymy, which are vehicles for expressing nonlinguistic relationships. Metaphor, as this excerpt from the *Poetics* makes abundantly clear, exploits relationships of similarity between things, not words:

. . . a cup stands in the same relationship to Dionysus as a shield to Ares, and one may therefore call the cup Dionysus's shield and the shield Ares's cup. Or again, old age is to life as evening is to day, and so one may call . . . old age the evening of life or the sunset of life. In some cases there is no name for some of the terms of the analogy, but the metaphor can be used just the same. For example, to scatter corn is called sowing, but there is no word for the sun's scattering of its flame; however, this stands in the same relationship to sunlight as sowing does to corn, and hence the expression, "sowing his god-created flame."[10]

In a parallel fashion, metonymy exploits relationships of contiguity between things, not words: between a thing and its attributes, its environment and its adjuncts. The first of the examples cited by Aristotle illustrates this trope as well as metaphor: Dionysus is metonymically related to his cup, and Ares to his shield. These objects could thus as effectively represent their owners as they could each other, despite the fact that in the first instance the association is based on proximity, and in the second on analogy. Since things are only available to us cognitively as concepts, metaphor is in essence the exploitation of conceptual similarity, and metonymy the exploitation of conceptual contiguity.

Both metaphor and metonymy are susceptible to a greater or lesser degree of secondarization. When these tropes come under the domination of the secondary process, the relationship between the terms which they compare or juxtapose is reciprocal. In other words, both concepts are present in the formulation; the formulation is mutually beneficial; and the grounds for their comparison or juxtaposition are evident.

When metaphor is subjected to the rationalizing operations of the secondary process, it takes the shape known as simile. *The Rime of the Ancient Mariner* provides a particularly striking example:

> And ice, mast-high, came floating by,
> As green as emerald. [53–54]

While "ice" is clearly a more privileged term in this equation than "emerald," neither is suppressed; this is a potential relationship of representation, but it has not been realized. The influence of the secondary process is apparent in the "as," which indicates, in a way that the primary process never does, the basis for a comparison between two distinct entities (i.e. greenness).

The opening of *French Connection I* supplies an analogous example of metonymy, one in which both terms are present, and the basis for the relationship between them established. Frog I is shown supervising the loading of a Continental automobile onto a ship at a French dock, and the adjacency of man to machine in this scene permits one subsequently to evoke the other.

Here both terms of the metonymic formulation would seem to be of equal importance; each derives value and significance from the initial relationship of contiguity, but neither subordinates the other. Thus while the car owes much of its fascination to its association with the dealer who is using it to transport drugs, its capture and deconstruction become obsessional preoccupations in the film, seemingly ends in themselves. Similarly, although the dealer's skill and intelligence are to some degree measured by the amount of time which elapses and the energy which is expended during the search of the car, his significance is not exhausted by his relationship with that object. Each recalls, but does not replace the other; the distance which separates them is as important as their initial juxtaposition.

When the figures of metaphor and metonymy come more under the influence of the primary than the secondary process, a definite hierarchy is established between their two terms. Paradoxically, the more privileged of the terms remains hidden; it falls to the position of the signified, while the other functions as its signifier or representative within the text. The "repression" of the privileged term indicates the incursion of desire into preconscious discourse, and the usurpation of difference by values which pass themselves off as positive (i.e. as self-sufficient). What is here described is the "classic" metaphoric situation, in which one term stands in for another which it in some way resembles, and the "classic" metonymic situation, in which one term stands in for another to which it is in some way contiguous. The principle of absence is thus central to the formulation.

Sometimes metaphor and metonymy are used by literary and cinematic texts to sustain the absence of a given term indefinitely (allegory, for instance, is often defined as an extended metaphor, one which never dissolves). On other occasions metaphor and metonymy are employed to create a dialectic of absence and presence; here the missing term always re-emerges after a time. The first stanza of William Butler Yeats's "The Circus Animals' Desertion," a poem which deals overtly with the relationship between concepts and their metaphoric elaboration, enacts precisely such a dialectic:

> I sought a theme and sought for it in vain,
> I sought it daily for six weeks or so,
> Maybe at last, being but a broken man,
> I must be satisfied with my heart, although
> Winter and summer till old age began
> My circus animals were all on show,
> Those stilted boys, that burnished chariot
> Lion and woman and the Lord knows what.

The privileged concept here is the poetic imagination and its vicissitudes, while the metaphoric one is the magic of the circus. The two concepts are never simultaneously manifest; rather, there is an oscillation, in which the presence of one militates against the presence of the other. However, whereas the circus spectacle represents poetic invention in the latter's absence, the reverse is not the case.

The privileging of one concept over another is the result of a psychic investment in it, an investment which can be extended to the terms which replace it in the metaphoric or metonymic construction. Thus in the stanza quoted above the metaphoric operation includes the displacement of affect from the failing of poetic invention to the collapse of the circus spectacle. That affect is of course transferred back again at the beginning of the next stanza ("What can I do but enumerate old themes?"), but in the process of these shifts it gains intensity. Freud notes that this kind of increase always occurs during displacement.

Raoul Walsh's *Pursued* provides an even more extreme example of metonymic substitution, one in which the privileged term remains absent for almost the duration of the narrative. Once again the substitution is accompanied by a psychic transfer. In that film a character played by Robert Mitchum suffers from hysterical amnesia about the early years of his life. His lapse of memory is triggered by the death of his father during a shootout with a sexual rival. The young boy hides during the fight in a kind of shelf below the trapdoor. All that he can see and hear is the movement of his father's spurs on the floor as he struggles with the other men. After those men leave, the boy lifts up the door and sees his father's corpse. He subsequently represses that memory, along with everything else pertaining to his family and childhood. Only the vision of the spurs, sharply hitting the floor, remains with him from that period of his life, and when he involuntarily recalls it he is always seized by intense fear.

The spurs are metonymically related to the father, and represent him in his protracted absence. They inspire both in his son and the viewer the desire for that missing figure, who dominates the film even though he does not appear in it until the very end, and then only briefly as the Mitchum character regains his childhood memories. This metonymic substitution involves the displacement of affect from the unconscious memory of the father's death to the conscious (but not voluntary) memory of his spurs, much like the shift of affect from the concept of poetic invention to that of the circus in the Yeats poem.[11]

The fact that the father dominates the film through his absence suggests that metaphor and metonymy can be used to increase the value of a given term by suppressing it. Desire, as Lacan is at pains to demonstrate, is created by absence—not only by the signifiers which "name" a missing signified, but by the other signifiers which replace those signifiers in the event of an additional metaphoric or metonymic elaboration.

It is evident from this short discussion of metaphor and metonymy that desire is somehow central to their operations and they to it. As we noted in Chapter 2, desire comes into existence only when the preconscious prevents a drive from cathecting with a particular mnemic trace—i.e. when it outlaws the expression and fulfillment of a certain impulse toward pleasure. At that moment, generally assumed to coincide with the Oedipus crisis, desire is born. This birth involves two things: the fixation of unconscious signification in relation to the mnemic trace whose access to consciousness has been denied, and the displacement of its affect onto a substitute which is acceptable to the censoring mechanism. In other words, it involves the repression of the prohibited and hence privileged term, and its replacement at the preconscious level by an uncensored term. What that replacement means is that the affect which belongs to the former is displaced onto the latter.

Displacement can only occur between two terms which are either similar or contiguous. Thus desire is in effect nothing more than a series of metaphors and metonymies, displacements away from an unconscious point of origin in which one term replaces another which it either resembles or adjoins, before being subjected to a similar fate.

When for some reason cathexis with the substitute is also blocked, fixation similar to that at the level of the unconscious results at the level of the preconscious. This fixation is normally not permanent, and yields in time to further displacement. However, while it lasts the element in question is treated as though desire originated with it.

Swann's attachment to Odette in the "Swann in Love" section of *Remembrance of Things Past* depicts these various stages in the preconscious course of desire with exemplary precision (it is, needless to say, impossible to exhume the original object around which his sense of lack organized itself). The fact that Odette's physical features are for Swann devoid of appeal clearly indicates that the desire of which she becomes the pivot originates elsewhere. It also dramatizes the distance between sexual gratification and desire. The middle section of *Swann's Way* renders equally transparent the metaphors and metonymies which constitute the history of desire, the displacement of affect away from one term onto another which either resembles or adjoins it, and which it thereafter represents.

We are told that Odette, the great love of Swann's life, leaves him "indifferent . . . [gives] him, indeed, a sort of physical repulsion; as one of those women of whom every man can name some, and each will name different examples, who are the converse of the type which our senses demand" (150). Yet having established the similarity between Odette's features and those of Zipporah in the Botticelli fresco of which he is so fond, he is eventually able to put Odette in the place of the beloved painting. In much the same way he effects an exchange between Odette and a little phrase of music of which he is passionately fond. This second event is facilitated by the fact that Swann has listened to the phrase of music so frequently in Odette's presence that it has become "a pledge, a token of his love" for her. Odette thus becomes a metaphoric signifier for the fresco, and a metonymic signifier for the musical phrase. By virtue of these signifying transactions she inherits their affective intensity. These signifying transactions are themselves facilitated by those which went before, and which comprise the sum total of Swann's amorous experiences:

> At this time of life a man has already been wounded more than once by the darts of love; it no longer evolves by itself, obeying its own incomprehensible and fatal laws, before his passive and astonished heart. We come to its aid; we falsify it by memory and by suggestion; recognizing one of its symptoms we recall and recreate the rest. Since we possess its hymn, engraved on our hearts in its entirety, there is no need of any woman to repeat the opening lines, potent with the admiration which her beauty inspires, for us to remember all that follows. And if she begin in the middle, where it sings of our existing, henceforward, for one another only, we are well enough attuned to that music to be able to take it up and follow our partner, without hesitation, at the first pause in her voice. [150]

In short, Swann is so familiar with the operations of desire as to be able to manipulate events on its behalf—to create ever new metaphoric and metonymic alliances.

However, until the moment that Odette's absence in the Verdurin house is felt as a lack, so that Swann begins at last actually to desire her, the relationship between her and the

Botticelli fresco is merely one of similarity; it has not yet become fully metaphoric. The phrase exists in an analogous position of conceptual contiguity to Odette, in whose presence Swann habitually listens to it, but she has not yet become a metonymic signifier for it.

Vinteuil's sonata enjoys a critical position in Swann's psychic existence. Prior to hearing it for the first time, Swann had suffered a crisis of belief in the authenticity of desirable objects. The little phrase rekindles that belief, which is ultimately a form of narcissism (i.e. a definition of the self in terms of ideal representations—self-love precedes object-love). Proust writes that Swann

> . . . had so long ceased to direct his course toward any ideal goal, and had confined himself to the pursuit of ephemeral satisfactions, that he had come to believe, though without ever formally stating his belief even to himself, that he would remain all his life in that condition, which death alone could alter. More than this, since his mind no longer entertained any lofty ideals, he had ceased to believe in . . . their reality. . . . But now, like a confirmed invalid whom, all of a sudden, a change of air and surroundings, or a new course of treatment . . . seems to have so far recovered from his malady that he begins to envisage the possibility, hitherto beyond hope, of starting to lead . . . a wholly different life, Swann . . . was conscious once again of a desire, almost, indeed, of the power to consecrate his life. [161]

Through its musical approximation of the familiar dialectic of absence and presence, the sonata sets the wheels of desire in motion once again. Its sensory intensity reawakens in Swann some long-buried reserve of affect, providing the necessary "fuel" for that psychic machine:

> With a slow and rhythmical movement it led him here, there, everywhere, towards a state of happiness noble, unintelligible, yet clearly indicated. And then, suddenly having reached a certain point from which he was prepared to follow it, after pausing for a moment, abruptly it changed its direction, and in a fresh movement, more rapid, multiform, melancholy, incessant, sweet, it bore him off with it toward a vista

of joys unknown. Then it vanished. He hoped, with a passionate longing, that he might find it again, a third time. And reappear it did, though without speaking to him more clearly, bringing him, indeed, a pleasure less profound. But when he was once more at home he needed it, he was like a man into whose life a woman, whom he has seen for a moment passing by, has brought a new form of beauty, which strengthens and enlarges his own power of perception, without his knowing even whether he is ever to see her again whom he loves already, although he knows nothing of her. . . . [160]

The extended simile at the conclusion of this passage lays bare the metaphoric relationship which enables the little phrase to assume such a privileged status in Swann's psychic economy— the similarities between it and some beloved woman from the days in which Swann still "believed" in ideal objects encourages the displacement of affect from her to it.

Because Vinteuil's sonata remains elusive, awakening desire without being in any way capable of assuaging it, Swann comes increasingly to substitute Odette for it. Proust describes this displacement as a signifying transaction ("those parts of Swann's soul in which the little phrase had obliterated all care for material interests, those human considerations which affect all men alike, were left bare by it, blank pages on which he was at liberty to inscribe the name of Odette" (182)). That transaction is facilitated not only by her constant proximity to the music, but by her reduplication of the same scenario of loss and recovery by means of which it seduces Swann.

For a long time after the evening when Swann discovers his desire for Odette the sonata remains the necessary antidote for her "vain presence"—for the disappointing discrepancy between the tangible woman and the ideal image which is the real focus of Swann's interest. The melody confers its seductive value on her, provides her with a significance which she would otherwise lack. In short, it remains the privileged term in the metaphoric equation ("where Odette's affection might seem ever so little abrupt and disappointing, the little phrase could come to supplement it, to amalgamate with it its own mysterious essence" (182)).

Eventually, however, Odette becomes even more inaccessible than the sonata, and supersedes it as the definitive object of desire in Swann's life. What then occurs is an odd reversal of the metaphoric relationship, in which the little phrase becomes a signifier for Odette, whose protracted absence has transformed her into the signified. Thus at the Saint-Euverte party, when the beloved melody emerges from the sonata to which Swann is listening, it "speaks" to him of Odette, evoking all of the pleasant memories from the early stages of their relationship:

> But suddenly it was as though she had entered, and this apparition tore him with such anguish that his hand rose impulsively to his heart. . . . And before Swann had had time to understand what was happening, to think: "It is the little phrase from Vinteuil's sonata. I mustn't listen!", all his memories of the days when Odette had been in love with him, which he had succeeded, up till that evening, in keeping invisible in the depths of his being . . . had awakened from their slumber, had taken wing and risen to sing maddeningly in his ears, without pity for his present desolation, the forgotten strains of happiness. [264–65]

The object of a new preconscious fixation becomes the starting point for additional displacements along the paths of metaphor and metonymy. Once Swann experiences Odette's absence as a lack, his desire radiates outward from her clothing, to her apartment, to the street on which she lives. This metonymic expansion is perhaps most striking in the carriage scene where Swann first kisses Odette, after virtually ravishing the flowers she is wearing. Indeed, even the cattleyas share to some degree in the fixation of his desire, since for many subsequent nights he feels compelled to follow the same ritual of straightening them on Odette's bodice, brushing away the pollen they have dropped, and smelling them before he kisses her.

Similarly, when he climbs the magnificent stairway to the Saint-Euverte residence he automatically compares it with the stairs of the little dressmaker's sordid flat where Odette goes once a week, and at the entry-way to the concert-room he thinks of the milk can which stands at the door of that other, very different residence. This rather complicated signifying transaction builds on the already established metonymic comparison between Odette and the dressmaker's apartment, adding to it a metaphoric opposition between that apartment and the Saint-Euverte mansion. As a consequence of these multiple displacements, the party episode becomes suffused with the melancholy which Swann experiences whenever he thinks about Odette. (Perhaps the most astonishing metonymic connection which is established during this evening is that between Odette and the woman with whom Swann has his next affair. The latter happens to be present during the party, and draws attention to herself by rescuing the piano from a dripping candle.)

These minor displacements—i.e. those from Odette to her belongings, surroundings, friends—are to be distinguished from the major one which accompanies the actual substitution of one object for another, in which the former assumes the position of the privileged term in a series of new signifying transactions. The shift of Swann's attention from Odette to her flowers, the glass of orangeade which she gives him, or the dressmaker she visits, does not in any way diminish his desire for her. On the contrary, these minor displacements increase Odette's appeal by extending her signifying network. The gifts Swann lavishes upon her only further elaborate that network.

The displacement of desire along metaphoric and metonymic lines reflects the intervention of the secondary process, which by insisting that the distinctions between similar and contiguous elements be maintained, permits desire a certain signifying flexibility upon which the primary process would prefer to foreclose. The signifying profligacy of the metaphoric and metonymic operations contrasts dramatically with the economy of the primary process, which would be much more inclined to conflate fourteen elements, representative of as many desires, into a single dream figure, than to project desire for one object onto fourteen similar and contiguous ones.

The secondary process exercises its influence over metaphor and metonymy in other ways as well. Freud draws our attention to the fact that even dreams exploit paths of similarity and contiguity established by the secondary process, condensing paradigmatic elements like "Flora," "blooming," and "Gartner" into the manifest element "botanical." The secondary process plays as central a role in the formation of metaphors and metonymies, creating those affinities which are exploited by the metaphoric substitution of Odette for the Botticelli fresco, and those contiguities which permit the metonymic exchange of the phrase of music for Odette. It is after all only the perception of differences which enables other sorts of relationships to be established, and we recall the inability of the primary process either to perceive differences, or to think relationally. Besides, similarities and contiguities are not inherent in objects, but in our perceptions of them, which are culturally shaped. The secondary process is one of the most important agencies for the transmission of cultural information. It is by means of that agency that Swann acquires the ability to make artistic or musical judgments, and learns to think in terms of the ideal.

The secondary process, which reflects the larger symbolic order both in the language it utilizes and in its refusal to give expression to forbidden psychic impulses, also helps to organize desire itself. Without preconscious censorship, which repeats larger cultural prohibitions, there would be no unconscious, and none of those displacements which give rise to metaphor and metonymy.

We have established that condensation and displacement are strategies for responding to similarity and contiguity in which the primary process exercises the largest control, while paradigm and syntagm are strategies for differentiating between similar and contiguous elements in which the secondary process predominates. Metaphor and metonymy offer a variety of mediating formations. If those formations come more under the influence of the secondary than the primary process, both of their terms will be present, as in a simile. However, if the primary process prevails, one of those terms will function as the signifier, and the other as signified. Moreover, the former will represent the latter in its absence, thus implying a much more intimate identification between the two parts of the equation.

The three sets of signifying clusters—condensation and displacement, paradigm and syntagm, and metaphor and metonymy—coexist in complex ways. Not only is each already the product of a certain facilitation between the primary and secondary processes, but they form additional accommodations and imbrications within discourse.

D) FACILITATIONS

Literary and cinematic texts, much like subjectivity, dramatize an elaborate series of exchanges between the primary and secondary processes. As we have already had numerous occasions to observe, neither operates independently of the other; the secondary process relies upon the primary one to "fix" or "anchor" signification by privileging certain terms over others, at least temporarily, and the primary process resorts to signification only as a result of secondary interference or blockage.

This is another way of saying that even dreams require syntagmatic support, and condensations and displacements can occur even within the most coherent of novels or films. Examples of condensation in such texts are numerous, ranging from puns to lap dissolves,* while displacement expresses itself not only through metaphors and metonymies, but as a much larger organizational principle: Since literary and cinematic texts always have a latent as well as a manifest level, displacement like condensation must be understood as an important agency of movement from one level to the other.

A passage from *Madame Bovary* which marks the transition from temptation to emotional surrender on the part of its heroine may help to indicate the complexity of the interactions between the primary and secondary processes in a classic narrative text. Emma and Rodolphe are seated together in the council-room of the town hall while the country fair progresses outside. Rodolphe has just concluded a rather mechanical seduction speech which thrills Emma because it corresponds so closely to the romantic novels which have structured her desires:

> She noticed in his eyes small golden lines radiating from the black pupils; she even smelt the perfume of the pomade which made his hair glossy. Then something gave way in her; she

---

*The brief superimposition of two cinematic shots.

recalled the Viscount who had waltzed with her at Vaubyessard, and whose beard exhaled a similar scent of vanilla and
lemon, and mechanically she half-closed her eyes the better to
breathe it in. But in making the movement, as she leant back
in her chair, she saw in the distance, right on the line of the
horizon, the old diligence the "Hirondelle," that was slowly de-
scending the hill of Leux, dragging after it a long trail of dust.
It was in this yellow carriage that Léon had so often come back
to her, and by this route down there he had gone forever. She
fancied she saw him opposite at his window; then all grew confused; clouds gathered; it seemed to her that she was again
turning in the waltz under the light of the lustres on the arm
of the Viscount, and that Léon was not far away, that he was
coming . . . and yet all the time she was conscious of Rodolphe's head by her side. The sweetness of this sensation re-
vived her past desires, and like grains of sand under the gust
of wind, they swirled around in the subtle breath of the perfume that diffused over her soul.[12]

The passage establishes a syntagmatic alternation between
sensory impressions (the brilliance of Rodolphe's eyes, the smell
of his pomade, the dusty procession of the yellow Hirondelle)
and recollection (the ball at Vaubyessard, the visits of Léon),
which is at first relatively leisurely, but which gains momentum
as it continues. The increasing rapidity of the alternations in
Emma's thoughts between these two sets of impressions is registered materially in the first part of the sentence beginning
"She fancied she saw him," with its abrupt clauses set apart by
semicolons.* The final clause of the same sentence reflects the
collapse of the distinction between memory and contemporary
detail in Emma's mind, with the ambiguous pronoun "he" and
the accompanying ellipsis.

The events Emma recalls constitute part of the larger syntagm of the novel. However, the relations between them are
increasingly distorted in this passage. Initially their sequence is
preserved—first Emma remembers the Viscount, then Léon—
although the other elements in the syntagmatic chain are ignored. However, ultimately even these elements are wrenched

---

*The punctuation differs slightly in the original.

out of their chronological context, and the Viscount, Léon, and Rodolphe are described as though they were simultaneously present.

The novel's syntagmatic organization collapses under the pressure of desire and its infinite capacity for displacement, manifested first in the guises of metaphor and metonymy, and finally that of condensation. The initial shift from present to past is achieved through an interesting collaboration of metaphor and metonymy. The second of these tropes is used to expand the field of desire from Rodolphe's voice to the light shining in his eyes, and the perfume he wears on his hair. The perfume then provides a metaphoric link between Rodolphe and the Viscount. Léon is evoked metonymically, through the glimpse Emma catches of the carriage in which he used to ride, and the transition from signifier (carriage) to signified (Léon) is made instantaneously. Almost as immediate is the displacement onto another metonymic substitution for Léon—the window of his apartment.

The associative links between the three men are by now so fully elaborated, and the force of Emma's accumulated desires so intense, that the metaphoric and metonymic relationships yield to an absolute identification. Needless to say, Rodolphe benefits greatly from this series of displacements and the resulting condensation, since when the secondary process inevitably intervenes and re-establishes difference, he becomes the sole repository of the affect which has in the meantime been so greatly intensified.

The moment at which conceptual distinctions seem most to blur for Emma, a new set of metaphoric terms are introduced for the reader, and they are so presented as to stress the distance between them. Emma's past desires, we are told, are *like* "grains of sand under a gust of wind." The narrator's recourse to simile in the context of Emma's surrender to condensation has the effect of re-establishing the differences which the preceding sentences have virtually eliminated, and returns us to narrative.

While at all points maintaining the interconnections between the categories "subject" and "signification," we have thus far focused more on the latter than the former. We have explored the discursive capacities of the subject, as well as the participation of both the primary and secondary processes in every signifying formation, but we have not yet examined in detail the production of the subject through discourse, or its place within a larger symbolic field.

The next chapter will comment on the central role played by the paternal signifier—i.e. by the Oedipal norm—both within the present cultural order in the West, and within the constitution of the subject. We will see that subjectivity is by no means an ideologically innocent condition, but one which reflects dominant cultural values. Those values are first and foremost patriarchal and they organize subjectivity, like signification, along lines of sexual difference. We will also discover in Chapter 4 that the subject lacks the coherence and autonomy attributed to it by humanism—that it is simultaneously partitioned and overdetermined.

4

The Subject

The term "subject" designates a quite different semantic and ideological space from that indicated by the more familiar term "individual." The second of these terms dates from the Renaissance, and it still bears the traces of the dominant philosophical systems of that time—systems which afforded to consciousness the very highest premium. The concept of subjectivity, as we shall see, marks a radical departure from this philosophical tradition by giving a more central place to the unconscious and to cultural overdetermination than it does to consciousness.

"Individual" is sometimes used as a noun, and sometimes as an adjective qualifying "man." However, the latter is implied even when it is not stated. Together the terms "individual" and "man" posit an entity that is both autonomous and stable. "Man" presupposes a human essence that remains untouched by historical or cultural circumstances—what the Renaissance was fond of calling "reason," but which in the twentieth century generally goes by the name of "consciousness." The attribution of individuality or privacy to this consciousness suggests that man's thinking processes are in no way coerced either by the material world or by the thoughts of other men; he is understood to be a free intellectual agent, except insofar as a greater mind—like God's—impinges upon him. In fact such an event cannot even be regarded as a disruption of his freedom, since individual man is understood to be most himself, truest to his nature, when he transcends materiality through religion, art, or philosophy, thereby approaching abstract values like the Divine, the Beautiful, and the Good.

René Descartes's *Discourse on Method* and *Meditations on the First Philosophy* are generally cited as the most classic demonstration of private consciousness, of a cognitive operation which believes itself to be both independent and authentic for all time. In those two works Descartes attempts to challenge all self-evident truths, to move beyond the bulk of opinions that make up human knowledge to eternal verities. He does not, however, call into question any of the commonly held assumptions about individual man, and consequently his interrogation leads only to the re-establishment of the Christian world.

The passage which is most pertinent to our present discussion can be found in Part IV of the *Discourse*. In it Descartes proves his own existence from his capacity to think:

> . . . as I . . . desired to give my attention solely to the search after truth, I thought that . . . I ought to reject as absolutely false all opinions in regard to which I could suppose the least ground for doubt, in order to ascertain whether after that there remained aught in my belief that was wholly indubitable. Accordingly, seeing that our senses sometimes deceive us, I was willing to suppose that there existed nothing really such as they presented to us; and because men err in reasoning . . . I, convinced that I was as open to error as any other, rejected as false all the reasonings I had hitherto taken for demonstrations; and finally, when I considered that the very same thoughts . . . which we experience when awake may also be experienced when we are asleep, while there is at that time not one of them true, I supposed that all the objects . . . that had ever entered into my mind when awake, had in them no more truth than the illusions of my dreams. But immediately upon this I observed that, whilst I thus wished to think that all was false, it was absolutely necessary that I, who thus thought, should be somewhat; and as I observed that this truth, I think, hence I am, was so certain and of such evidence that no ground of doubt . . . could be . . . capable of shaking it, I concluded that I might, without scruple, accept it as the first principle of the Philosophy of which I was in search.[1]

Descartes's next step is of course to assert, on the basis of the ideas of perfection which he finds within his own mind, a divine being who corresponds to them. And once the creator is back in place, the creation soon follows. The operative belief here is that ideas correspond in an unmediated way to real objects and values. The notion that meaning emerges from the play of differences within a closed system could not be more alien to Descartes's logic. This last issue would seem to require a further clarification, particularly in relation to the speaker's own status.

The first person pronoun is ubiquitous in the passage quoted above. It is on each occasion used as if it transparently reflected the identity of the speaker rather than, as Benveniste would argue, constructing that identity. Moreover, Descartes's "I" assumes itself to be fully conscious (nothing can be more false, he tells us, than dreams), and hence fully self-knowable. It is not only autonomous but coherent; the concept of another psychic territory, in contradiction to consciousness, is unimaginable. In other words, the *Discourse on Method* projects a continuous presence behind its own exfoliation, a stable point of authorial origin. It offers us a narrator who imagines that he speaks without simultaneously being spoken, who believes himself to exist outside of discourse.

The pronoun "I" here functions as the key term in what is seen to be a solitary enterprise, a point Descartes underscores when he dismisses all other human knowledge as irrelevant. The individual, he suggests, need only close out all other voices and turn within in order to arrive at a direct apprehension of the truth. This truth exists independently of discourse, as does man. It can be discovered by means of certain ideas which transparently reflect things as they really are. For Descartes, both God and man transcend cultural definition; the concepts of goodness and perfection which the latter discovers within his own mind are not time-bound or specific to a given civilization, but eternal and immutable. They confer identity not only on things external to man, but on man himself.

Some remarks made by Michel Foucault in *The Order of Things,* which have achieved a kind of notoriety, are calculated to call into question the values of autonomy and stability which define the position of the individual within what is commonly called the humanist tradition. Foucault insists that man as we know him is the product of certain historically determined discourses, and that by challenging those discourses we can "dissolve" him. Foucault does not suggest that we will thereby eliminate the category of the human, but that we will deconstruct the conceptions by means of which we have so far understood that category. He isolates ethnology and psychoanalysis as two of the most important recent discourses for effecting that deconstruction because of the double focus they place on cultural overdetermination and the unconscious. By constantly locating the production of human reality beyond the boundaries of consciousness, they dismantle concepts like "individual" and "man," deny the possibility of a timeless human essence:

> [Ethnology and psychoanalysis never] come near to a general concept of man: at no moment do they come near to isolating a quality in him that is specific, irreducible and uniformly valid wherever he is given to experience. . . . Not only are they able to do without the concept of man, they are also unable to pass through it, for they always address themselves to that which constitutes his outer limits . . . since *Totem and Taboo,* the establishment of a common field for these two, the possibility of a discourse that could move from one to the other without discontinuity, the double articulation of the history of individuals upon the unconscious of culture, and of the historicity of those cultures upon the unconscious of individuals, has opened up, without doubt, the most general problems that can be posed with regard to man. . . . [they show that] the signifying chain by which the unique experience of the individual is constituted is perpendicular to the formal system on the basis of which the significations of a culture are constituted. . . .[2]

Foucault here stresses the interconnectedness of ethnology, psychoanalysis, and semiotics. He indicates, that is, that neither culture nor the unconscious can be approached apart from a theory of signification, since it is by means of historically circumscribed signifying operations that both are organized. The close alignment of semiotics and ethnology has also been strongly emphasized by the French anthropologist Claude Lévi-

Strauss,[3] while both Sigmund Freud and Jacques Lacan have demonstrated that psychoanalysis is in effect a branch of semiotics.

The term "subject" foregrounds the relationship between ethnology, psychoanalysis, and semiotics. It helps us to conceive of human reality as a construction, as the product of signifying activities which are both culturally specific and generally unconscious. The category of the subject thus calls into question the notions both of the private, and of a self synonymous with consciousness. It suggests that even desire is culturally instigated, and hence collective; and it de-centers consciousness, relegating it (in distinction from the preconcious, where cognitive activity occurs) to a purely receptive capacity. Finally, by drawing attention to the divisions which separate one area of psychic activity from another, the term "subject" challenges the value of stability attributed to the individual.

This chapter is concerned with what might be called the "interior" of the subject. However, we will be obliged to grasp that interiority in relation to the exteriority of what Jacques Lacan calls the "symbolic order." We have already had occasion to note the cultural organization of the preconscious, an organization which is implicit in the operations of the secondary process, but we will discover that the unconscious and even the drives also succumb to a cultural orchestration. The writings of Lacan, the psychoanalytic theoretician who has done more than anyone else to establish Freud's importance for semiotics, suggests that no aspect of human existence escapes the structuration of the symbolic order. We will pay close attention to the models elaborated by both Freud and Lacan, models which have gained wide theoretical currency.

Psychoanalysis has shown the family, like language, to be a vital relay between the various territories that make up subjectivity and the larger cultural field. Both Freud and Lacan place a heavy emphasis on those events in the life of the subject which could be grouped under the Oedipal rubric. Freud insists that not only the subject's sexuality, but its very identity is entirely determined by these events. Lacan reiterates this point, translating it into more recognizably semiotic terms: he asserts that the signifying activities of both the unconscious and the pre-conscious are centered on the Oedipal experience, and that the Western symbolic order derives its coherence from the phallus or paternal signifier.

The discussion which follows will therefore pay particular attention to what might be called the Oedipalization of the sub-ject, and the phallocentricity of that symbolic order. It will con-sequently scrutinize those aspects of Freud's and Lacan's argu-ments which are themselves congruent with phallocentricity—which attempt to justify or naturalize the privileged position of the paternal within our culture. We will endeavor to create a space for the female subject within these pages, even if that space is only a negative one—one, that is, which reflects the marginality to which she has been confined for centuries.

It must be here observed, at the risk of stating the obvious, that the term "man" is gender-specific, although it purports to include all humanity. Its double application permits the phal-locentricity of our philosophical heritage to go unquestioned, creating the illusion that any case which is made for man au-tomatically includes woman. In fact, however, the definition of man which we inherit from the Renaissance does not apply to woman. The same philosophical tradition—Christian, Platonic, humanist—which associates man with reason and transcend-ence associates woman with irrationality and the Fall. Semiotics must include a careful examination of the ways in which sexual difference has determined signifying practice, both at the level of the larger symbolic order and at that of subjectivity, if it wants to progress beyond the epistemological limits of that philosophical tradition.

One additional caveat should be noted: Although the theo-retical systems to which this chapter are devoted present them-selves as relevant to any cultural situation, they must be under-stood as applying in the strict sense only to the dominant Western model. It must be additionally stressed, although it falls beyond the very limited dimensions of the present study to do more than make note of the fact, that this cultural model and the theories which describe it have very precise historical and economic determinants.[4]

A) THE FREUDIAN MODEL

The Freudian subject is above all a partitioned subject, incapable of exhaustive self-knowledge. Its parts do not exist harmoniously; they speak different languages and operate on the basis of conflicting imperatives. The analyst functions as a kind of interpreter, establishing communication between the various sectors, although his loyalties are always engaged more fully by one than the others (because the analyst "normalizes," introducing the patient into an acceptable cultural position, he is within this framework necessarily "male"—i.e. aligned with the father, the law, discursive power).

We examined one version of this partitioned subject in Chapter 2—that offered in *The Interpretation of Dreams*. The subject there described houses two major compartments: the unconscious and the preconscious/conscious. The sympathies of the young Freud would seem to be very much engaged by the unconscious, and he elaborates an analytic model calculated to establish a flow from it to the conscious subject. Indeed, the young Freud is at pains to circumvent the censorship of the preconscious, to lift the bar of repression.

The Freud of *The Ego and the Id* (1923), or the late essays on female sexuality, takes a very different attitude toward the subject, and has recourse to a topographical model within which Oedipal values play a much more central role. This model also reformulates the unconscious in ways which diminish its complexity and appeal. *New Introductory Lectures* (1933) provides the clearest diagram of this mature topography: [5]

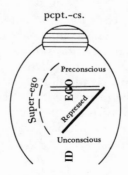

As the diagram suggests, the terms "id," "ego," and "super-ego" all enjoy a prominent position in Freud's final conceptualization of the subject. They coexist in a somewhat uneasy alliance with the categories "unconscious" and "preconscious," overlapping with them in certain respects but by no means all.

"Id" designates that part of the psychic apparatus which is most rudimentary; it predates the development both of the ego and the superego. It is unconscious, but only portions of it are repressed. In this respect, it differs strikingly from the unconscious of *The Interpretation of Dreams,* which consists exclusively of repressed materials. The id differs from that unconscious in other respects as well: It lacks the latter's signifying capacities, seeming to be little more than an area of instinctual anarchy. Freud associates it with the passions, and he attributes to it qualities like unruliness and lack of control. The id always obeys the dictates of the pleasure principle, no matter what the consequence. Finally, unlike the unconscious of *The Interpretation of Dreams,* the id is not a product of the same cultural prohibitions which establish the preconscious, but is rather a primordial category.

Whereas the id operates at the behest of the pleasure principle, the ego carries out the commands of the reality priniple. Indeed, the ego consists of what used to be a part of the id, but which has under the influence of the reality principle been transformed into a "coherent organization of mental processes,"[6] including the systems known as perception and the preconscious in the earlier topography, and part of the unconscious or id. It is sharply differentiated only from that part of the id which has been repressed. Freud associates the ego with reason and common sense, and he describes its relation to the id as one of intelligent guidance and severe restraint:

> The functional importance of the ego is manifested in the fact that normally control over the approaches to motility devolves upon it. Thus in its relation to the id it is like a man on horseback, who has to hold in check the superior strength of the horse; with this difference, that the rider tries to do so with his own strength while the ego uses borrowed forces. The analogy may be carried a little further. Often a rider, if he is

not to be parted from his horse, is obliged to guide it where it
wants to go; so in the same way the ego is in the habit of
transforming the id's will into action as if it were its own. [XIX.
25]

This relationship contrasts strikingly with the notion of "facilitation," which as we recall is used by Freud to explain the interactions of the primary and secondary processes. It brings
together brute strength and superior wisdom instead of two
equally complex signifying operations.

The ego is formed through a series of identifications with
objects external to it. Freud argues that each of these identifications follows the same pattern, a pattern whereby an object is
first loved and then taken inside the ego in the guise of a visual
image, a voice, a set of values, or some other key features. That
introjection provides the means whereby the id can be persuaded to renounce an object which has for one reason or another proved inaccessible. The ego refashions itself after that
object, and offers itself to the id as a substitute ("the character
of the ego is a precipitate of abandoned object-cathexes and
. . . it contains the history of those object-choices. . . . When
the ego assumes the features of the object, it is forcing itself
. . . upon the id as a love-object and is trying to make good
the id's loss by saying: 'Look, you can love me too—I am so like
the object' " (XIX. 29–30)). We will return to the issues of identification and narcissism in our discussion of Lacan.

The super-ego emerges from the first and most important
of these identifications, that with the father. By taking the image of the father into himself, the male subject resolves both
his original erotic feelings for that figure, and his subsequent
hostility and jealousy. (Freud insists here and elsewhere on the
subject's initial bisexuality, a bisexuality which is subsequently
repressed but which results in an early version of the Oedipus
complex in which the father is both loved and hated, and in
which the mother is both desired and resented.) The male subject's identification with the father also sanctions his continued,
albeit diminished, affection for the mother.

However, this first identification is not a simple one; it differs quite profoundly from those that follow. Not only does the

son identify with the father, he also accepts that there are ways in which he can never be like him. In other words, the male subject internalizes along with the image of the father an image of his own distance from the father. That distance is expressed through the creation of a psychic construct which stands to one side of the ego, as a kind of ideal version of it. This ego ideal or superego functions throughout the history of the subject as the mirror in which the ego sees what it should be, but never can be.

The inability of the ego to identify as completely with the father as it will identify with later objects has to do with the decisive role played by that figure in the Oedipal crisis. He is not only the pivot of the son's desires, but the agency whereby those desires are inhibited:

> The superego is . . . not simply a residue of the earliest object-choices of the id; it also represents an energetic reaction-formation against these wishes. Its relation to the ego is not exhausted by the precept: "You *ought* to be like this (like your father)." It also comprises the prohibition: "You *may not be* like this (like your father)—that is, you may not do all that he does; some things are his prerogative." This double aspect of the ego ideal derives from the fact that the ego ideal had the task of repressing the Oedipus complex; indeed, it is to that revolutionary event that it owes its existence. . . . The superego retains the character of the father, while the more powerful the Oedipus complex was and the more rapidly it succumbed to repression (under the influence of authority, religious teaching, schooling and reading), the stricter will be the domination of the superego later on. . . . [XIX. 34–35]

Freud here draws attention not only to those values which define the paternal position—repressiveness, privilege, potency—but its institutional supports: the state, the church, the educational system and texts. In so doing he anticipates Lacan's notion of the symbolic father.

We have been obliged to confine most of our remarks so far to the male subject for two reasons, the first of which is that sexual difference plays an absolutely central role within the Freudian model, necessitating a separate treatment of male and female subjects, and the second of which is that Freud himself concentrates almost exclusively on the former. In "Some Psychical Consequences of the Anatomical Distinction Between the Sexes (1925)," Freud acknowledges his neglect of the female subject, but the attempt which he there makes to remedy that neglect only intensifies the lines of division. The importance of sexual difference within the Freudian scheme can perhaps best be indicated through an exploration of that scheme's chronological dimension.

The metaphor of a path which has been traveled many times before and which leads to a familiar destination occurs again and again in Freud's discussions of subjectivity. For instance, in *Beyond the Pleasure Principle* we are told that the drives are conservative in nature, and that they strive to "return by the circuitous paths along which [their] development leads" to an old state of things (XVIII.39). Similarly, in *Three Essays on Sexuality* oral and anal sexuality are designated as "pre-genital," as if to suggest that they are preliminary stages in a larger narrative. Even the adult sexual encounter resembles a road whose destination is all-important—since the logical culmination of such an encounter is procreation, excessive lingering (i.e. foreplay) along the way is to be discouraged. The Oedipus complex is perhaps the most frequently traversed path of all; we learn in "Dissolution of the Oedipus Complex" (1924) that it is "a phenomenon which is determined and laid down by heredity and which is bound to pass away according to programme when the next pre-ordained phase of development sets in" (XIX. 174). The "normal" Western subject is fully contained within a predetermined narrative.

That narrative begins for both the male and the female subject with the oral and anal stages of sexuality, during which the boundaries are not as yet clearly drawn between self and other. Erotic gratification, which is first localized at the mouth and then at the anus, takes the form of the introjection and extrojection of objects which seem to constitute a part of the subject. These two stages are characterized by a self-sufficiency with which Freud is never altogether comfortable, as his concern in *Three Essays on Sexuality* for their speedy and unobtrusive culmination would indicate:

These phases of sexual organization are normally passed
through smoothly, without giving more than a hint of their
existence. It is only in pathological cases that they become active and recognizable to superficial observation. [VII.198]

The transition which Freud anticipates is that from autoerotism
to sexually differentiated object-love.

Within the Freudian framework the subject does not assume its cultural identity until the genital phase of infantile
sexuality. At this point all sorts of boundaries are established—
not only those between self and other, but between male and
female. Lacan focuses much more fully on the first of these
than does Freud, who concentrates his chief attention on the
delineation of sexual difference (a delineation which would obviously crystalize the opposition of self and other).

In "Some Psychical Consequences of the Anatomical Distinction Between the Sexes," Freud describes a critical moment
in infantile sexuality, one which establishes the concepts of
maleness and femaleness and determines a very different history for each. It is a moment in which vision plays a central
role, in which the male and female subjects first "see" each other.
However, as we shall discover, that vision is culturally mediated:

> There is an interesting contrast between the behaviour of
> the two sexes. . . . when a little boy first catches sight of a
> girl's genital region, he begins by showing irresolution and lack
> of interest; he sees nothing or disavows what he has seen . . .
> It is not until later, when some threat of castration has ob-
> tained a hold upon him, that the observation becomes impor-
> tant to him. . . .
> A little girl behaves differently. She makes her judgment
> and her decision in a flash. She has seen it and knows that she
> is without it and wants to have it. [XIX. 252]

Before attempting to situate this moment within the larger
narrative of male and female subjectivity, it would seem important to clarify exactly what is at issue. As this passage makes
evident, sexual definition means definition in relation to the
penis. In the same essay Freud refers to the male sex organ as

"large" and "superior," and what he takes to be the female equivalent (i.e. the clitoris) as "stunted" and "inferior." Not only does the male subject possess the privileged appendage, but the female subject acknowledges the importance which that possession confers. Thus the value of the penis depends entirely upon the twin assumptions of female lack and envy.

Freud uses the penis/clitoris opposition as the basis for other oppositions as well. He associates the male subject with aggressivity, voyeurism, and sadism, and the female subject with the antithetical but complementary qualities of passivity, exhibitionism, and masochism.

There are more than a few traces within the Freudian argument of an attempt to root these oppositions in biology. For instance, in *Three Essays on Sexuality* he suggests that "The sexuality of male human beings contains an element of aggressiveness—a desire to subjugate; the biological significance of it seems to lie in the need for overcoming the resistance of the sexual object by means other than the process of wooing" (VII. 157–58); and elsewhere in the same work he insists that "moral ideas"—ideas which bear directly on the diverse sexual attitudes and behavior of the two sexes—derive from organic rather than cultural sources:

> . . . in reality this development [i.e. that of moral ideas] is organically determined and fixed by heredity, and it can occasionally occur without any help from education. Education will not be trespassing beyond its appropriate domain if it limits itself to following the lines which have already been laid down organically and to impressing them somewhat more clearly and deeply. [VII.177–78]

However, on other occasions Freud indicates that male and female subjects are made, not born. In "An Outline of Psychoanalysis (1940)," one of his last works, he reverts once again to the original bisexuality of the subject, and suggests that it is never completely eliminated, even in the most conventional of cases, thereby suggesting that sexual identity is cultural, not organic. Moreover, he isolates the Oedipus complex as the agency for producing male and female subjects, the juncture at which they are compelled to follow separate paths (XXIII.188).

Freud also notes in "An Outline of Psychoanalysis" the difficulty of attributing any absolute value to the terms "male" and "female" because they do not correspond to any human essence. In so doing he comes very close to suggesting that the categories of male and female only acquire meaning through their opposition to each other—in other words, that they comprise a binary set analogous to antonyms in language, and must be understood as belonging to a closed system of signification rather than to what Peirce would call "reality." It is only within the confines of this system that the oppositions aggressivity/passivity, voyeurism/exhibitionism, and sadism/masochism designate two different sexual positions, just as if it is there and there alone that the penis signifies "plenitude," and the vagina or clitoris signifies "lack."

Lacan has extended the notion of lack to include the male subject as well as the female through his insistence on the distinction between the penis and the phallus. For him the term "penis" refers quite simply to an anatomical appendage, while "phallus" designates the privileges of the symbolic, privileges from which the son is temporarily excluded. However, even the Freudian paradigm makes clear the inadequacy of the male subject, acknowledging as it does that he relies for his authentication upon the felt inferiority of the female subject. Hollywood melodramas show how easily the male subject's potency can be challenged by putting it into crisis again and again. *Rebel Without a Cause, Bigger than Life, Written on the Wind,* and *Magnificent Ambersons* all revolve in one manner or another around the weakness or inadequacy of a male character.

The first of these films states the problem of male potency in unusually sensitive terms. Nicholas Ray's *Rebel Without a Cause* dramatizes a young man's search for the normative family which can accommodate his Oedipal yearnings. Since his own father wears an apron and cannot be persuaded to "be a man," while his mother occupies a traditionally masculine position, Jimmy finds two other teen-agers as determined to be culturally subjected as he is, and the three of them play at housekeeping in an abandoned villa. When hostile forces threaten this little family, and when Jimmy proves incapable of holding it together, his own father steps into the breach and promises that he will

thereafter function in an authoritarian capacity. All of the mel-
odramatic energies of the film are generated by the failure of
the father to achieve a perfect match between himself and the
values which define the paternal function, a failure which he
inevitably transmits to the son. *Rebel Without a Cause* locates the
blame at a predictable site. The mother is shown to have pre-
cipitated the entire crisis by refusing to stay in her culturally
sanctioned place. The conclusion is clear: men can only be aggressive and potent if women are passive and impotent.

All of this is another way of saying that the moment isolated
by Freud as inaugurating the division of the sexes must be
understood as the product of intense cultural mediation, as an
event which is experienced retrospectively by both male and
female subjects. The perceptual model which Freud elaborates
for the little boy ("he sees nothing. . . . It is not until later . . .
that the observation becomes important to him") must be extended as well to the little girl. Both refer back their cultural
status to their anatomical status after the former has been consolidated, and they do so at the suggestion of the society within
which they find themselves. Since at the Oedipal juncture the
male and female subjects go their separate but mutually dependent ways, we will be obliged to effect a similar division in our
analysis.

For a time the male child merely loves and respects the paternal parent, but if he is properly responsive he soon feels the
cultural imperative to *be* his father, and adopts a competitive
and hostile attitude toward him. Simultaneously, he learns to
make his mother the object of his desire. The conflicting feelings of aggressivity toward the mother and attraction for the
father will "normally" be understated.

The male child draws attention to his competition with his
father for his mother's love either through excessive demands
or public masturbation, and is consequently threatened by his
parents in a way which he interprets as a castration warning.
This threat does not make much of an impression upon him
until he remembers the glimpse he earlier enjoyed of the female anatomy. Freud insists that the boy now understands this
difference to be the result of castration for some wrong-doing.

Afraid that the same will happen to himself, he overcomes his hatred for his father and abandons his mother as a love-object.

The means by which the male subject "dissolves" his Oedipal desires are important. If everything goes according to cultural plan, he identifies with his father by internalizing the latter's authority or "voice." This operation is in essence an assimilation of cultural prohibition, and it forms the superego. The male child will henceforth measure and define himself in relation to this repressive paternal representation, and thus to his society's dominant values. As a consequence of his successful Oedipalization, he will find himself "at home" in those discourses and institutions which define the current symbolic order in the West, and will derive validation and support from them at a psychic if not at an economic or social level. In other words, he will "recognize" himself within the mirror of the reigning ideology, even if his race and economic status place him in contradiction to it.[7]

The history of the female subject differs from that of the male subject in many respects. One of the most important of these has to do with the radical discontinuity between the libidinal investments of her infancy, and those which she is required to make at the Oedipal juncture. Because she is usually the source of infantile warmth and nourishment, the mother constitutes the first love object for both male and female subjects. Since the male subject is encouraged to select her as the locus of his Oedipal desires, and later to replace her with members of the same sex, there are no major interruptions in his erotic life. However, the female subject is obliged to renounce her first object choice, to effect a quite violent break with the source of her earliest pleasures. The Oedipus complex functions not to maintain and reinforce an already existing emotional bond, but to replace one parent with the other in the daughter's psychic register.

Another, closely related difference between the male and female versions of the Oedipus complex is that whereas the former is dissolved by the castration threat, the latter only begins with the "discovery" of an already realized "castration." As we noted above, for Freud that discovery is coterminous with the little girl's first glimpse of the male genitalia ("She makes her decision and her judgment in a flash. She has seen it and knows she is without it and wants to have it"). In short the female subject immediately and spontaneously reads her anatomical difference as a deficiency. However, as we have already had occasion to remark in relation to the male subject, anatomy only acquires meaning and value as the consequence of intense cultural mediation. What is at issue here is not the female subject's biological inferiority, but her symbolic exclusion or lack—her isolation, that is, from those cultural privileges which define the male subject as potent and sufficient.

We must consequently understand the attribution of superiority to the penis and inferiority to the clitoris as occurring from a point fully within patriarchal culture. It is only after the subject has arrived at an understanding of the privileged status afforded men and the de-privileged status afforded women within the current symbolic order that sexual difference can be read in the way suggested by Freud. In short, it is only retroactively that anatomy is confused with destiny. That confusion performs a vital ideological function, serving to naturalize or biologize what would otherwise be open to queston.

Freud indicates that the female subject's felt lack "ideally" results in anti-feminism. This rejection begins with the mother, who is not only perceived as deficient herself, but as the cause of her daughter's deficiency. Subsequently, however, it is extended to the entire female sex:

> When she has passed beyond her first attempt at explaining her lack of a penis as being a punishment personal to herself and has realized that the sexual character is a universal one, she begins to share the contempt felt by men for a sex which is the lesser in so important a respect, and, at least in holding that opinion, insists on being like a man. [XIX.253]

The other classic feature of the female Oedipus complex is of course a reification of the father. "Normally" the little girl not only turns away from her mother, but turns toward her father. It is important to note both the extremity of the means by which that transfer is effected, and what it implies for the

future of the female subject. As Freud is the first to admit, the
female subject will only make the culturally requisite investment in her father once she has acceded to the belief that she
is "castrated" or "lacking." Moreover, the form which that investment most legitimately takes—i.e. the desire for a child—
suggests that what she is thereby "buying" is not just a heterosexual rather than a homosexual relationship, but the nuclear
family, and by extension the whole of patriarchal culture:

> So far there has been no question of the Oedipus complex,
> nor has it up to this point played any part. But now the girl's
> libido slips into a new position along the line—there is no other
> way of putting it—of the equation "penis-child." She gives up
> her wish for a penis and puts in place of it a wish for a child:
> and *with that purpose in view* she takes her father as a love-
> object. Her mother becomes the object of her jealousy. The
> girl has turned into a little woman. [XIX.256]

Yet another way in which the development of the little girl
diverges sharply from that of the little boy is that she is not
encouraged to move beyond her Oedipal desires. The most exemplary female subject is one who continues to idealize procreation, and within whose psychic economy the father remains
absolutely central. Freud writes in *An Outline of Psychoanalysis*
that

> It does little harm to a woman if she remains in her feminine
> Oedipus attitude. . . . She will in that case choose her hus-
> band for his paternal characteristic and be ready to recognize
> his authority. Her longing to possess a penis, which is in fact
> unappeasable, may find satisfaction if she can succeed in com-
> pleting her love for the organ by extending it to the bearer of
> the organ. . . . [XXIII.194]

The ideological bases of the Oedipus complex become even
more startlingly evident at this point in Freud's argument. The
properly Oedipalized female subject can find relief from her
crippling sense of inadequacy only through a heterosexual,
procreative cathexis, and by aligning herself with the qualities
of passivity, exhibitionism, and masochism which make her the
perfect "match" for the properly Oedipalized male subject. This

is in fact the "recipe" for female subjectivity provided by He-
lene Deutsch, one of Freud's foremost followers, in *Psychology
of Women: A Psychoanalytic Interpretation.*[8]

(Given the extraordinary demands which it makes upon her,
it is not surprising that the female subject often fails to conform to the scenario described by Freud, that she declines in
particular either to effect or to sustain the critical displacement
of her erotic interest away from her mother to her father. Many
heavily traversed paths diverge from the straight and narrow
one leading to Oedipal normalization, including frigidity, les-
bianism, hysteria, and paranoia. Because of the intimate links
between the Oedipus complex and the larger symbolic order,
links which we will examine in greater detail in our discussion
of Lacan, each of these psychic "disorders" can be read as a
point of female resistance to patriarchal culture.)

In *New Introductory Lectures* and "Some Psychical Consequences of the Anatomical Distinction Between the Sexes" Freud
suggests that because the female subject never overcomes her
Oedipal fixation she fails to acquire the superego which is its
precipitate. The failure to acquire a superego results in a further cultural deprivation—a moral deprivation:

> I cannot evade the notion . . . that for women the level of
> what is ethically normal is different from what it is in men.
> Their super-ego is never so inexorable, so impersonal, so in-
> dependent of its emotional origins as we require it to be in
> men. Character-traits which critics of every epoch have brought
> up against women—that they show less sense of justice than
> men, that they are less ready to submit to the great exigencies
> of life, that they are more often influenced in their judge-
> ments by feelings of affection or hostility—all these would be
> amply accounted for by the modification in the formation of
> their super-ego which we have inferred above. [XIX. 257–58]

These assumptions warrant close attention, since this is one occasion where Freud's prejudices unwittingly lead him to an important feature of female subjectivity.

We recall that the superego is set up inside the male subject
as a means of bringing his Oedipal crisis to a conclusion. Since
the female subject is discouraged from bringing her Oedipal

desires to a similar termination, the superego would seem irrelevant to her psychic existence. However, the notion that the female subject lacks a superego seems inconsistent with other things Freud tells us about her, such as his assertion that she suffers from a much stronger sense of guilt than the male subject, or that masochism plays a determinative part in her construction. *The Ego and the Id* attributes both experiences to the interactions of the ego with the superego; not only does guilt issue from the sense of inadequacy felt by the ego in its relations with the superego, but these relations are described by Freud as masochistic on the part of the ego, and sadistic on the part of the superego (XIX. 47–59).

These inconsistencies can only be resolved by looking once again at the divergent histories of the male and female subjects, and at the role played by the superego in the first of these. The superego is formed through the son's internalization of the father. It provides him with the mirror in which he discovers his own ideal identity—an image which defines him, even if it always exceeds him. In short, the superego is part of the paternal legacy, passed on from father to son. The female subject is not entitled to any share in this inheritance. She lacks that thing which would enable her to be like the father, and to carry his voice inside her; it is only "just," then, that she be marked by another lack. The missing superego functions as the moral equivalent and "consequence" of the missing penis. (There is even a linguistic "impossibility" here, given the equation both within Freud's writings and the larger cultural order of the terms "superior" or "super" and "male.")

It would seem reasonable to assume that female identity is constructed through the initial assimilation of a very different image and voice than those internalized by the male subject— that the female subject takes into herself the values of inferiority and powerlessness embodied by the mother rather than those of superiority and power embodied by the father. It is only by looking into this mirror that she discovers her "castration." (Any notion that the female subject therefore lacks ethical sensitivity must of course be abandoned since she takes up cultural residence within the same symbolic field as the male subject. The "moral ideas" to which Freud frequently returns are nothing other than the values and prohibitions of that field, and given the powerlessness of her position in it the female subject can only be presumed to be even more receptive to them than is her male counterpart.)

The fact that the female subject learns of her "castration" only by means of a cultural mediation in which the mother plays a key role can perhaps best be demonstrated by a text which dramatizes the breakdown of that operation, Alfred Hitchcock's *Marnie*. The title character of that film is presented as a deviant in many respects, of which three would seem particularly important: she successfully robs a number of male businessmen, she manipulates her own social identity, and she manifests not the slightest interest in marriage or children. This unorthodox behavior is shown from the very beginning of the film to be linked in some vital way to Marnie's passionate attachment to her mother, on whom she lavishes gifts after each robbery.

The central male character in the film, Mark Rutland, takes it upon himself to normalize Marnie. He is well equipped to do so since he incorporates all of the ideal paternal attributes; he has monetary, legal, visual, discursive, and sexual control, and he functions within the narrative as a composite of father, detective, and psychoanalyst. He is further assisted in his enterprise by the complex of hysterical symptoms with which the film burdens Marnie—she becomes incapacitated whenever she sees the color red, finds herself in the middle of an electrical storm, or is sexually "handled." These symptoms ultimately lead Mark Rutland to the traumatic episode responsible for the rather unusual turn taken by Marnie's subjectivity.

The events which Marnie recalls under pressure from Rutland occurred one evening when she was a small child, and they are presented to us in the form of a flashback. We watch while Mrs. Edgar, Marnie's mother, rouses her from sleep and moves her from the bedroom to the living-room couch. Mrs. Edgar, clad only in a slip, then returns to the bedroom with a sailor, who the film implies is a sexual customer. An electrical storm is in progress, and Marnie calls to her mother in fear. The sailor comes out of the bedroom and begins drunkenly to fondle the child. A struggle ensues between him and Mrs. Edgar, and he falls to the floor on top of her. Marnie reaches for the poker and hits him fatally on the head. These events are subsequently suppressed by Mrs. Edgar, and repressed by Marnie. The former proves herself thereafter to be an outspoken critic of men, romance, and marriage. Indeed throughout the rest of the film Mrs. Edgar more closely approximates a puritanical feminist than a prostitute, reverting obsessively to the theme of "decency."

What the flashback sequence brings to the manifest level both of the film and of Marnie's psychic existence is a "perversion" of the Oedipal scenario, in which the hostile energies both of the mother and of the daughter are directed against a male figure who temporarily occupies the place of the father, resulting in his death. Marnie not only indulges in the "masculine" wish to kill the father, but she fulfills that wish; she thus violates the Oedipal norm in two ways. In addition, and perhaps most radically, she organizes her desires not around the father, but around the mother.

Earlier moments of the film show the Edgar household to be a small matriarchy, a sub-culture of three members: Marnie, her mother, and Jessie, a young neighborhood girl who spends her afternoons there. At one point Mrs. Edgar suggests to Marnie that the sub-culture be extended to include Jessie's mother, who is also husbandless, but Marnie opposes the idea. Mrs. Edgar is the dominant figure in this miniature matriarchy. She is perceived as powerful and adequate in spite of a prominent leg injury, and there is considerable vying for her affections. Moreover, both Marnie and Jessie turn to Mrs. Edgar to validate their appearance, indicating that she functions as the mirror within which they find their own identities. When Mrs. Edgar, Marnie, and Jessie sit together in the living room the blondeness which all three share creates the momentary impression that we are looking at photographs of the same person taken at twenty-year intervals. It is evident, even at this preliminary juncture, that Marnie's transgressive impulses have their origin in her adoration of her mother, and the latter's usurpation of the paternal position. As a consequence of the "perverted" Oedipal scenario which they have together enacted, Marnie has internalized values of potency and what the film calls "resourcefulness" instead of the requisite impotence and dependency.

Mrs. Edgar's leg injury was inflicted upon her the night of the murder, and like Marnie's hysterical symptoms it is the film's way of telling us that after all she really is weak and mutilated, that all we have to do is look for ourselves and we will see the compelling visual testimony. Indeed, both Marnie and her mother are presented by the film as "sick," and their story reads like a case history. At the same time Hitchcock's text renders absolutely transparent what might be described as the "technology" whereby the female subject is conventionally produced, i.e. an obligatory identification with a "castrated" and insufficient mother, and an erotic acquiescence to a potent and more-than-sufficient father. Marnie removes herself from the assembly line by refusing to accede to the usual Oedipal imperatives, and by focusing her desires on her mother instead of on one of the numerous "fathers" who offer themselves to her. Because she does not displace her affections away from her mother to a paternal figure, she never learns the crucial lesson of her "castration." As a result, she shows herself capable of exercising control in areas—guns, money, identity papers, inter-sexual relations, and even narrative—where that control is traditionally denied to women. Marnie is "cured"—put back on the assembly line—only when she encounters a paternal representative with sufficient institutional support to discredit her mother.

Both of Freud's major topographical models have a great deal to teach us. The one advanced in *The Interpretation of Dreams* encourages us to think of the subject as a complex of signifying processes, with quite extraordinary mnemic and discursive capacities. It demonstrates the absolute inseparability of the terms "subject" and "discourse," and it does so in a manner which enriches both. The fascination which the early model continued to hold for Freud is evidenced by the fact that he returned to it as late as 1925, in "A Note Upon the Mystic Writing Pad." Consequently, we should understand it to be not so much superseded as supplemented by the final topography.

The psychic model proposed in *The Ego and the Id,* and further elaborated in the *New Introductory Lectures,* has very different uses, although once again it generates valuable strategies for dealing with texts as well as subjects. It alerts us to the central role played by the Oedipal scenario in the development of the subject, and to that scenario's sexually differentiating function. It also establishes important connections between the paternal position and other agencies of cultural repression—between the family and the broader social field. It was, after all, Freud's pioneering work in this area which permitted Wilhelm Reich in *The Mass Psychology of Fascism* to discuss the family as the factory within which patriarchal culture reproduces itself, even if Reich's political attitudes are very different from those which inform *The Ego and the Id.* Finally, it offers us a remarkably coherent theory of identification, one which anticipates not only the work of Lacan but much recent writing on film.

The prescriptive or normalizing value of the late model is intimidating, and may at first glance appear to outweigh its descriptive uses. However, if we attend closely to those features of Freud's mature argument which are most defensive, those areas in which he seems most at pains to justify or naturalize the technology whereby subjects are currently produced, we can learn a great deal about the mechanisms that prevent cultural change. We can discover, for instance, that Oedipalization creates sexual difference, that it is culturally induced, that it prevents subjects from determining their own desires, and that it sustains the symbolic field in its present phallocentricity. All of these lessons will be repeated in the next section of this chapter, which will look at what Jacques Lacan has to say about the subject.

B) THE LACANIAN MODEL

French psychoanalyst Jacques Lacan has exercised an enormous influence over the direction recently taken by semiotic theory. He has initiated the return of psychoanalysis to Freud's early writing, which for years was neglected in favor of his later works, and in so doing he has deflected therapeutic attention away from the ego to the unconscious. In addition, he has encouraged the re-reading of Freud's writings in relation to the

contributions of Saussure and Lévi-Strauss, thereby demonstrating the profound but previously unnoticed affinities between psychoanalysis on the one hand, and linguistic and anthropological semiotics on the other. Finally, Lacan has extended
and enriched the Freudian model, further consolidating the
theoretical interconnections between subject, signifier, and cultural order. His writings and seminars have provided the inspiration for much interesting work in the area of film theory, and
they are increasingly playing the same role in the related field
of literary theory.

An unusually large number of difficulties attend a serious
reading of Lacan. To begin with, although two volumes of his
essays have been published under the title *Ecrits,* much of his
work remains unavailable for the simple reason that it was dis-
seminated in the form of seminars. Those seminars have been
held annually in Paris since 1953, and transcripts of them have
only begun to be printed. Second, Lacan's prose is notoriously
remote, and his presentation deliberately a-systematic. Many of
the terms to which he most frequently returns constantly shift
meaning. These qualities make it almost impossible to offer definitive statements about the Lacanian argument; indeed, Lacan himself almost never agreed with his commentators. Finally, although Lacan insists that everything he says has its
origins in Freud's writings, his followers have been hard pressed
to reconcile Lacan's pronouncements on certain key issues, such
as the unconscious, with those made by Freud. We will consequently not attempt a comprehensive survey of the Lacanian
argument, but will focus instead on those parts of it which have
proved most assimilable to a broader psychoanalytic theory,
while at the same time extending that theory in the direction
of semiotic linguistics and anthropology.

Lacan's theory of the subject reads like a classic narrative—
it begins with birth, and then moves in turn through the territorialization of the body, the mirror stage, access to language,
and the Oedipus complex. The last two of these events belong
to what Lacan calls the symbolic order, and they mark the subject's coming of age within culture. Since each of the stages of
this narrative is conceived in terms of some kind of self-loss or
lack, we will first attempt to determine exactly what is implied
by that notion, particularly in relation to the subject's birth and

the zoning of its body. We will then progress with that subject through the mirror stage, the acquisition of language, and the adventures of the Oedipal.

i. *Birth, territorialization, and lack.* The concept of lack appears again and again in Lacan's writings and in the transcripts of his seminars, figuring centrally at every moment in the development of the subject. Indeed, one could say of the Lacanian subject that it is almost entirely defined by lack.

This point emerges with particular clarity in *Four Fundamental Concepts of Psycho-Analysis* (Seminar XI), which more than once invokes the story told by Aristophanes in Plato's *Symposium* about the birth of desire:

> . . . in the beginning we were nothing like we are now. For one thing, the race was divided into three . . . besides the two sexes, male and female, which we have at present, there was a third which partook of the nature of both. . . .
> And secondly . . . each of these beings was globular in shape, with rounded back and sides, four arms and four legs, and two faces. . . . And such . . . were their strength and energy, and such their arrogance, that they actually tried . . . to scale the heights of heaven and set upon the gods.
> At this Zeus took counsel with the other gods as to what was to be done. . . . At last . . . after racking his brains, Zeus offered a solution.
> I think I can see my way, he said, to put an end to this disturbance. . . . What I propose to do is to cut them all in half, thus killing two birds with one stone, for each one will be only half as strong, and there'll be twice as many of them. . . .
> Now, when the work of bisection was complete it left each half with a desperate yearning for the other, and they ran together and flung their arms around each other's necks, and asked for nothing better than to be rolled into one. So much so, that they began to die. . . . Zeus felt so sorry for them that he devised another scheme. He moved their privates round to the front . . . . and made them propagate among themselves. . . . So you see . . . how far back we can trace our innate love for one another, and how this love is always trying to reintegrate our former nature, to make two into one, and to bridge the gulf between one human being and other.[9]

I have quoted this passage at length because it contains a surprisingly large number of critical Lacanian assumptions. One of these assumptions is that the human subject derives from an original whole which was divided in half, and that its existence is dominated by the desire to recover its missing complement. Another of these assumptions is that the division suffered by the subject was sexual in nature—that when it was "sliced" in half, it lost the sexual androgyny it once had and was reduced to the biological dimension either of a man or a woman. This biological dimension is seen by Lacan, if not by Plato, as absolutely determining the subject's social identity. Finally, Lacan shares with Aristophanes the belief that the only resolution to the loss suffered by the subject as the consequence of sexual division is heterosexual union and procreation. We will examine each of these points in greater detail.

Lacan situates the first loss in the history of the subject at the moment of birth. To be more precise, he dates it from the moment of sexual differentiation within the womb, but it is not realized until the separation of the child from the mother at birth. This lack is sexual in definition; it has to do with the impossibility of being physiologically both male and female. Lacan refers to this lack as "real," by which he indicates that it occurs outside of signification. He tells us that it anticipates further divisions experienced by the subject within signification:

> Two lacks overlap here. The first emerges from the central defect around which the dialectic of the advent of the subject to his own being in relation to the Other turns—by the fact that the subject depends on the signifier and that the signifier is first of all in the field of the Other. This lack takes up the other lack, which is the real, earlier lack to be situated at the advent of the living being, that is to say, at sexed reproduction. The real lack is what the living being loses, that part of himself *qua* living being, in reproducing himself through the way of sex. This lack is real because it relates to something real, namely, that the living being, by being subject to sex, has fallen under the blow of individual death.[10]

The notion of an original androgynous whole, similar to that projected by Aristophanes, is absolutely central to Lacan's ar-

gument. The subject is defined as lacking because it is believed
to be a fragment of something larger and more primordial.

Lacan tells us that the only way the subject can compensate
for its fragmentary condition is by fulfilling its biological destiny—by living out in the most complete sense its own "maleness" or "femaleness," and by forming new sexual unions with
members of the opposite sex. It is by means of such unions that
the subject comes closest to recovering its lost wholeness.

Italo Calvino provides a witty and amorous account of that
state of imagined primordial wholeness in the story "Mitosis,"
which narrates from the point of view of a multicellular organism what life was like when it was only a single cell:

> . . . And when I say "dying of love,"—*Ofwfq went on,*—I mean
> something you have no idea of, because you think falling in
> love has to signify falling in love with another person, or thing,
> or what have you, in other words I'm here and what I'm in
> love with is there, in short a relationship connected to the life
> of relationships, whereas I'm talking about the times before I
> had established any relationships between myself and anything
> else, there was a cell and the cell was me, and that was that.
> Now we needn't wonder whether there were other cells around
> too, it doesn't matter, there was the cell that was me, and it
> was already quite an achievement, such a thing is more than
> enough to fill one's life, and it's this very sense of fullness I
> want to talk to you about, I don't mean fullness because of the
> protoplasm I had, because even it if had increased to a consid-
> erable degree it wasn't anything exceptional, cells of course are
> full of protoplasm, what else could they be full of; no, I'm
> talking about a sense of fullness that was, if you'll allow the
> expression, quote spiritual unquote, namely, the awareness that
> this cell was me, this sense of fullness, this fullness of being
> aware was something that kept me awake nights, something
> that made me beside myself, in other words the situation I
> mentioned before, I was "dying of love." [11]

As in the Lacanian scenario, the loss of this perfect fullness
finds inevitable expression in heterosexual object-love—in the
desire for one "Priscilla Langwood, chez Madame Lebras, cent-
quatre-vingt-treize rue Vaugirard, Paris quinzième." However,
the ironies of the passage are manifold, suggesting that the no-

tion of an original and unqualified wholeness is a cultural dream. Not only does the narrator achieve a kind of materialist reduction of that idealist concept by attributing spirituality to protoplasm, but he demonstrates the impossibility of talking about the self in other than relational terms, even when that self is assured to be whole and sufficient. In addition, he describes the condition of the single cell in ways which closely resemble the condition of cultural subjectivity; both are characterized by restlessness, the sense of being "beside" oneself, and the yearning for something else.

According to the Lacanian argument, the sexually differentiating scenarios of the culture into which the subject is later assimilated show it the "way" to "sexual fulfillment," the path to personal salvation. The Oedipus complex plays a particularly important role:

> Only this division [the sexual division] . . . makes necessary what was first revealed by analytic experience, namely, that the ways of what one must do as man or as woman are entirely abandoned to the drama, to the scenario, which is placed in the field of the Other—which, strictly speaking, is the Oedipus complex.
>
> I stressed this last time, when I told you that the human being has always to learn from scratch from the Other what he has to do, as man or as woman. I referred to the old woman in the story of Daphnis and Chloe, which shows us that there is an ultimate field, the field of sexual fulfillment, in which, in the last resort, the innocent does not know the way. [204]

What Lacan here suggests is that human "nature" finds its logical expression and complement in the cultural definitions of "male" and "female." However, at the same time he draws attention to the coerciveness of those definitions, and of the sexually differentiated narratives into which the subject is inserted. The word "innocent" is particularly revealing, indicating that the Oedipus complex effects the sexual differentiation which Lacan locates at birth, and that the notion of "lack" is something which the subject learns only after its entrance into the symbolic order.

The second loss suffered by the Lacanian subject occurs after birth, but prior to the acquisition of language. Although it takes place before the assimilation of the subject into the symbolic order, it can be viewed as the result of a cultural intervention. The loss in question is inflicted by what might be called the "pre-Oedipal territorialization" of the subject's body—by the preparation of the human body for the sexually differentiated scenarios into which it will later be accommodated.

For a time after its birth, the child does not differentiate between itself and the mother upon whose nurture it relies, or the blanket whose warmth it enjoys, or the pillow whose softness supports its head. Its libidinal flow is directed toward the complete assimilation of everything which is experienced as pleasurable, and there are no recognized boundaries. At this point the infant has the status of what Freud describes as an "oceanic self," or what Lacan punningly refers to as "l'homme-lette" (a human omelette which spreads in all directions).

However, the partitioning of the subject begins almost immediately. The child's body undergoes a process of differentiation, whereby erotogenic zones are inscribed and libido is canalized (i.e. encouraged to follow certain established routes). Specific somatic areas are designated as the appropriate sites of pleasure, and the areas which are so designated are all ones which open onto the external world—most importantly the mouth, the anus, the penis and the vagina. The mother is the usual agent of this inscription, defining the erotic zones through the care she lavishes upon them.

The territorialization of the infant's body provides the means whereby the outpouring of libido can be directed and contained. By indicating the channels through which that libido can move, the mother or nurse performs a social service, assists in the conversion of incoherent energy into coherent drives which can later be culturally regulated. Indeed, by organizing the infant's body in relation to its reproductive potential, the mother or nurse already indicates the form which that cultural regulation will take: the orchestration of the drives around sexual difference.

The drives possess a coherence which needs do not have because they are attached to particular corporal zones—because they in effect represent those zones (mouth, anus, penis, vagina). As a result of this attachment, the drives provide only an indirect expression of the original libidinal flow. Thus very early in its history the subject loses unmediated contact with its own libidinal flows, and succumbs to the domination of its culture's genital economy. In "From Love to the Libido" Lacan underscores both the deprivation experienced by the subject as a consequence of this mapping operation, and the fact that it is thereby brought under the symbolic rule of the reproductive organs:

> . . . the libido, *qua* pure life instinct, that is to say, immortal life, or irrepressible life, life that has need of no organ, simplified, indestructible life . . . is precisely what is subtracted from the living being by virtue of the fact that it is subject to the cycle of sexed reproduction. [198]

The erotogenic zones or somatic gaps become the points through which the child attempts to introject into itself those things which give it pleasure, and which it does not yet distinguish from itself. The first such object is generally the breast, and it is of course inserted into the orifice of the mouth. The child perceives the breast as its missing complement, that thing the loss of which has resulted in a sense of deficiency or lack ("The breast—as equivocal, as an element characteristic of the mammiferous organization, the placenta, for example—certainly represents that part of himself that the individual loses at birth, and which may serve to symbolize the most profound lost object" (198)). Other objects which enjoy the same privileged status are the feces, and the gaze and voice of another, such as the mother.

There will be many such objects in the life of the subject. Lacan refers to them as *"objets petit a,"* which is an abbreviation for the more complete formula *"objets petit autre."* This rubric designates objects which are not clearly distinguished from the self and which are not fully grasped as other (*autre*). The object (a), as we will henceforth refer to it, derives its value from its identification with some missing component of the subject's self, whether that loss is seen as primordial, as the result of a bodily organization, or as the consequence of some other division.

Orson Welles gives us a conspicuous example of the object (a) in *Citizen Kane;* indeed, he organizes the entire film around it. That object is of course the sled named "Rosebud" with which the young Charles Kane is seen playing early in the film, as his mother watches him from the window of their house. At that point in the story Charles obviously identifies strongly both with the sled and his mother, whose gaze he seems to solicit as he plays. The events which follow rupture his relationship with both, and constitute Rosebud, at least at the manifest level, as "the most profound lost object." Throughout the rest of the film he is shown obsessively collecting objects in a vain attempt to compensate for its loss, a loss which he experiences as an amputation.

The register within which these identifications are sustained—within which the objects (a) acquire their privileged status—is called by Lacan the "imaginary."

ii. *The imaginary.* "Imaginary" is the term used by Lacan to designate that order of the subject's experience which is dominated by identification and duality. Within the Lacanian scheme it not only precedes the symbolic order, which introduces the subject to language and Oedipal triangulation, but continues to coexist with it afterward. The two registers complement each other, the symbolic establishing the differences which are such an essential part of cultural existence, and the imaginary making it possible to discover correspondences and homologies. The imaginary order is most classically exemplified by the mirror stage.

Lacan tells us that somewhere between the ages of six months and eighteen months the subject arrives at an apprehension of both its self and the other—indeed, of its self *as other*. This discovery is assisted by the child seeing, for the first time, its own reflection in a mirror. That reflection enjoys a coherence which the subject itself lacks—it is an *ideal* image:

> This jubilant assumption of his specular image by the child at the *infans* stage, still sunk in his motor incapacity and nursling dependence, would seem to exhibit in an exemplary situation the symbolic matrix in which the *I* is precipitated in a

primordial form, before it is objectified in the dialectic of identification with the other, and before language restores to it, in
the universal, its function as subject.

This form would have to be called the Ideal-I, if we wished
to incorporate it into our usual register, in the sense that it will
also be the source of secondary identifications, under which
term I would place the functions of libidinal normalization.
But the important point is that this form situates the agency
of the ego, before its social determination, in a fictional direction, which will always remain irreducible for the individual
alone. . . .[12]

This self-recognition is, Lacan insists, a mis-recognition; the
subject apprehends itself only by means of a fictional construct
whose defining characteristics—focus, coordination—it does not
share. It must also be stressed that the mirror stage is one of
those crises of alienation around which the Lacanian subject is
organized, since to know oneself through an external image is
to be defined through self-alienation.

The situation here closely resembles that in which the subject identifies with the mother's breast, voice, gaze, or whatever
other object is perceived as its missing complement. The mirror
image can no more be assimilated than can any of those other
privileged objects, yet the subject defines itself entirely in relation to it. As a consequence of the irreducible distance which
separates the subject from its ideal reflection, it entertains a
profoundly ambivalent relationship to that reflection. It loves
the coherent identity which the mirror provides. However, because the image remains external to it, it also hates that image.

This radical oscillation between contrary emotions in respect to the same object characterizes all of the relationships of
the imaginary order. As long as the subject remains trapped
within that order, it will be unable to mediate between or escape from the binary oppositions which structure all of its perceptions; it will fluctuate between the extremes of love and hate
toward objects which will undergo corresponding shifts in value.
Moreover, the subject will itself be capable of identifying alternately with diametrically opposed positions (victim/victimizer,
exhibitionist/voyeur, slave/master).[13]

The binary extremes of the imaginary order are vividly

evoked by a passage from the "Combray" section of *Swann's Way*, where Marcel meets Gilberte for the first time. She makes what he believes to be an insulting gesture in his direction, and he promptly falls passionately in love/hate with her:

> I loved her; I was sorry not to have had the time and the inspiration to insult her, to do her some injury, to force her to keep some memory of me. I knew her to be so beautiful that I should have liked to be able to retrace my steps so as to shake my fist at her and shout, "I think you are hideous, grotesque; you are utterly disgusting!" [109]

The same emotional ambivalence can be seen in the relationship of Catherine and Heathcliffe in *Wuthering Heights,* or Gilda and Johnny in the film *Gilda.* The last two instances dramatize as well the tendency of the subject in thrall to imaginary identifications to occupy in turn both sides of a dyad. Catherine's most famous remark is "Nelly, I *am* Heathcliffe," and with it she draws attention to the narcissistic bases of their association. Gilda does the same thing when she tells Johnny: "I hate you so much I'd destroy myself to bring you down."

The important role played by visual images in the identifications of the imaginary order has made this part of Lacan's model particularly rich in implications for the study of film. Indeed, as we noted earlier, Christian Metz in *Le Signifiant imaginaire* has defined the cinematic signifier as an imaginary one—as one which induces by means of visual images the same sorts of identifications which occur early in the subject's life, and within which absence plays the same structuring role. However, it would seem important to understand that the images which figure so centrally in the imaginary register exceed any strictly specular definition, and that they can be generated by many other sources. Anika Lemaire indicates the range of those sources in her study of Lacan:

> The imaginary is an infinitely supple conceptual category. It covers everything in the phantasy which is an image or representation of a lived experience pertaining to the castration complex before its formalization—forever incomplete, of course—becomes petrified in the symbol of the "Phallus." At

the level of our example, the imaginary concerns the intuitive lived experience of the body (the receptive hollow, the erectile form, for example), of the affects (dependence, welcome, gift, etc.), of activity, of passivity, of the will to power, etc., lived experiences which overlap, accumulate, and overflow into infinite successions of sensorial, emotional and conceptual jugglings.[14]

A closely related issue which would seem to warrant some additional clarification is the relationship between the mirror stage and the Oedipus complex, i.e. between pre- and post-symbolic identifications. Lacan suggests that the image which the child discovers in the mirror is ideologically neutral, that it has no social determination. At the same time he tells us that the child's identification with that image takes exactly the same form as subsequent identifications with images which *are* socially determined. During the Oedipus complex, for instance, the male subject identifies with an ideal paternal representation which exceeds him in much the same way as the mirror image exceeds the child, and he entertains the same ambivalent feelings toward that representation. The question we are thus obliged to ask is whether the mirror stage is not in some manner culturally induced.

Careful scrutiny of the account given to us of the mirror stage reveals undeniable traces of cultural intervention, most notably in the term "ideal" by means of which Lacan qualifies the pronoun "I." "Ideal" is a term which has meaning only within a system of values. It indicates that social norms play an important role in the mirror stage, and that the child's identity is from the very beginning culturally mediated. That mediation may be as simple and direct as the mother's interpretation of the mirror image for the child, or as complex and diffuse as the introduction into the child's environment of various representations (dolls, picture-books, trains, or toy guns) which determine the way in which it will eventually regard itself. As most readers of "The mirror stage" are quick to point out, we cannot interpret the reflection within which the child finds its identity too literally; it must be understood at least to some degree as a cultural construct. There are even theoreticians like Benveniste who go so far as to assert that language provides the only medium within which the subject finds itself.

It is probably most helpful to think of the mirror stage as always occurring from within the symbolic order, and as an event which is in some way culturally orchestrated. Lacan himself encourages us to conceptualize the mirror stage along these lines, since he describes it as a moment which is only retrospectively realized—realized from a position within language, and within the symbolic.

Since *Madame Bovary* places such an insistent emphasis on the cultural sources from which ideal images derive—churches, schools, the marketplace, literature—a passage from that novel may help to clarify for us the fact that ideal representations are always socially mediated. It should also serve to indicate the broad sense in which we must understand the term "image." Finally, this passage will remind us that the identity of the subject is sustained only through the constant repetition of the same identifications by means of which it first finds itself. The excerpt in question is taken from a conversation between Emma and Léon which makes explicit what is everywhere implicit in the novel: that both Emma's identity and her desires have been almost entirely structured by the romantic novels she has read obsessively since she was a schoolgirl:

> "One thinks of nothing," [Léon] continued; "the hours slip by. Without having to move, we talk through the countries of our imagination, and your thought, blending with the fiction, toys with the details, follows the outlines of the adventures. It mingles with the characters, and it seems you are living their lives, that your own heart beats in their breast."
>
> "That is true! that is true!" she said.
>
> "Has it ever happened to you," Léon went on, "to discover some vague idea of one's own in a book, some dim image that comes back to you from afar, and as the fullest expression of your own slightest sentiment?"
>
> "I have experienced it," she replied.
>
> "That is why," he said, "I especially love the poets. I think verse more tender than prose, and that it makes one weep more easily."
>
> "Still in the long run it is tiring," continued Emma, "and

now, on the contrary, I have come to love stories that rush breathlessly along, that frighten one. I detest commonplace heroes and moderate feelings, as one finds them in nature." [59]

Emma constantly discovers familiar ideas and images in the books she devours because each reading is in effect a re-reading. Since these sorts of books earlier defined her identity, it is hardly surprising that in turning to them once again she finds that identity reconfirmed.

The novels in question not only endlessly project the same images of women, but they repeat the same masochistic narratives ("They were all about love, lovers, sweethearts, persecuted ladies fainting in lonely pavilions, postilions killed at every relay, horses ridden to death on every page, sombre forests, heartaches, vows, sobs, tears and kisses" (26). To identify with these images of women is simultaneously to take up residence in their masochistic narratives, as Léon himself implies ("it seems you are living their lives"). This conversation between Emma and Léon once again suggests that the imaginary order—the order of equations and identifications—and the symbolic order—the order of language, discourse, narrative—are so closely imbricated as to be virtually inseparable.

As we noted above, there can be no resolution of the emotional extremes of the original narcissistic relationship so long as the subject remains within the imaginary order. That resolution comes only with the subject's access to language and its accommodations within the triangular configuration of the Oedipal paradigm—in other words, with its entry into the symbolic order. However, both these events result in additional self-losses, alienate the subject even more fully from its own needs. We will deal first with those losses inflicted by language, and then with those suffered by the subject as the consequence of its Oedipalization.

iii. *Signification.* We will begin our discussion of the subject's acquisition of language with a brief account of Lacan's theory of signification. A passage from "The freudian thing" in which Lacan offers an unusually explicit and comprehensive series of remarks about signification will assist us in that task. This passage equates the signifier with the paradigmatic, and the signified with the syntagmatic. It also opposes signification to reality. As we shall see, the two sets of assumptions are intimately connected:

> A psychoanalysis should find it easy enough to grasp the fundamental distinction between signifier and signified, and to begin to use the two non-overlapping networks of relations that they organize.
>
> The first structure, that of the signifier, is the synchronic structure of the language material in so far as in that structure each element assumes its precise function by being different from the others; this is the principle of distribution that alone governs the function of the elements of the language (*langue*) at its different levels, from the phonematic pair of oppositions to the compound expressions to disengage the stable forms of which is the task of the most modern research.
>
> The second network, that of the signified, is the diachronic set of the concretely pronounced discourses, which reacts historically on the first, just as the structure of the first governs the pathways of the second. The dominant factor here is the unity of signification, which proves never to be resolved into a pure indication of the real, but always refers back to another signification. That is to say, the signification is realized only on the basis of a grasp of things in their totality.[15]

When Lacan refers to the synchronic network he invokes the Saussurean tenet that every signifying element assumes value in relation to all of the other signifying elements with which it is paradigmatically classed. In other words, he reminds us that meaning emerges as the result of the play of differences within a closed system. However, whereas Saussure indicates that both signifiers and signifieds enjoy paradigmatic relationships, Lacan associates those relationships exclusively with the signifier.

Lacan establishes a corresponding connection between syntagmatic relationships and the signified. He argues that meaning emerges only through the temporal or diachronic unfolding of a signifying chain. Since it does not pre-exist the syntagmatic alignment of signifiers, the signified *is* that syntagmatic alignment. Lacan thus denies the possibility of meaning inhering in any isolated unit, attributing signifying capabilities only to the discursive complex.

Coexisting with the definition of signifier as paradigm and signified as syntagm is another, equally important conceptualization of those terms. Although Lacan repeatedly emphasizes the linguistic status of the signifier—i.e. its formal properties— many passages in his writings project a more inclusive understanding of it—an understanding which encompasses what Saussure would call the signified. He conceives of the relationship between the formal and conceptual dimensions in determinedly abstract ways; he tells us that the concept "insists" within the form or "letter." The Lacanian signifier is thus an elusive blend of idea and form.

"Function and field of speech and language" suggests that what is really at issue in this super-subtle definition is the signifier's liberation from any obligation to represent the world of real objects. The only means by which such a liberation can be effected is to tie the signifier to a concept which is as much a part of a closed system as is the material "letter":

> In order for the symbolic object freed from its usage to become the word freed from the *hic et nunc,* the difference resides not in its material quality as sound, but in its evanescent being in which the symbol finds the permanence of the concept.[16]

Within the Lacanian argument the signifier is the mark of the subject's radical alienation from the real—from its organic nature, from actual mothers or fathers, or from any phenomenal experience. Thus the signifier "father" has no relation whatever to the physical fact of any individual father. Instead, that signifier finds its support in a network of other signifiers, including "phallus," "law," "adequacy," and "mother," all of which are equally indifferent to the category of the real.

For Lacan, the definitive criterion of a signifier is that it abandon all relation to the real, and take up residence within a closed field of meaning, not that it partake of a given materiality. Language is consequently not the only source of signifiers; dietary rituals, marriage ceremonies, hysteria, conventions of dress, and neuroses all generate signifiers. Indeed, since signification constitutes the matrix within which the subject resides after its entry into the symbolic order, nothing escapes cultural value. In a celebrated passage from "Function and field of speech and language," Lacan describes the subject as entirely contained within a network of signification:

> Symbols . . . envelop the life of man in a network so total that they join together, before he comes into the world, those who are going to engender him "by flesh and blood"; so total that they bring to his birth . . . the share of his destiny; so total that they give the words that will make him faithful or renegade, the law of the acts that will follow him right to the very place where he *is* not yet and even beyond his death; and so total that through them his end finds its meaning in the last judgement, where the Word absolves his being or condemns it. . . . [68]

At the same time as we indicate the range of signifying materials, it is important to note the privileged position enjoyed by language. For Lacan, as for Barthes, languages mediates all other signifiers. This means that we have access to the signifiers generated by dietary rituals, marriage ceremonies, hysteria, conventions of dress, or neuroses only through linguistic ones. It also means that the subject participates in signification only after the acquisition of language. Prior to that acquisition, the subject engages in representation, but not what Lacan calls the "non-representative representation" which constitutes signification.

This last distinction is a critical one within the Lacanian argument. It is used to differentiate iconic and indexical signifiers from purely conventional ones—to distinguish, that is, between a mirror image or a photograph, which refers in some way (albeit indirectly) to an actual object, and a word, which has abandoned any such association and refers only to other elements within the same system. A consequence of the non-representational status of language is that the signified is always provisional—that it is never "resolved back into a pure indication of the real." Every signified functions in turn as a signifier; in short, every signified is commutable. Lacan is not as explicit as one might like him to be about the subject's entrance into language. However, he does return repeatedly to three points: He tells us that language isolates the subject from the real, confining it forever to the realm of signification; he indicates that the unconscious comes into existence at the moment of the subject's access to language; finally, he insists that the unconscious is organized around an irreducible signifier, otherwise called the "unary" signifier.

The real from which language excludes the subject consists of both the subject's own "being" (its libidinal resources or needs) and the phenomenal world. Once the subject has entered the symbolic order its organic needs pass through the "defiles" or network of signification and are transformed in a way which makes them thereafter impossible to satisfy. The drives offer only a partial and indirect expression of those needs, but language severs the relationship altogether. It is, as we have just observed, *non-representative*. Moreover, since language speaks no more to the reality of objects than it does to that of subjects, it effects as complete a rupture with the phenomenal world.

With the subject's entry into the symbolic order it is reduced to the status of a signifier in the field of the Other. It is defined by a linguistic structure which does not in any way address its being, but which determines its entire cultural existence. Lacan insists that the subject is linguistically coerced not only at the level of the preconscious, as Freud would argue, but at that of the unconscious as well. Within his scheme "the unconscious is the discourse of the Other"; its desires are those of an already constituted social order, and it is organized by means of the same language as the preconscious.

Lacan conceives of the unconscious not as an inarticulate and chaotic region, but as a signifying network. He observes in "Agency of the letter in the unconscious" that it is "neither primordial nor instinctual; what it knows about the elementary is no more than the elements of the signifier."[17] Within the Lacanian scheme the unconscious is split off not only from the undifferentiated needs which comprise the subject's being, but from the drives, which as we indicated earlier are themselves already the product of a cultural mediation, i.e. of the territorialization of the body. Indeed, the unconscious is as sharply partitioned from the drives as the preconscious/conscious system is from the unconscious. It is thus altogether opposed to the area designated as the "id" in the late Freudian topography, an area which is virtually synonymous with the drives. It much more closely resembles the unconscious elaborated by *The Interpretation of Dreams,* in that it too can only be defined through its signifying activities.

Within the Lacanian account both the subject's entrance into the symbolic and the formation of the unconscious are effected through a single signifying event. This event involves only two signifiers—what Lacan calls the "unary" and the "binary" signifiers. Together they inaugurate a closed system of signification, one which excludes both the phenomenal world and the drives. Lacan pays particular attention to the second of these exclusions, and he illustrates it through the story Freud tells about his grandson in *The Interpretation of Dreams* and *Beyond the Pleasure Principle.* Although we have already had occasion to discuss this story briefly, I will quote the second version of it in full here:

> The child was not at all precocious in his intellectual development. At the age of one and a half he could say only a few comprehensible words; he could also make use of a number of sounds which expressed a meaning intelligible to those around him. He was, however, on good terms with his parents and their one servant-girl, and tributes were paid to his being a "good boy." He did not disturb his parents at night, he conscientiously obeyed orders not to touch certain things or go into certain rooms, and above all he never cried when his mother left him for a few hours. At the same time, he was greatly attached to his mother, who had not only fed him herself but had also looked after him without any outside help. This good little boy, however, had an occasional disturbing habit of taking any small objects he could get hold of and throwing them away from him into a corner, under the bed, and so on, so that hunting for his toys and picking them up was often quite a business. As he did this he gave vent to a long-drawn-out "o-o-o—," accompanied by an expression of interest and satisfaction. His mother and the writer of the present account were agreed in thinking that this was not a mere interjection but represented the German word *"fort"*

[gone]. I eventually realized that it was a game and that the only use he made of any of his toys was to play "gone" with them. One day I made an observation which confirmed my view. The child had a wooden reel with a piece of string tied round it. It never occurred to him to pull it along the floor behind him, for instance, and to play at its being a carriage. What he did was to hold the reel by the string and very skill-fully throw it over the edge of his curtained cot, so that it disappeared into it, at the same time uttering his expressive "o-o-o-o." He then pulled the reel out of the cot again by the string and hailed its reappearance with a joyful "*da*" [there]. This, then, was the complete game—disappearance and re-turn. [XVIII. 14–15]

There are significant differences between the Lacanian and Freudian approaches to this important episode in the history of an exemplary subject. Whereas Freud describes the child's actions as an attempt to diminish the unpleasure caused by his mother's absences, Lacan stresses instead the self-alienation which those actions dramatize. In other words, Lacan identifies the toy with which the child plays as an object (a), one of those privileged items which the subject perceives as its own missing complement. Lacan thus interprets the story more as a parable about the disappearance of the self than the disappearance of the mother. In "Tuché and Automaton" he asserts that

This reel is not the mother reduced to a little ball by some magical game worthy of the Jivaros—it is a small part of the subject which detaches itself from him while still remaining his, still retained. . . . If it is true that the signifier is the first mark of the subject, how can we fail to recognize here—from the very fact that this game is accompanied by one of the first oppositions to appear—that it is in the object to which the op-position is applied in act, the reel, that we must designate the subject. To this object we will later give the name it bears in the Lacanian algebra—the *petit a*. [18]

What Lacan here suggests is that at this stage in its history the subject does not yet distinguish between itself and an exter-nal realm; it is still caught up in the imaginary register, the register of identification and emotional ambivalence. It identifies the toy with itself, just as it identifies parts of the mother or its own mirror image with itself, and it directs toward the toy the same conflicting emotions that crystallize around those other objects. The young subject, here represented by Freud's grandson, stages a drama ideally suited to express these conflicting emotions—a drama of presence and absence, appearance and disappearance.

The notion that what the child thereby acts out are not so much his mother's entrances and departures as his own was unwittingly suggested by Freud himself, in a footnote to the final account of the game:

> One day the child's mother had been away for several hours and on her return was met with the words "Baby o-o-o-o!" which was at first incomprehensible. It soon turned out, however, that during this long period of solitude the child had found a method of making *himself* disappear. He had discovered his reflection in a full-length mirror which did not quite reach to the ground, so that by crouching down he could make his mirror-image "gone." [XVIII .15]

Not only does a mirror image play a prominent role in this version of the game, but the child manifests in relation to that image precisely the combination of love and hate described by Lacan. The whole of the Lacanian theory of the imaginary register, complete with the mirror stage and the object (a), is thus contained within the simple story about his grandson which Freud tells twice. So, as we shall see, is Lacan's theory of signification.

Like Freud, Lacan reads the *"fort"/"da"* episode as an allegory about the linguistic mastery of the drives. However, whereas Freud connects that mastery with the binding activity which helps to bring the *preconscious* into existence, Lacan associates it with a signifying transaction by means of which the *unconscious* is established. This signifying transaction involves the terms *"fort"* and *"da,"* and the play of differences between them which has the effect of eliminating any outside reference.

Rather than focusing, as Freud does, on the compulsively repetitive aspects of the game, Lacan emphasizes the phonemic opposition between the "o" and "a" in the words uttered by the child. He sees that formal opposition as ushering in a conceptual one, and in the process creating a self-enclosed signifying system. Moreover, since they are not only paradigmatically related terms, but syntagmatically connected in the game, they also constitute a self-enclosed discourse. These signifying alliances function to exclude altogether both the speaker's lost complement, represented in the game by the toy, and the hostile and erotic drives which find expression in the actions of throwing away and recovering that toy. The mechanisms of this exclusion, and its consequences for the subject, warrant further clarification.

Freud tells us that prior to the episode in question his grandson knew only a few words. Because of their isolation from each other, these words did not enjoy the status of signifiers; they lacked both paradigmatic and syntagmatic relationships. The complete version of the *"fort"*/*"da"* game—the one which involves both words—must thus be seen as the child's first signifying chain, and hence his entry into language.

However, we learn in *Beyond the Pleasure Principle* that the child enacted an incomplete version on numerous occasions before he ever enacted the complete one—a version, that is, in which only the word *"fort"* was uttered. Lacan refers to this solitary signifier, this signifier which as yet lacks any paradigmatic or syntagmatic "company"—as the "unary" signifier. The unary signifier can best be described as that thing which intervenes between the drives and meaning, and it is indicated in the following diagram by the rubric "non-meaning":

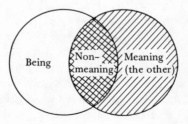

The unary signifier does not itself participate in meaning because there is neither a linguistic system nor a discourse to support it. It is both nonsensical and irreducible—nonsensical because there is no other signifier into which it can be translated, or to which it can be referred, and irreducible because it does not represent, cannot be reduced to the drives.

The situation is altogether different when the child utters "*da*," since it refers back to "*fort*" both paradigmatically and syntagmatically. Lacan calls this second signifier "binary," and he attributes to it a number of momentous and closely connected events: the creation of meaning; the exclusion of the drives; the formation of the unconscious; the emergence of the subject into the symbolic order, otherwise known as the field of the Other; and the inauguration of desire.

With the addition of "*da*" to "*fort*," the latter falls to the position of a signified to the former. In other words, "*da*" henceforth means "*fort*," just as any signifying term in effect means those other terms upon which it depends for all its value and significance. (When we attempt to define a word, for instance, we often list its synonyms or its antonyms.) However, "*fort*" is inscribed in the psyche in its original, nonsensical form, and the unconscious takes shape around it. (It is, of course, reinscribed in the preconscious as a word which signifies like any other. This is the principle of double inscription with which Freud familiarizes us.)

Since the binary signifier ("*da*") refers back to the unary signifier ("*fort*") instead of to the drives, it effects a complete rupture with them. Lacan describes this rupture as the "fading" of the subject's being in the face of its meaning:

> . . . that first signifying coupling . . . enables us to conceive that the signifier appears first in the Other, in so far as the first signifier, the unary signifier, emerges in the field of the Other and represents the subject for another signifier, which other signifier has as its effect the *aphanisis* of the subject. Hence the division of the subject—when the subject appears somewhere as meaning, he is manifested elsewhere as "fading," as disappearance. There is, then, one might say, a matter of life and death between the unary signifier and the subject, *qua* binary signifier, cause of his disappearance.[19]

This fading or "aphanisis" represents the most extreme and permanent of the alienations by means of which the Lacanian subject is constituted. Not only is the subject thereby split off or partitioned from its own drives, but it is subordinated to a symbolic order which will henceforth entirely determine its identity and desires. It will from this point forward participate in the discourse of the Other, and regard itself from the space of the Other.[20] Moreover, it will do so at two non-communicating levels, one unconscious and the other preconscious.

The extreme formulation "a signifier is that which represents the subject for another signifier" indicates the degree to which the subject is dependent upon—indeed secondary to— the meaning which constitutes it. This is Lacan's way of saying once again that subjectivity is the product of a signifying transaction which excludes the drives, that it is the effect of a relationship between two signifiers. Benveniste makes the same point in different and more accessible terms when he asserts that subjectivity finds its locus in the pronoun "I," which derives all of its value and significance from the pronoun "you."

Because it is not assimilable to the closed system of meaning inaugurated by the binary signifier, the unary signifier might be conceptualized as the trace of the repression suffered by the drives—as the mark of the subject's rupture with its being. Indeed, Lacan refers to it as embodying a "traumatic" non-meaning, suggesting that it is there that the reverberations of the conflict between being and meaning are registered. This nonsensical signifier attests too fully to the terms upon which the subject enters the symbolic order to be available to the conscious subject, and it is hidden away in the unconscious.

Although the unary signifier remains external to meaning, it plays a vital supporting role. Because it is nonsensical, it sets in motion an absolutely fluid play of signification, one which has no fixed reference point. The unary signifier permits the establishment of a signifying system within which there are no positive values, only differences. It is thus the antithesis of the transcendental signified, which functions to control and arrest meaning. In "From Interpretation to the Transference" Lacan compares the unary signifier to a zero in the position of a mathematical denominator:

> Everyone knows that if zero appears in the denominator,
> the value of the fraction no longer has meaning, but assumes
> by convention what mathematicians call an infinite value. In a

way, this is one of the stages in the constitution of the subject. In so far as the primary signifier is pure non-sense, it becomes the bearer of the infinitization of the value of the subject, not open to all meanings, but abolishing them, which is different. . . . What, in effect, grounds, in the meaning and radical non-meaning of the subject, the function of freedom, is strictly speaking this signifier which kills all meanings.

That is why it is untrue to say that the signifier in the unconscious is open to all meanings. It constitutes the subject in his freedom in relation to all meanings, but this does not mean that it is not determined in it. For, in the numerator, in the place of zero, the things that are inscribed are significations, dialectized significations in the relation of the desire of the Other, and they give a particular value to the relation of the subject to the unconscious.[21]

The nonsensicality of the unary signifier frees the linguistic system from any obligation to defer to it, just as a zero in the position of the denominator frees the numerator from any obligation to defer to it. In other words, the non-meaning of the unary signifier initiates the process of endless displacements and substitutions which comprise signification within the Lacanian scheme. At the same time, it deprives the subject of any autonomy. As a consequence of the central part played by the unary signifier in the organization of the subject, the latter has no meaning of its "own," and is entirely subordinated to the field of social meaning and desire.

The unary signifier is not the only signifying element within the Lacanian unconscious, merely the focal point. Numerous other signifiers are later assimilated into the unconscious, drawn there by the first one:

This signifier constitutes the central point of the *Urverdrängung*—of what, from having passed into the unconscious will be . . . the point of attraction, through which all the other repressions will be possible, all the other similar passages in the locus of the *Unterdrückt,* of what has passed underneath as signifier.[22]

The signifiers which subsequently enter the unconscious all do so through repressions of the sort to which first the drives, and then the unary signifier, are subjected. It is imperative to understand that these primary repressions involve self-losses, losses which are even more profound than those incurred through the territorialization of the body or the mirror stage. Within the Lacanian argument the drives represent the final and already elaborately mediated contact which the subject entertains with its being. The unary signifier attests to the permanent disappearance of that being—to the fact that with the inauguration of meaning it is irretrievably "gone" (*"fort"*). The unconscious is the area where these self-losses—as well as future ones—are inscribed.

This extremely difficult and abstract part of the Lacanian argument would seem to require a second illustration. Werner Herzog's film, *Everyman for Himself and God Against All,* which recounts the famous story of Kaspar Hauser, a "wild child" or *"enfant sauvage,"* dramatizes the acquisition of language in ways which conform with startling precision to the *"fort"*/*"da"* episode. It would thus seem ideally suited further to clarify the relationship between signification and the real.

At the beginning of the film Kaspar is wrenched out of the cave in which he has spent the thirty years of his life, given a brief and violent lesson in walking, taught a few words which suggest nothing more than sound to him, and abandoned in the central square of a small German town. After vainly interrogating him about his past, the townspeople put him in the local prison. Kaspar's entry into language occurs during his first visit to the dinner table, after the jailer and his wife have decided that he should be treated as an oversized child.

Kaspar's body is molded into the requisite shape for sitting at the table, and a spoon is placed in his hand. Everyone coaxes him to eat, but the food tastes alien to him and he spits it out. However, he enthusiastically consumes water when it is offered to him, and turns the cup upside down to extract more when he has exhausted the contents. The following exchange occurs:

> Child: Look, it's empty. There isn't anything else in-
> side. Nothing else will come out of it.

Jailer: Empty.

Child: Empty.

Kaspar: Empty. (*his face is animated*)

Jailer: Nothing else will come out of it.
(*The child turns the container upside down and taps on the bottom.*)

Kaspar: (*articulating with difficulty*): Empty.
(*The child puts the container back on the table and resumes eating.*)

Kaspar: (*reaching for a different container*): Empty.

Jailer: No, that pot isn't empty. There's beer inside. There's beer. Look, it's full.
(*He puts his finger in the container of beer.*) It isn't empty. (*He reaches for the empty container and puts his finger inside it.*) This pot is empty. There's nothing inside it, it's empty.

Kaspar: Empty.

Jailer: (*satisfied*): Yes, it's empty.

Like Freud's grandson, Kaspar is here confronted by the absence of a beloved object, an absence which makes palpable the separateness of the object from the self. The signifier which emerges in the gap opened up by that absence does not "name" the object (water), any more than *"fort"* designates the toy reel; the word which Kaspar learns, "empty," signifies the *absence* of the beloved object and hence of his drives, and it does so not through any existential reference, but through an interaction with its binary opposite, "full."

Kaspar's entry into meaning—into the symbolic order of nineteenth-century Germany—confines him inside what Fredric Jameson would call "the prisonhouse of language." Not only does this episode take place inside an actual jail, but as soon as the language lesson is over the camera cuts to a caged bird. Kaspar is thereafter as fully alienated from his being, and from the world of actual objects, as was Freud's grandson after he uttered the word *"da."*

However, unlike the latter, who proved to be an exemplary cultural subject, Kaspar does not altogether acquiesce to the loss of his being in signification. In one of the film's most poignant scenes, he transforms the signifier which confers subjectivity upon him into a plot of grass; he plants his name in cress

seeds, and watches it grow. In other words, he attempts to replace a set of signifying relationships with an existential one.
Afterwards he tells us that this brief rapprochement between
being and meaning gave him a "joy which I can't describe,"
suggesting the inability of language to survive such an extreme
dislocation.

Within the Lacanian account of subjectivity one other momentous event is linked to these others—to the inauguration of
meaning, the loss of the real, the formation of the unconscious,
and the entry into the symbolic—and that event is the birth of
desire. Desire commences as soon as the drives are split off
from the subject, consigned forever to a state of non-represen-
tation and non-fulfillment. In short, it begins with the subject's
emergence into meaning. Desire has its origins not only in the
alienation of the subject from its being, but in the subject's perception of its distinctness from the objects with which it earlier
identified. It is thus the product of the divisions by means of
which the subject is constituted, divisions which inspire in the
subject a profound sense of lack.

Lacan characterizes desire as "impossible"—impossible both
because it derives its energy from the drives, and because it
derives its goals from the symbolic. As Lacan suggests in "Direction of treatment and principles of its power," desire is fueled
by drives which can never be satisfied because they have been
denied any expression within the subject's psychic economy:

> Desire is produced in the beyond of the demand, in that, in
> articulating the life of the subject according to its conditions,
> demand cuts off the need from that life . . . In this embodied
> aporia, of which one might say that it borrows, as it were, its
> heavy soul from the hardy shoots of the wounded drive, and
> its subtle body from the death actualized in the signifying se-
> quence, desire is affirmed as the absolute condition.[23]

Moreover, desire is directed toward ideal representations which
remain forever beyond the subject's reach. The first of these
representations, as we have already observed, is the mirror image in which the subject initially "finds" its identity. The identifications which the subject is encouraged to make immediately
upon its entry into the symbolic order, and which exercise a
kind of retroactive influence over the mirror stage, are calcu-

lated to induce in the subject an even more radical sense of inadequacy and lack. It is as a consequence of these identifications—identifications, that is, with maternal and paternal representations—that the subject discovers itself to be "castrated."

The Oedipus complex will not only determine the subject's future relations with itself, but those it entertains with others. Desire will therefore always be impossible, whether it pertains to the self or to an other. Indeed, since others will be loved only if they are believed to be capable of completing the subject, desire must be understood as fundamentally narcissistic.

Proust indicates the continuity between narcissistic and object love when he attempts in *Within a Budding Grove* to account for the points of coincidence between Gilberte, Marcel's first girl friend, and Albertine, his second. We discover there that object love is nothing more than the continued search for the lost complement—that it is, in fact, a form of self-love:

> If in this craze for amusement Albertine might be said to echo something of the old original Gilberte, that is because a certain similarity exists, although the type evolves, between all the women we love, a similarity that is due to the fixity of our own temperament, which it is that chooses them, eliminating all those who would not be at once our opposite and our complement, fitted that is to say to gratify our senses and to wring our heart. They are, these women, a product of our temperament, an image inversely projected, a negative of our sensibility. [342–43]

This passage from the second volume of *Remembrance of Things Past* not only demonstrates the narcissistic bases of desire, but reminds us of the vital part played by ideal representations in defining for the subject what it lacks. Not only does language provide the agency of self-loss, but cultural representations supply the standard by which that loss is perceived. We look within the mirror of those representations—representations which structure every moment of our existence—not only to discover what we are, but what we can never hope to be and (as a consequence) hopelessly desire. Proust also reminds us that each of these ideal images derives its value and significance from its opposite or "inverse"—i.e. that it is culturally defined.

The subject not only learns to desire within the symbolic

order; it learns *what* to desire. It is there taught to value only
those objects which are culturally designated as full and complete. Its desires, like its identity, originate from the place of
the Other. This is a point upon which Lacan insists in "The direction of the treatment and the principles of its power":

> —if desire is an effect in the subject of the condition that is
> imposed on him by the existence of the discourse, to make his
> need pass through the defiles of the signifier;
> —if, on the other hand . . . we must establish the notion of
> the Other . . . as being the locus of the deployment of
> speech . . .
> —it must be posited that, produced as it is by an animal at the
> mercy of language, man's desire is the desire of the Other.[24]

What Lacan here suggests is that desire results from the cultural co-optation of the subject's libidinal resources—that the
subject supplies the raw materials, but is barred access to the
site of production. In short, Lacan indicates that the subject's
desires are manufactured for it. The factory—the site of production—is the symbolic. As we shall see, the family plays as
central a role there as signification does. Indeed, within the Lacanian argument, language and the Oedipus complex always
work in tandem.

  iv. *The symbolic.* The concept of a symbolic register has its
origins in the writings of the French anthropologist Claude Lévi-
Strauss, although Lacan has considerably enriched it. In *Elementary Structures of Kinship*, Lévi-Strauss attempts to account
for what he takes to be the universal imposition of the incest
taboo through the symbolic network which it articulates. Of
crucial importance here is the distinction which he makes between nature and culture: In the former, mating is unregu-
lated, whereas in the latter it is subordinated to certain rules.
The essence of the incest taboo is its regulatory status, and that
status makes it virtually synonymous with culture. Indeed, the
simple imposition of the incest taboo transforms a state of nature into a state of culture:

The *fact of being a rule,* completely independent of its modalities, is indeed the very essence of the incest prohibition. If nature leaves marriage to chance and the arbitrary, it is impossible for culture not to introduce some sort of order where there is none. The prime role of culture is to ensure the group's existence as a group, and consequently, in this domain as in all others, to replace chance by organization. The prohibition of incest is a certain form, and even highly varied forms, of intervention. But it is intervention over and above anything else; even more exactly, it is *the* intervention. [32]

Lévi-Strauss argues that every negative stipulation implies a positive stipulation, and that in all cases the prohibition against marrying a member of one group involves the obligation to marry a member of another group—the individual thus surrenders a taboo object in exchange for an acceptable one. The prohibited group varies from culture to culture, but in a society in which brothers were forbidden to marry their biological sisters the incest regulation would work like this: each brother would be obliged to give up his sister to someone else's brother, and to choose his own wife from among another man's sisters.

Thus for Lévi-Strauss the incest taboo is really an exogamy rule, and it has the effect of establishing a grid of structural relationships, not only among members of the family but members of the group. It sets up a system of marital exchange which provides the basis for all of the other systems of exchange upon which culture depends. Women are the privileged commodity within this rudimentary system of exchange:

. . . exogamy should be recognized as an important element . . . in that solemn collection of manifestations which, continually or periodically, ensures the integration of partial units within the total group, and demands the collaboration of outside groups. Such are the banquets, feasts and ceremonies of various kinds which form the web of social life. But exogamy is not merely one manifestation among many others. . . . The law of exogamy . . . is omnipresent, acting permanently and continually; moreover, it applies to valuables—viz., women . . . without which life is impossible. . . . It is no exaggeration, then, to say that exogamy is the archetype of all other manifestations based upon reciprocity, and that it provides the fun-

damental and immutable rule ensuring the existence of the
group as a group. [480–81]

Lévi-Strauss encourages a broadly structural understanding
of kinship ties. Biological connections have much less importance than do social relationships and classifications within his
scheme, and the family is perceived primarily in terms of its
capacity to confer identity upon its members. That identity is
determined strictly on the basis of sexual and generational distinctions. The family is thus the agency whereby an entire symbolic network can be elaborated. Lévi-Strauss insists that it is
not the social state which creates the rules of kinship and marriage, but the rules of kinship and marriage which create the
social state, by "reshaping biological relationships and natural
sentiments, forcing them into structures implying them as well
as others, and compelling them to rise above their original
characteristics" (490).

The rules of kinship and marriage dictate the positions and
possibilities open to all members of the group. Each individual
is thus born into an already defined symbolic system, and inserted into a fully articulated familial diagram. Consanguinity
is irrelevant, except insofar as its categories overlap with cultural ones. The positions of "father," "mother," "daughter," and
"son" all exceed the individuals who temporarily occupy them.
Those positions also determine a wide range of things, such as
appropriate responses to other members of the familial diagram, acceptable mates, the names and attitudes with which the
subject identifies, the distribution of power, legal and economic
status, etc.

Lévi-Strauss concludes his lengthy analysis of primitive marriage rules with a comparison between the ordering capacities
of exogamy and language, and he stresses the far greater precision and stability of the latter. Language, even more than kinship rules, ensures that all of the members of a group inhabit
the same psychic territory, and regiments the exchanges which
take place between them.

Lacan's theory of the subject pushes the analogy much farther. He suggests a close affinity—indeed a virtual collaboration—between the structuring agency of the family and that of

the signifier. In "Field and function of speech and language"
Lacan attributes to the Oedipus complex the same determinative role as that of language in the constitution of the unconscious, subjectivity and the symbolic order:

> . . . the Oedipus complex—in so far as we continue to recog-
> nize it as covering the whole field of our experience with its
> signification—may be said . . . to mark the limits that our dis-
> cipline assigns to subjectivity: namely, what the subject can know
> of his unconscious participation in the movement of the com-
> plex structures of marriage ties, by verifying the symbolic ef-
> fects in his individual existence of the tangential movement
> towards incest that has manifested itself ever since the coming
> of a universal community.
>
> The primordial Law is therefore that which in regulating
> marriage ties superimposes the kingdom of culture on that of
> a nature abandoned to the law of mating. The prohibition of
> incest is merely its subjective pivot, revealed by the modern
> tendency to reduce to the mother and the sister the objects
> forbidden to the subject's choice, although full licence outside
> of these is not yet entirely open.
>
> This law, then, is revealed clearly enough as identical with
> an order of language. For without kinship nominations, no
> power is capable of instituting the order of preferences and
> taboos that bind and weave the yarn of lineage through suc-
> ceeding generations.[25]

Toward the end of this passage Lacan indicates that the Oedipus complex and language do not merely resemble each other,
but that they are "identical." He supports this claim by pointing
out that the incest taboo can only be articulated through the
differentiation of certain cultural members from others by
means of linguistic categories like "father" and "mother," and
he indicates that those differentiations bring the subject within
the Oedipal matrix even before the moment of "crisis." Lacan
further consolidates the relationship between the Oedipus complex and language by defining the paternal signifier—what he
calls the "Name-of-the-Father" as the all-important one both in
the history of the subject and the organization of the larger
symbolic field. In short, he conceptualizes the Oedipus complex
as a linguistic transaction.

Lacan describes the family as a set of symbolic relations which always transcend the actual persons who are defined by means of them. "Mother" and "father" signify cultural positions, and hence have no necessary correlation to biological realities. Those positions may be occupied by persons who have no "natural" claim to them. Moreover, even when actual mothers and fathers strive to fulfill their symbolic roles, they can never be equal to the task. This is because "mother" and "father" are binary terms within a closed system of signification; each sustains its value and meaning through its relation to the other, and not through any reference to the real.

That value and that meaning can only be realized within discourse, within a syntagmatic chain which includes "daughter" and/or "son." The latter two signifiers also constitute a paradigmatic set at the level of the abstract system, and also rely upon discourse for their realization. Each of these four terms—"mother," "father," "daughter," and "son"—operates much like the personal pronouns discussed by Benveniste. Like "I" or "you," these familial signifiers are activated only when subjects identify with them. The discourse of the family—a discourse which is absolutely central to the perpetuation of the present, phallocentric symbolic order—needs subjects.

The discourse of the family produces the subjects it needs by aligning them with the symbolic positions of "father" and "mother," an operation which is considerably more complex within the Lacanian argument than it is within the Freudian one. That operation begins when the subject confuses its actual parents with their symbolic representations, and concludes at the unhappy moment of a fully realized lack or inadequacy. Some of the more important intervening stages involve the organization of the subject's desires in relation to the mother, the identification of the subject with the ideal image of the parent of the same sex, and the subordination of the subject to the law of the father. Sexual difference provides the informing principle of this discourse, its major structuring opposition.

Lacan gives us a very different account of sexual difference from that provided by Freud, one in which the privileged term is no longer the penis but the *phallus*. "Phallus" is a word used by Lacan to designate all of those values which are opposed to lack, and he is at pains to emphasize its discursive rather than its anatomical status. However, it must be noted that this signifier, like the one to which it is opposed, sustains two radically different meanings, neither of which at all points maintains its autonomy from the penis. Since those contradictory meanings have not only been the source of enormous confusion to Lacan's listeners and readers but have fostered a radical misapprehension of female subjectivity, we will attempt to place a maximum distance between them.

On the one hand, the phallus is a signifier for those things which have been partitioned off from the subject during the various stages of its constitution, and which will never be restored to it, all of which could be summarized as "fullness of being." In his seminars on *Hamlet*, Lacan stresses in particular the castrating effect of language, associating the phallus with those losses inflicted by signification.

> This is our starting point: through his relationship to the signifier, the subject is deprived of something [:] of himself, of his life, which has assumed the value of that which binds him to the signifier. The phallus is our term for the signifier of his alienation in signification. When the subject is deprived of this signifier, a particular object becomes for him an object of desire. . . .
>
> The object of desire is essentially different from the object of any need [*besoin*]. Something becomes an object in desire when it takes the place of what by its very nature remains concealed from the subject: that self-sacrifice, that pound of flesh which is mortgaged [engagé] in his relationship to the signifier.[26]

The phallus is thus a signifier for the organic reality or needs which the subject relinquishes in order to achieve meaning, in order to gain access to the symbolic register. It signifies that thing whose loss inaugurates desire.

On the other hand, the phallus is a signifier for the cultural privileges and positive values which define male subjectivity within patriarchal society, but from which the female subject remains isolated. It is thus closely aligned with two other very privileged terms within the Lacanian grammar, "symbolic father" and "Name-of-the-Father." All three are signifiers of paternal power and potency.

The relation of the phallus to the penis, or the symbolic to the actual father, requires a very precise formulation. The first point which should be made about this relation is that it involves an irreducible disequivalence. The penis can never approximate the phallus, just as the actual father can never conform to the epic proportions of the symbolic father. As Lacan observes in "Function and field of speech and language," "Even when . . . it is represented by a single person, the paternal function concentrates in itself both imaginary and real relations, always more or less inadequate to the symbolic relation that essentially constitutes it."[27]

The inevitable failure of the actual father to correspond to the symbolic father, or the penis to embody the phallus, in no way jeopardizes the existing cultural order. The ideal paternal representation to which those two signifiers refer remains determinedly abstract and diffuse, finding expression less through individual human agents than through the institutional supports with which it is finally synonymous. Those supports include not only the patriarchal family, but the legal, medical, religious, technological, and educational systems, and the dominant political and economic organizations. The concept of "panopticism," extensively theorized by Foucault, may perhaps assist us in grasping the degree to which the phallus exceeds the penis, and the symbolic the actual father.

In *Discipline and Punish* Foucault describes the replacement during the eighteenth century of a punitive system predicated on corporal punishment with one which addressed itself much more fully to the psyche. He isolates Bentham's panoptical prison as the perfect realization of this new punitive system because it subordinated its inmates more to an idea than to a physical constraint. That prison consisted of a circle of individual cells with a watch tower in the middle. The interior of each cell was immediately visible to anyone situated in the watch tower, but the great "virtue" of the plan was that the prisoners so fully internalized the prison's scopic regime that it worked even when no one was looking. In much the same way the paternal signifier goes on working even when the actual father inevitably falls short of his symbolic function. That function not only transcends any individual subject but is inscribed into the very fabric of Western culture—into both its infra- and super-structure. Thus the symbolic order, like the Panopticon, is a machine which can be operated by "Any individual, taken almost at random . . . in the absence of the [father], his family, his friends, his visitors, even his servants."[28] Moreover, no matter who actually assumes responsibility for operating the machine, that person—even if it is the mother—will always represent the phallus.

In spite of these institutional supports, however, we will see that the desire of the son proves indispensable to the maintenance of the current symbolic order. What this means is that the actual father must be identified with the symbolic father, and that the son must believe him to be in possession of the phallus. The mother plays a critical part in this project, since it is her "lack" which defines the father as potent, and her desire which awakens in the son the impossible wish to supply her with the missing phallus.

Before we proceed to a discussion of the centrality of Oedipal desire to the operations of patriarchal culture, some further explanation of the relation of the phallus to the penis must be offered. We have noted that the phallus is a signifier both for those things which are lost during the male subject's entry into culture, and those things which are gained, but we have not accounted for the role played by the penis in that transition, nor for the mysterious exclusion of the female subject from not only the second half of this scenario, but the first.

Despite Lacan's repeated assertions that the penis is not the phallus, it is clear that there is a very intimate and important relation between the two. Lacan suggests in the passage already quoted that the male subject "pays" for his symbolic privileges with a currency not available to the female subject—that he "mortgages" the penis for the phallus. In other words, during his entry into the symbolic order he gains access to those privileges which constitute the phallus, but forfeits direct access to his own sexuality, a forfeiture of which the penis is representative. The problems with this formulation are manifold, and they are further compounded by the assumptions it makes about female subjectivity.

In *Séminaire livre XX* Lacan indicates his belief that the female subject neither succumbs to as complete an alienation from the real, nor enjoys as full an association with the symbolic as does the male subject.[29] She thus has a privileged relation to the real, but a de-privileged relation to the symbolic. The female subject escapes that "castration" which alone assures the male subject his symbolic potency. We are told by Lacan and his commentators that she "lacks lack," and that while signifying "castration" within the symbolic order she nonetheless continues (unlike her male counterpart) to "be" the phallus.[30]

As the preceding paragraph would suggest, the contradictory meanings of "lack" and "phallus" always become particularly evident when Lacan speaks about the female subject. His language doubles back upon itself in the form of paradoxes and repetitive tropes, no sooner acknowledging woman's cultural deprivation than nullifying the importance of that observation with assertions about the *jouissance* (ecstatic pleasure) she supposedly enjoys elsewhere.

In "Inquiry into Femininity," Michèle Montrelay provides an intelligent and coherent account of female subjectivity as Lacan conceives it, one which should enable us to obtain a firm grasp on the problems implicit in his account not only of the female but of the male entry into the symbolic order. Montrelay's exposition hinges on the maintenance of two sets of oppositions, those between the categories "woman" and "femininity," and those between the categories "repression" and "censorship."[31]

For Montrelay "femininity" designates a complex of drives which remain outside of cultural structuration, whereas "woman" refers to the female subject who, like the male subject, is an effect of repression. Those drives which constitute "femininity" are able to escape repression because the latter only occurs as the consequence of representation, and female sexuality remains unrepresented within patriarchal culture. In other words, because both male and female sexuality are defined in relation to the phallus, and because the symbolic order provides a positive representation of male sexuality, but a negative one of female sexuality (female sexuality as the "not-phallus"), the latter is *censored* rather than *repressed.*

Montrelay explains that repression involves the setting in place within the unconscious of a representation which structures sexuality in a particular way. Censorship, however, excludes without representation, and consequently has no structuring effect upon sexuality. Because male sexuality is both represented and repressed by the phallus, the male subject is simultaneously more alienated from the real and more integrated within the symbolic than is his female counterpart. Female sexuality, on the other hand, is censored rather than repressed by the phallus—covered over but not represented or structured by the paternal signifier. For that reason it remains a "dark continent," a real which threatens to submerge not only the female subject but the entire order of signification.

It is evident that this paradigm relies upon a view of representation which is diametrically opposed to that presented earlier in this chapter. Whereas in his account of the binary signifier Lacan stresses the *non-representational* nature of the signifying event which inaugurates subjectivity, in his elaboration of the phallus he invokes the concept of a *representational representation.* *"Fort"* and *"da"* signify only in relation to each other, rather than to the toy which Freud's grandson threw away, or the mother who disappeared and reappeared. However, we are asked not only to understand the phallus as the signifier *par excellence,* but to conceive of it as having been motivated by the real. It is after all a very specific pound of flesh which the male subject exchanges for his symbolic legacy, one which the female body conspicuously lacks. The inevitable conclusion to which Lacan's argument pushes us is that the phallus somehow mirrors or resembles the penis. The fundamental symmetry between the penis and the phallus within the Lacanian scheme is nowhere more startling evidently than in his seminars on *Hamlet,* where he remarks that "Claudius's real phallus is always somewhere in the picture" (50).

The phallus thus comes to refer not only to the privileges of the symbolic and the fullness of being which can never coexist with those privileges, but to the penis whose sacrifice ac-

tivates them. The first and third of these meanings—privileges
of the symbolic and "mortgaged" penis—are brought together
to define male subjectivity in terms which rigorously exclude
woman both at the anatomical and cultural levels, an exclusion
which is further overdetermined at the theoretical level by her
association with the second of them—fullness of being.

We are now in a position to decode the paradoxes and repetitive tropes cited earlier, and having done so to leave them
behind. What woman lacks within the Lacanian scheme is the
phallus-as-lost-penis, the "amputated" or "castrated" appendage which assures the male subject access to the phallus-as-
symbolic-legacy. She thus continues to "be" the phallus as full-
ness-of-being long after the male subject has been alienated
from the real. This phenomenal plenitude precludes her ever
having the phallus, i.e. ever acquiring symbolic power and potency, but it provides her with a *jouissance* denied to man.

In fact, however, both sides of this subjective coin have been
stamped within the symbolic treasury; woman as plenitude and
woman as lack are merely two alternative cultural projections
by means of which man can always be assured of having the
phallus—in the first instance through appropriation, and in the
second through an oppositional definition. These two equations are also signifying strategies for justifying the exclusion
of the female subject from symbolic authority and privilege.

The phallus, like any other signifier, derives its meaning and
value entirely from its relation to the other terms in the closed
systems and concrete discursive events of which it is a part. It
has no more foundation in reality than does any other semantic
unit. There is thus a radical impossibility inherent in Lacan's
use of the word "phallus." It cannot apply simultaneously to
the privileges of the symbolic and to a phenomenological plenitude, any more than it can denote both a real pound of flesh
and the signifier which usurps it, or anatomical difference and
the discourse of sexual difference. All of these dual applica-
tions imply a continuity between those very realms which Lacan
is otherwise at such pains to keep distinct, collapse the symbolic
into the real.

If we are to benefit from Lacan's discovery that the phallus

is not the penis but a signifier we must remember the conditions under which it can function as such. Like any other signifier it can be activated only within discourse, and like any
other signifier it is defined by those terms with which it is paradigmatically connected, whether through similarity or opposition. The discourse of the family serves constantly to activate
the paternal signifier, and one of the most important ways in
which it does so is through the evocation of its binary complement, i.e. "lack." In short the paternal signifier finds its support
in what might be called the "maternal" signifier. It is only
through the mother's desire that the cultural primacy of the
phallus can be established and maintained, and that the discourse of the patriarchal family can be perpetuated. Finally,
and at the risk of a tautology which is endemic to the symbolic
order, it must be stated that the mother will desire the phallus
only if her own relation to it is negative, i.e. if she has been
defined as lacking.

Before turning to the discourse of the family, a few final
remarks about the female subject should be added. It is preposterous to assume either that woman remains outside of signification, or that her sexuality is any less culturally organized
or repressed than that of her male counterpart. If the entry
into language is understood as effecting an automatic breach
with the real—and the Lacanian argument is very persuasive
on this point—then the female subject's linguistic inauguration
must be seen as locating her, too, on the side of meaning rather
than being. She makes the same "sacrifice" as does the male
subject, a sacrifice which cannot be localized in the way suggested by Lacan. Secondly, while it is unquestionably true that
her sexuality is negatively rather than positively defined, it does
not for that reason escape structuration. On the contrary, female sexuality would seen to be even more exhaustively and
intensively "spoken" than is male sexuality, to be a site where
numerous discourses converge. "Lack" is inscribed not only at
the orifices, but across the entire surface of the female body,
and it is precisely at the level of that (constructed) surface that
woman is obliged to live a great deal of her cultural existence.[32]

Within the Lacanian account, as within the Freudian one,

the mother functions as the initial object of desire both for the male and female objects—the first object, that is, which is loved as something distinct from the self. There would seem to be two main reasons why she, rather than the father, represents the first love object. One of these is that she is more likely to have supplied the infantile subject with warmth and nourishment and so is already perceived as a source of pleasure. Another closely related reason, and one more congruent with the Lacanian argument, is that the mother is an important "source" of objects (a) during the imaginary moments of the subject's history—even before she is perceived as a discrete object, her breasts, her voice, and her gaze are likely to have been the pivot of important identifications.

However, with the subject's entry into the symbolic the father quickly replaces the mother as the central object of desire. Lacan tells us that the child wants to be desired by the mother— that it desires the mother's desire. The mother, on the other hand, desires what she lacks, i.e. the phallus. Since she associates the phallus with the father, she consequently desires him. The child's desire for the mother is therefore displaced onto what she desires, and the paternal signifier emerges as the definitive one in the history of the subject. Lacan illustrates this displacement with the following diagram: [33]

$$\frac{\text{Name-of-the-father}}{\text{Desire of the mother}} \cdot \frac{\text{Desire of the mother}}{\text{Signified to the subject}} \rightarrow \text{Name-of-the-father} \left(\frac{\text{O}}{\text{Phallus}} \right)$$

This signifying transaction, whereby the child makes the mother's meaning and desires its own, is not just one among many. It is of crucial importance in the constitution of the Lacanian subject, and when it does not occur (either because of the failure of the mother's desire, as in *Hamlet,* or because of the failure of the child's) psychosis occurs. In other words, the subject's desires fail to conform to the larger symbolic order, a deviance which threatens the perpetuation of that order. If, however, this metaphoric event is successfully consummated— if, that is, the child identifies the actual with the symbolic father—then he or she will henceforth be structured in relation to the phallus. That structuration will be positive for the male subject and negative for the female subject. In other words, the son will identify with the father as the possessor of the phallus, and the daughter with the mother as the one who lacks the phallus. (This sexual differentiation implies the additional identification of the penis with the phallus, and the female genitalia with a lack.)

It must be stressed once again that the desire of the mother, like that of the daughter or son, has its origins elsewhere, finds its inspiration and support in a symbolic field which is invested at all points with the desire for paternal authority. If she desires the phallus, and identifies it with the father, that is because she too finds herself subjected to the desire of the Other— to a cultural network which reifies the father by inserting his "name" into a signifying chain in which it enjoys close proximity to other privileged signifiers: "law," "money," "power," "knowledge," "plenitude," "authoritative vision," etc. It is also because she is defined in opposition to these signifiers.

When the child internalizes the image of the parent of the same sex at the end of the Oedipal crisis, it compounds misrecognition upon mis-recognition. The result can only be a brutalizing sense of inadequacy both for male and female subjects—for the former because he can never be equivalent to the symbolic position with which he identifies, and for the latter because she is denied even an identification with that position.

Lacan thus projects a subject who is from the very beginning alienated from itself, and whose organic deficiency anticipates subsequent losses. The assumption of a primordial lack justifies him in locating the mirror stage prior to the symbolic order: it is only "natural," after all, that the first self-confrontation on the part of a mutilated subject should involve both a compensatory vision of plenitude and coherence, and a sense of exclusion from that vision.

It seems equally inevitable that culture should wean the subject away from this morbid self-meditation through an alternative set of ideal representations (mother, father), and a system of signification which achieves an even more extreme alienation from any fullness of being. And all the time, we are told, the search for perfection and wholeness is urged forward by libidinal forces which cannot be ignored. Thus although there are numerous ruptures within the Lacanian scheme between being and meaning, and between the imaginary and the symbolic, the continuity of lack from one regime to another ultimately overrides everything else, and makes impossible any real critique of the present cultural order.

However, once we deny this primordial lack, we are free to understand all ideal representations as culturally manufactured, and to relocate the mirror stage inside the boundaries of the symbolic. We can then see that the desire which initiates the search for the ideal subject is the same as that which initiates the search for the ideal object, and that it is the desire of the Other. Finally, we are able to conceptualize that desire as belonging to a culturally and historically determinate Other— to a particular symbolic order, and not one which is universal or absolute.

It would thus seem imperative to understand both the Freudian and the Lacanian models of the subject in relation to the dominant discursive practices which defined their immediate context, and which still largely prevail. It would also seem important to challenge any attempt made by either author to predicate the cultural system on something outside of and prior to it such as the instinctual, the natural, or the real; these categories are culturally fabricated, and they function to seal off criticism and change. If either Freud or Lacan is read without these precautions, the subjectivity which they describe assumes the proportions of an axiom, which cannot be refuted and whose very rigors seduce.

However, if read with these precautions, their interlocking theoretical models can clarify for us not only the relation of signification and subjectivity to the present symbolic order, but the part played by sexual difference in the determination of each. Turned around upon themselves, these models can even help us to conceive of a different signification, a different subjectivity, and a different symbolic order.

The next two chapters will deal first with the intersection of subject and text, and then with that between text and symbolic order. The first of these explorations will focus on cinematic texts, and the second on literary ones. However, the models should be understood as reversible; the theory of suture, which has been elaborated in relation to film, has obvious relevance to literature, while Barthes's theory of codes, which has been formulated in relation to literature, can be fruitfully extended to film.

5

Suture

We are now much better prepared than we were in Chapter 1 to explore Emile Benveniste's claim that "the foundation of 'subjectivity' . . . is determined by the linguistic status of 'person',"[1] and to witness the extension of that claim to the subject positions generated by classic cinema. The intervening chapters have indicated in a variety of ways that the terms "subject" and "signification" are at all points interdependent, and that psychoanalysis must consequently be understood as a branch of semiotics.

We have learned, for instance, that all signifying formations are the product of a facilitation between two psychic processes (the primary and the secondary), and that the sets metaphor and metonymy and paradigm and syntagm can no more be divorced from subjectivity than can condensation and displacement. We have discovered that the discourse within which the subject finds its identity is always the discourse of the Other— of a symbolic order which transcends the subject, and which orchestrates its entire history. The preceding chapters have also alerted us to the conspicuous part played by sexual difference within that order, making us aware of the phallocentricity of our current signifying practices. Finally, we have looked at those discursive instances which inaugurate subjectivity, and which mediate even the earliest of the subject's identifications: the alignment of the subject with the binary signifier, and its subordination to the Name-of-the-Father.

It would now seem to be the moment to examine some of the textual strategies whereby subjectivity is constantly *reactivated*. We have chosen cinema as our example because its combination of images and linguistic sounds renders particulary vivid the dual parts played in that reactivation by the imaginary and symbolic registers.

"Suture" is the name given to the procedures by means of which cinematic texts confer subjectivity upon their viewers. These procedures have been exhaustively theorized by a number of writers on film, each of whom has modified and expanded upon the psychoanalytic definition of suture originally offered by Jacques-Alain Miller. Before we turn to this theoretical complex, however, some restatement of Benveniste's notions about discourse and subjectivity would seem appropriate.

A) DISCOURSE AND SUBJECTIVITY

We noted earlier in this study that Saussure leaves unexplored the relation of subject to signifying chain; his semiotics includes the subject only as a generator of *paroles* (speech acts). He consequently perceives the relationship between signifiers and signifieds as stable and predictable, unaffected by individual speakers. While insisting upon the vital role played both by paradigmatic and syntagmatic relationships in determining the value of all signifying elements, he nevertheless argues for the possibility of anchoring particular signifiers to particular signifieds in order to form linguistic signs.

Lacan has suggested that there can be no such anchoring of particular signifiers to particular signifieds—that meaning emerges only through discourse, as the consequence of displacements along a signifying chain. Moreover, like Peirce, Derrida, and Barthes, he insists upon the commutability of the signified, upon its capacity to function in turn as a signifier. Finally, by defining the signifier as that which "represents the subject for another signifier," Lacan indicates that signification cannot be considered apart from the subject.

Benveniste verifies all three of these assertions at once when he draws our attention to a group of words which has no meaning at the level of the abstract system or *langue*. The group in question includes "I," "you," "here," "there," "then," "when," and conjugated verbs, whose tenses always function indexically. These signifiers have no stable signifieds, are activated only within discourse, and assume meaning only in relation to a subject. Moreover, they are not predictable, but vary from discursive instance to discursive instance, and even within the same signifying chain. "I" and "you," and "here" and "there" are endlessly reversible signifiers; the signifier "you" addressed by one person to another immediately translates in the mind of the second person into "I," and "here" and "there" function in much the same way.

We must emphasize that these signifiers do not connect up with real persons and objects any more than do other signifiers; the term "I" has no reference to the organic reality of the subject who uses it, nor does "there" coincide with a physical place. They are fully contained within a closed system of signification; "I" derives its value from "you," and "here" from "there," just as "black" refers to "white," or "male" to "female."

Benveniste in no way qualifies the distinction between being and signification which is so central to the Lacanian scheme. Not only does he carry over that distinction into his own more specifically linguistic discussion, but he formulates it with greater precision. We recall that the gap which separates being from signification manifests itself in Benveniste's writings as the division between the speaking subject (*le sujet de l'énonciation*) and the subject of the utterance or speech (*le sujet de l'énoncé*):

> *I* signifies "the person who is uttering the present instance of the discourse containing *I.*" . . . *I* can only be identified by the instance of discourse that contains it and by that alone. It has no value except . . . . in the act of speaking in which it is uttered. There is thus a combined double instance in this process: the instance of *I* as referent and the instance of the discourse containing *I* as the referee. The definition can now be stated precisely as: *I* is "the individual who utters the present instance of discourse containing the linguistic instance *I.*" [218]

The speaking subject belongs to what Lacan would call the domain of the real, but it can attain subjectivity or self-apprehension only through the intervention of signification. Since signification results in an aphanisis of the real, the speaking subject and its discursive representative—i.e. the subject of the speech—remain perpetually dissimultaneous, at odds.

The reason that the signifiers isolated by Benveniste are activated only within discourse is that they require both a subject who will fill them up conceptually (i.e. supply them with a signified) and one who will identify with the most important of them: the "I." (The first-person pronoun acquires its privileged status from the fact that it determines the meaning of the signifiers "here," "there," "then," "when," as well as the tenses of all verbs in a given syntagmatic cluster. The notions of space and time implied by these various terms are keyed to the subject of the speech.)

In ordinary conversational situations, the speaking subject performs both of these actions; that subject automatically connects up the pronouns "I" and "you" with those mental images by means of which it recognizes both itself and the person to whom it speaks, and it identifies with the former of these. However, when a subject reads a novel or views a film it performs only one of these actions, that of identification. The representations within which we recognize ourselves are clearly manufactured elsewhere, at the point of the discourse's origin. In the case of cinema, that point of origin must be understood as both broadly cultural (i.e. as the symbolic field) and as specifically technological (i.e. as encompassing the camera, the tape-recorder, the lighting equipment, the editing room, the script, etc.).[2]

Benveniste shows himself fully cognizant of the fact that discourse involves the "match" of the linguistic signifiers "I" and "you" to ideal representations, and that it is through those representations that the subject finds itself. In "Language in Freudian Theory" he describes discourse in precisely these terms:

> All through Freudian analysis it can be seen that the subject makes use of the act of speech and discourse in order to "represent himself" to himself as he wishes to see himself and as he calls upon the "other" to observe him. His discourse is appeal and recourse: a sometimes vehement solicitation of the

other through the discourse in which he figures himself desper-
ately, and an often mendacious recourse to the other in order
to individualize himself in his own eyes. Through the sole fact
of addressing another, the one who is speaking of himself in-
stalls the other in himself and thereby apprehends himself,
confronts himself, and establishes himself as he aspires to be,
and finally historicizes himself in this incomplete or falsified
history. Language ("*langage*") is thus used here as the act of
speech ("*parole*"), converted into that expression of instantaneous and elusive subjectivity which forms the condition of
dialogue. The subject's language ("*langue*") provides the in-
strument of a discourse in which his personality is released
and creates itself, reaches out to the other and makes itself be
recognized by him. [67]

Benveniste here emphasizes that the signifier "I" is activated
not through its reference to an actual speaker, but through its
alignment with the ideal image in which that speaker sees him
or herself. "You" functions in an analogous way, referring not
so much to another person as to an image of that person. Benveniste finds it necessary to posit only two discursive subjects:
the speaking subject and the subject of the speech. This is because he focuses so exclusively on the conversational situation;
as we noted above, the speaker in a conversational situation is
closely associated both with the production of the signified, and
the operation of identification, and that dual association serves
to blur the differences between those activities.

However, even in our preliminary discussion of cinematic
texts we were obliged to add a third subject—what we decided
to call the "spoken subject" or projected viewer. Cinema clarifies for us, in a way which the conversational model cannot, the
distance which separates the speaking subject from the spoken
subject, since it locates the first of these "behind" the discourse,
and the second "in front" of the discourse. In other words, the
speaking subject of the cinematic text is always situated at the
site of production, while the spoken subject of that same text is
most exemplarily found instead at the site of consumption.[3] The
cinematic model also helps us to understand that it is the spoken subject who activates those signifiers isolated by Benveniste, since it is this subject who "agrees" to be signified by them.

It is the spoken subject who, by identifying with the subject of the speech, permits the signifier "I" to represent a subject to another signifier (i.e. "you").

As we shall see, some of the theoreticians of suture concentrate their attention on the relationship between the spoken subject and the subject of the speech, while others focus instead on that between the speaking subject and the subject of the speech. In other words, some address the connections between the viewer and the fictional character with whom that viewer identifies, while others explore the connections between the level of the enunciation and that of the fiction.

Although it constitutes itself through speaking, the Lacanian subject is always simultaneously spoken. It inherits its language and its desires from the Other, and its identity and history are culturally written before it is even born. Despite his conflation of the speaking and spoken subjects, Benveniste never loses sight of the fact that subjectivity is constructed within discourse; for him, as for Lacan, the subject cannot be distinguished from signification.

Indeed, the subject has an even more provisional status in Benveniste's writings than it does in Lacan's, since it has no existence outside of the specific discursive moments in which it emerges. The subject must be constantly reconstructed through discourse—through conversation, literature, film, television, painting, photography, etc.

Curiously, this very transience results in a much less totalized view of subjectivity than that advanced by Lacan. Benveniste's discontinuous subject may depend for its emergence upon already defined discursive positions, but it has the capacity to occupy multiple and even contradictory sites. This descriptive model thus enables us to understand the subject in more culturally and historically specific ways than that provided by Lacan—i.e. in terms of a range of discursive positions available at a given time, which reflect all sorts of economic, political, sexual, artistic, and other determinants, instead of in terms of a monolithic symbolic order. It also holds open the possibility of change, since the generation of new discursive positions implies a new subjectivity as well.[4]

The concept of suture attempts to account for the means by

which subjects emerge within discourse. As I have already indicated, although that concept has been most intensely theorized in relation to cinematic texts, its initial formulation comes
from Jacques-Alain Miller, one of Lacan's disciples. We will look
briefly at that formulation before turning to the cinematic one.

Miller defines suture as that moment when the subject in-
serts itself into the symbolic register in the guise of a signifier,
and in so doing gains meaning at the expense of being. In "Suture (elements of the logic of the signifier)," he writes:

> Suture names the relation of the subject to the chain of its
> discourse . . . it figures there as the element which is lacking,
> in the form of a stand-in. For, while there lacking, it is not
> purely and simply absent. Suture, by extension—the general
> relation of lack to the structure of which it is an element, in-
> asmuch as it implies the position of a taking-the-place-of.[5]

Miller's account of suture locates the emphasis in orthodox Lacanian places; the key terms in his definition of it are "lack"
and "absence." Indeed, as Miller describes it, suture closely resembles the subject's inauguration into language, illustrated by
Lacan with the *"fort"/"da"* game. A given signifier (a pronoun,
a personal name) grants the subject access to the symbolic order, but alienates it not only from its own needs but from its
drives. That signifier stands in for the absent subject (i.e. absent
in being) whose lack it can never stop signifying.

The French theoretician Jean-Pierre Oudart subsequently
transported the concept of suture into film studies, where it has
been used to probe the precise nature of cinematic signification—to answer the frequently pondered questions "What is the
cinematic equivalent for language in the literary text?" and
"What is cinematic syntax?" These formal speculations have not
pre-empted those about subjectivity but have been integrated
into them. The theory of suture has been rendered more complex with each new statement about it, so that it now embraces
a set of assumptions not only about cinematic signification, but
about the viewing subject and the operations of ideology. Rather
than retracing each argument in turn, we will here attempt to
provide a synthesis of the contributions made by Jean-Pierre

Oudart, Daniel Dayan, Stephen Heath, Laura Mulvey, and Jacqueline Rose. We will conclude with a discussion of the ideological underpinnings of the theory of suture.

B) SUTURE: THE CINEMATIC MODEL

Theoreticians of cinematic suture agree that films are articulated and the viewing subject spoken by means of interlocking shots. They are thus in fundamental accord with Noel Burch's remark that "Although camera movements, entrances into and exits from frame, composition and so on can all function as devices aiding in the organization of the film object . . . the shot transition [remains] the basic element [of that organization]." [6] Shot relationships are seen as the equivalent of syntactic ones in linguistic discourse, as the agency whereby meaning emerges and a subject-position is constructed for the viewer.

However, some theoreticians conceptualize those relationships differently from others. Whereas Oudart and Dayan find the shot/reverse shot formation to be virtually synonymous with the operations of suture, Heath suggests that it is only one element in a much larger system, and emphasizes features of the editing process which are common to all shot transitions. We will begin by discussing the shot/reverse shot formation, and then extend the theory of suture in the directions indicated by Heath.

The shot/reverse shot formation is a cinematic set in which the second shot shows the field from which the first shot is assumed to have been taken. The logic of this set is closely tied to certain "rules" of cinematic expression, in particular the 180° rule, which dictates that the camera not cover more than 180° in a single shot. This stricture means that the camera always leaves unexplored the other 180° of an implicit circle—the half of the circle which it in fact occupies. The 180° rule is predicated on the assumption that a complete camera revolution would be "unrealistic," defining a space larger than the "naked eye" would normally cover. Thus it derives from the imperative that the camera deny its own existence as much as possible, fostering the illusion that what is shown has an autonomous existence, independent of any technological interference, or any coercive gaze.

However, the viewing subject, unable to sustain for long its belief in the autonomy of the cinematic image, demands to know whose gaze controls what it sees. The shot/reverse shot formation is calculated to answer that question in such a manner that the cinematic illusion remains intact: Shot 1 shows a space which may or may not contain a human figure (e.g. the wall of a building, a view of the ocean, a room full of people), being careful not to violate the 180° rule. Shot 2 locates a spectator in the other 180° of the same circular field, thereby implying that the preceding shot was seen through the eyes of a figure in the cinematic narrative.* As a result, the level of enunciation remains veiled from the viewing subject's scrutiny, which is entirely absorbed within the level of the fiction; the subject of the speech seems to be the speaking subject, or to state it differently, the gaze which directs our look seems to belong to a fictional character rather than to the camera.

Theoretically, the filmmaker would be obliged to achieve an exact match between the two parts of the shot/reverse shot formation (i.e. shot 1 would delineate precisely half of a circle, and shot 2 the other half; moreover, in shot 1 the camera would take up a position identical with that of the spectator in shot 2). In practice, however, such precision is rarely observed. A simple display of a fictional character looking in shot 2 usually proves sufficient to maintain the illusion that shot 1 visually "belongs" to that character. The camera may even adopt an oblique position, slightly to one side of the actor, rather than directly facing him or her.

Filmmakers are generally no more literal with shot 1 of the shot/reverse shot formation. Often we are shown the shoulders or head of the character through whose eyes we are ostensibly looking. In fact, mathematical exactitude provides a much less successful approximation of "reality" than does the loose application of the shot/reverse shot convention.

In "Notes on Suture" Stephen Heath cautions against too restrictive an identification of suture with the shot/reverse shot

* This paradigm may be reversed.

formation, which statistical studies have shown to be symptomatic of only about one-third of the shots in a classical Hollywood film.[7] Actually, the suture argument relies much less
centrally on the notion of syntagmatic progression, and the
question of whether it is achieved through the shot/reverse shot
formation or by some other means, than on the process of cinematic signification, and its relationship to the viewing subject.

Consequently, the shot/reverse shot formation derives its real
importance and interest for many of the theoreticians of suture
because it demonstrates so lucidly the way in which cinema operates to reduplicate the history of the subject. The viewer of
the cinematic spectacle experiences shot 1 as an imaginary
plenitude, unbounded by any gaze, and unmarked by difference. Shot 1 is thus the site of a *jouissance* akin to that of the
mirror stage prior to the child's discovery of its separation from
the ideal image which it has discovered in the reflecting glass.

However, almost immediately the viewing subject becomes
aware of the limitations on what it sees—aware, that is, of an
absent field. At this point shot 1 becomes a signifier of that
absent field, and *jouissance* gives way to unpleasure. Daniel
Dayan offers a very clear summary of this transition in "The
Tutor Code of Classical Cinema":

> When the viewer discovers the frame—the first step in
> reading the film—the triumph of his former *possession* of the
> image fades out. The viewer discovers that the camera is hid-
> ing things, and therefore distrusts it and the frame itself which
> he now understands to be arbitrary. He wonders why the frame
> is what it is. This radically transforms his mode of participa-
> tion—the unreal space between characters and/or objects is no
> longer perceived as pleasurable. It is now the space which sep-
> arates the camera from the characters. The latter have lost
> their quality of presence. The spectator discovers that his pos-
> session of space was only partial, illusory. He feels dispossessed
> of what he is prevented from seeing. He discovers that he is
> only authorized to see what happens to be in the axis of the
> gaze of another spectator, who is ghostly or absent.[8]

Jean-Pierre Oudart refers to the spectator who occupies the
missing field as the "Absent One." The Absent One, also known

as the Other, has all the attributes of the mythically potent symbolic father: potency, knowledge, transcendental vision, self-sufficiency, and discursive power. It is of course the speaking subject of the cinematic text, a subject which as we have already indicated finds its locus in a cluster of technological apparatuses (the camera, the tape-recorder, etc.). We will see that this speaking subject often finds its fictional correlative in an ideal paternal representation.

The speaking subject has everything which the viewing subject, suddenly cognizant of the limitations on its vision, understands itself to be lacking. This sense of lack inspires in that subject the desire for "something else," a desire to see more.

However, it is equally important that the presence of the speaking subject be hidden from the viewer. Oudart insists that the classic film text must at all costs conceal from the viewing subject the passivity of that subject's position, and this necessitates denying the fact that there is any reality outside of the fiction.

The shot/reverse shot formation is ideally suited for this dual purpose, since it alerts the spectator to that other field whose absence is experienced as unpleasurable while at the same time linking it to the gaze of a fictional character. Thus a gaze within the fiction serves to conceal the controlling gaze outside the fiction; a benign other steps in and obscures the presence of the coercive and castrating Other. In other words, the subject of the speech passes itself off as the speaking subject.

For Oudart, cinematic signification depends entirely upon the moment of unpleasure in which the viewing subject perceives that it is lacking something, i.e. that there is an absent field. Only then, with the disruption of imaginary plenitude, does the shot become a signifier, speaking first and foremost of that thing about which the Lacanian signifier never stops speaking: castration. A complex signifying chain is introduced in place of the lack which can never be made good, suturing over the wound of castration with narrative. However, it is only by inflicting the wound to begin with that the viewing subject can be made to want the restorative of meaning and narrative.

Stephen Heath emphasizes the process of negation which

occurs concurrently with a film's positive assertions—its structuring absences and losses. In "Narrative Space," he writes:

> Film is the production not just of a negation but equally, simultaneously, of a negativity, the excessive foundation of the process itself, of the very movement of the spectator as subject in the film; which movement is stopped in the negation and its centring positions, the constant phasing in of subject vision ("this but not that" as the sense of the image in flow).[9]

The unseen apparatuses of enunciation represent one of these structuring losses, but there are others which are equally important. The classic cinematic organization depends upon the subject's willingness to become absent to itself by permitting a fictional character to "stand in" for it, or by allowing a particular point of view to define what it sees. The operation of suture is successful at the moment that the viewing subject says, "Yes, that's me," or "That's what I see."

Equally important to the cinematic organization are the operations of cutting and excluding. It is not merely that the camera is incapable of showing us everything at once, but that it does not wish to do so. We must be shown only enough to know that there is more, and to want that "more" to be disclosed. A prime agency of disclosure is the cut, which divides one shot from the next. The cut guarantees that both the preceding and the subsequent shots will function as structuring absences to the present shot. These absences make possible a signifying ensemble, convert one shot into a signifier of the next one, and the signified of the preceding one.

Thus cinematic coherence and plenitude emerge through multiple cuts and negations. Each image is defined through its differences from those that surround it syntagmatically and those it paradigmatically implies ("this but not that"), as well as through its denial of any discourse but its own. Each positive cinematic assertion represents an imaginary conversion of a whole series of negative ones. This castrating coherence, this definition of a discursive position for the viewing subject which necessitates not only its loss of being, but the repudiation of alternative discourses, is one of the chief aims of the system of suture.

Most classic cinematic texts go to great lengths to cover over these "cuts." Hitchcock's *Psycho,* on the other hand, deliberately exposes the negations upon which filmic plenitude is predicated. It unabashedly foregrounds the voyeuristic dimensions of the cinematic experience, making constant references to the speaking subject, and forcing the viewer into oblique and uncomfortable positions both *vis-à-vis* the cinematic apparatuses and the spectacle which they produce.

Psycho not only ruptures the Oedipal formation which provides the basis of the present symbolic order, but declines to put it back together at the end. The final shot of Norman/mother, which conspicuously lacks a reverse shot, makes clear that the coherence of that order proceeds from the institution of sexual difference, and the denial of bi-sexuality.

Finally, *Psycho* obliges the viewing subject to make abrupt shifts in identification. These identifications are often in binary opposition to each other; thus the viewing subject finds itself inscribed into the cinematic discourse at one juncture as victim, and at the next juncture as victimizer. These abrupt shifts would seem to thwart the process of identification, as would all the other strategies just enumerated. However, quite the reverse holds true. The more intense the threat of castration and loss, the more intense the viewing subject's desire for narrative closure.

Psycho's opening few shots take in the exterior of a group of city buildings, without a single reverse shot to anchor that spectacle to a fictional gaze. The transition from urban skyline to the interior of a hotel room is achieved by means of a trick shot: the camers appears to penetrate the space left at the bottom of a window whose venetian blind is three-quarters closed. The viewing subject is made acutely aware of the impossibility of this shot—not just the technical but the "moral" impossibility, since the shot in question effects a startling breach of privacy.

Our sense of intruding is accentuated by the first shot inside the hotel room, which shows us a woman (Marion), still in bed, and her lover (Sam) standing beside the bed, half-undressed,

with a towel in his hands. His face is cropped by the frame, so
that he preserves a certain anonymity denied to Marion, who
will be the object of numerous coercive gazes during the film.
From the very outset, the viewer is not permitted to forget that
he or she participates in that visual coercion.

Marion and Sam exchange a series of embraces before leaving the hotel room. Their love-making is interrupted by a discussion about Sam's marital status, and the strain imposed by
their clandestine meetings. Marion expresses an intense desire
to have their relationship "normalized"—to be inserted through
marriage into an acceptable discursive position. Sam comments
bitterly on the economic obstacles in the way of such a union.
Later in the same day when Marion is entrusted with $40,000
which is intended to buy someone else's marital bliss, and when
the man who gives it to her announces that he never carries
more money that he can afford to lose, Marion decides to
achieve her culturally induced ambitions through culturally taboo means.

The sequence which follows is an extremely interesting one
in terms of suture. In the first shot of that scene Marion stands
in the doorway of her bedroom closet, her right side toward
the camera, wearing a black brassiere and half-slip. A bed separates the camera from her, and in the left far corner there is
a vanity-table and mirror. Suddenly the camera moves backward to reveal a corner of the bed not previously exposed, on
which lies the envelope of stolen money. It zooms in on the
money, then pans to the left and provides a close-up of an open
suitcase, full of clothing. During all of this time, Marion is facing the closet, unable to see what we see.

There is a cut to Marion, who turns and looks toward the
bed. Once again the camera pulls back to reveal the packet of
money. In the next shot, Marion adjusts her hair and clothes
in front of the vanity-table and mirror. She turns to look at the
bed, and we are given a reverse shot of the stolen envelope.
This particular shot/reverse shot formation is repeated. Finally,
Marion sits down on the bed, puts the money in her purse,
picks up the suitcase, and leaves.

This sequence achieves a number of things: It establishes
the fascination of the money, not only for Marion but for us

(we can't help looking at it, even when Marion's back is turned). It delimits a claustral transactional area, an area from which all mediating objects (i.e. the bed) are eventually removed, from which Marion can no longer emerge. The film resorts more and more obsessively to shot/reverse shots in the following episodes, suggesting Marion's absolute entrapment within the position of a thief. Finally, it associates the money with a transcendental gaze, a gaze which exceeds Marion's, and that can see her without ever being seen—one which knows her better than she knows herself.

The privileged object in the shot/reverse shot formations which punctuate the second half of this episode is the packet of money, not Marion. Indeed, the entire spatial field is defined in relation to that spot on the bed where the $40,000 lies; positioned in front of it, we look for a long time at the contents of the room before its human inhabitant ever casts a significant glance at anything. By privileging the point of view of an inanimate object, Hitchcock makes us acutely aware of what Oudart would call the "Absent One"—i.e. of the speaking subject. Our relationship with the camera remains unmediated, "unsoftened" by the intervention of a human gaze.

Far from attempting to erase our perception of the cinematic apparatus, the film exploits it, playing on the viewing subject's own paranoia and guilt. We enjoy our visual superiority to Marion, but at the same time we understand that the gaze of the camera—that gaze in which we participate—exceeds us, threatening not only Marion but anyone exposed to the film's spectacle.

It would appear that the system of suture cannot be too closely identified with that shot/reverse shot formation in which the function of looking is firmly associated with a fictional character, since by violating that convention Hitchcock throws a much wider net over his audience. He thereby forces the viewing subject to take up residence not only within one of the film's discursive positions (that of victim), but a second (that of sadistic and legalistic voyeur). The whole operation of suture can be made *more* rather than less irresistible when the field of the speaking subject is continually implied. Two other episodes in *Psycho* demonstrate the same point.

The earlier of these inscribes the law into the fictional level of the film through the figure of a highway patrolman. An opening long-shot shows Marion's car pulled over to the side of a deserted road. A police car pulls into frame and parks behind it. In the next shot the patrolman climbs out of his car, walks over to the driver's side of Marion's automobile, and looks through the window. A third shot shows us what he sees—a sleeping Marion. A succession of almost identical shot/reverse shot formations follow, by means of which the superiority of the legal point of view is dramatized. The patrolman knocks on Marion's window and at last she wakes up. We are now provided with a shot/reverse shot exchange between the two characters, but although Marion does in fact look back at the person who has intruded upon her, his eyes are concealed by a pair of dark glasses.

The policeman interrogates Marion about her reasons for sleeping in her car, and she explains that she pulled over because of fatigue. She asks: "Have I broken a law?" The conversation is as oblique as the exchange of looks—rather than answering her question, the patrolman asks: "Is there anything wrong?" His question is neither casual nor solicitous; it is a threat, backed up by a series of quick shot/reverse shots which expose Marion yet further to the scrutiny of a law which it seems impossible to evade, and impossible to decipher.

The police officer asks to see Marion's license. Again the question is far from innocent; "license" has as broadly existential a meaning as the word "wrong" in the earlier question. After she gives him her driver's license, the patrolman walks around to the front of the car to write down the license plate number. We see him through the windshield, still protected by his dark glasses from any personal recognition. The reverse shot discloses not Marion, but the license plate which seems to speak for her with greater authority, and to do so through a legal discourse which renders her even more passive.

The policeman permits Marion to resume her journey, but he tails her for several miles. Her paranoia during this period is conveyed through a group of alternating frontal shots of her driving, and reverse shots of her rear-view mirror. The patrol car is clearly visible in both—Marion is now doubly inscribed.

Several sequences later, as Marion continues on her journey in the rain and darkness, the voices of her boss, of the man whose money she has stolen, and of a female friend are superimposed on the sound track, speaking about Marion and defining her even more fully. This device is the acoustic equivalent of all those shots which we have seen, but which Marion has been unable to see because her back was turned, because she was looking in another direction, or because she was asleep. It serves, like those shots, to reinforce the viewing subject's consciousness of an Other whose transcendent and castrating gaze can never be returned, and which always sees one thing: guilt.

The famous shower sequence not only further disassociates the film's spectacle from any of its characters but suggests how much larger the system of suture is than any shot formation. The scene begins with Marion undressing in a motel bedroom, watched through a peephole by Norman, her eventual killer. She goes into the bathroom and flushes down the torn pieces of paper on which she has just taken stock of her financial situation (she has decided to return the stolen money, and wants to calculate how much of it she has spent). Marion then closes the bathroom door, effectively eliminating the possibility of Norman or anyone else within the fiction watching her while she showers. Once again the camera insists on the primacy of its own point of view.

Marion steps inside the bath, and we see her outline through the half-transparent curtain. Then, in a shot which parallels the earlier one in which we seem to slip through the bottom of the hotel window, we penetrate the curtain and find ourselves inside the shower with Marion. The film flaunts these trick shots, as if to suggest the futility of resisting the gaze of the speaking subject.

There are nine shots inside the shower before Marion's killer attacks. They are remarkable for their brevity, and for their violation of the 30° rule (the rule that at least 30° of space must separate the position of the camera in one shot from that which follows it in order to justify the intervening cut). Some of the theoreticians of suture argue that the narrative text attempts to conceal its discontinuities and ruptures, but the shower sequence repeatedly draws our attention to the fact of the cinematic cut. This episode also includes a number of obtrusive and disorienting shots—shots taken from the point of view of the shower head at which Marion looks. When the stabbing begins, there is a cinematic cut with almost every thrust of the knife. The implied equation is too striking to ignore: the cinematic machine is lethal; it too murders and dissects. The shower sequence would seem to validate Heath's point that the coherence and plenitude of narrative film are created through negation and loss.

We have no choice but to identify with Marion in the shower, to insert ourselves into the position of the wayward subject who has strayed from the highway of cultural acceptability, but who now wants to make amends. The vulnerability of her naked and surprisingly small body leaves us without anything to deflect that transaction. Marion's encounter with the warm water inside the shower not only suggests a ritual purification, but a contact so basic and primitive as to break down even such dividing lines as class or sexual difference. Finally, the whole process of identification is formally insisted upon by the brevity of the shots; the point of view shifts constantly within the extremely confined space of the shower, making Marion the only stable object, that thing to which we necessarily cling.

That identification is not even disrupted when the cutting activity is mirrored at the level of the fiction, and a bleeding, stumbling Marion struggles to avoid the next knife wound. It is sustained up until the moment when Marion is definitively dead, an inanimate eye now closed to all visual exchanges. At this point we find ourselves in the equally appalling position of the gaze which has negotiated Marion's murder, and the shading of the corners of the frame so as to simulate the perspective of a peep-hole insists that we acknowledge our own voyeuristic implication.

Relief comes with the resumption of narrative, a resumption which is effected through a tracking shot from the bathroom into the bedroom. That tracking shot comes to rest first upon the packet of money, then upon an open window through which Norman's house can be seen, and finally upon the figure of Norman himself, running toward the motel. When Norman emerges from his house, adjacent to the motel, the full extent of our complicity becomes evident, since we then realize that for the past five or ten minutes we have shared not his point of view, but that of a more potent and castrating Other. But the envelope of money rescues us from too prolonged a consideration of that fact.

The $40,000 assures us that there is more to follow, and that even though we have just lost our heroine, and our own discursive position, we can afford to finance others. What sutures us at this juncture is the fear of being cut off from narrative. Our investment in the fiction is made manifest through the packet of money which provides an imaginary bridge from Marion to the next protagonist.

Psycho is relentless in its treatment of the viewing subject, forcing upon it next an identification with Norman, who with sober face and professional skill disposes of the now affect-less body of Marion, cleans the motel room, and sinks the incriminating car in quicksand. Marion is subsequently replaced in the narrative by her look-alike sister, and Norman's schizophrenia dramatizes the same vacillation from the position of victim to that of victimizer which the viewing subject is obliged to make in the shower sequence and elsewhere. *Psycho* runs through a whole series of culturally overdetermined narratives, showing the same cool willingness to substitute one for another that it adopts with its characters. Moreover, the manifest context of these narratives yields all too quickly to the latent, undergoing in the process a disquieting vulgarization. We understand perfectly the bourgeois inspiration of Marion's marital dreams, and the spuriousness of the redemptive scenario she hopes to enact by returning the money. Similarly, Norman's Oedipal crisis is played more as farce than melodrama, replete with stuffed birds and hackneyed quarrels in which he plays both parts.

The film terrorizes the viewing subject, refusing ever to let it off the hook. That hook is the system of suture, which is held up to our scrutiny even as we find ourselves thoroughly ensnared by it. What *Psycho* obliges us to understand is that we want suture so badly that we'll take it at any price, even with the fullest knowledge of what it entails—passive insertions into pre-existing discursive positions (both mythically potent and mythically impotent); threatened losses and false recoveries; and subordination to the castrating gaze of a symbolic Other.

In fact, the more the operations of enunciation are revealed to the viewing subject, the more tenacious is its desire for the comfort and closure of narrative—the more anxious it will be to seek refuge within the film's fiction. In so doing, the viewing subject submits to cinematic signification, permits itself to be spoken by the film's discourse. For the theoreticians of suture, the viewing subject thereby re-enacts its entry into the symbolic order.

We have seen how central a role narrative plays in determining the viewer's relationship to *Psycho*, but we have not yet attempted a general formulation of the ways in which suture overlaps with story. It is once again Stephen Heath to whom we must turn for such a formulation.

Heath argues that narrative not only makes good the losses and negations which result from classic cinema's editing operations, but that its coherence is made possible through them. He points out that fragmentation is the basis of diegetic unity—that narrative integration is predicated not so much on long takes and invisible cuts as on short takes which somehow foreground their own partial and incomplete status. The narrative moves forward and acts upon the viewer only through the constant intimation of something which has not yet been fully seen, understood, revealed; in short, it relies upon the inscription of lack:

> . . . the work of classical continuity is not to hide or ignore off-screen space but, on the contrary, to contain it, to regularise its fluctuation in a constant movement of reappropriation. It is this movement that defines the rules of continuity and the fiction of space they serve to construct, the whole functioning according to a kind of metonymic lock in which off-screen space becomes on-screen space and is replaced in turn by the space it holds off, each joining over the next. The join is conventional and ruthlessly selective (it generally leaves out of account, for example, the space that might be supposed to be masked at the top and bottom of the frame, concentrating much more on the space at the sides of the frame or on that

"in front", "behind the camera," as in variations of field/reverse
field), and demands that the off-screen space recaptured must
be "called for," must be "logically consequential," must arrive
as "answer," "fulfilment of promise" or whatever (and not as
difference or contradiction)—must be narrativised.[10]

Heath here suggests that the shot/reverse shot formation is
merely one device among many for encoding anticipation into
a film, and for regularizing the difference which might otherwise emerge as contradiction. Camera movement, movement
within the frame, off-screen sound, and framing can all function in a similar indexical fashion to a fictional gaze, directing
our attention and our desire beyond the limits of one shot to
the next. Narrative, however, represents a much more indispensable part of the system of suture. It transforms cinematic
space into dramatic place, thereby providing the viewer not just
with a vantage but a subject position.
    Cinematic suture is thus largely synonymous with the oper-
ations of classic narrative, operations which include a wide variety of editing, lighting, compositional and other formal elements, but within which the values of absence and lack always
play a central role. Those values not only activate the viewer's
desire and transform one shot into a signifier for the next, but
serve to deflect attention away from the level of enunciation to
that of the fiction, even when as in *Psycho* the cinematic apparatus is constantly implied. As Heath observes,

The suturing operation is in the process, the give and take of
presence and absence, the play of negativity and negation, flow
and bind. Narrativisation, with its continuity, closes, and is that
movement of closure that shifts the spectator as subject in its
terms. . . .[11]

A closely adjacent passage from "Narrative Space" emphasizes the never ending nature of the suture process, the fact
that the subject's "construction-reconstruction has always to be
renewed." What seems to us a stable world is actually nothing
more than the effect of this constant renewal, of the ceaseless-
ness of the discursive activities which provide us with our sub-

jectivity. As we will see in a moment, those discursive activities serve a very important ideological function.

C) SUTURE AND IDEOLOGY

The Israeli theoretician Daniel Dayan was the first writer on film to attempt to use the suture argument as a means of examining ideological coercion. For him suture effects this coercion by persuading the viewer to accept certain cinematic images as an accurate reflection of his or her subjectivity, and because it does this *transparently* (i.e. it conceals the apparatuses of enunciation). These two processes are connected, since if the viewer were aware of the film as discourse, he or she would presumably be less willing to be spoken by it. Like Oudart, Dayan isolates shot-to-shot relationships as the strategy whereby both of these tasks are accomplished:

> What happens in systematic terms is this: the absent one of shot one is an element of the code that is attracted into the message by means of shot two. When shot two replaces shot one, the absent one is transferred from the level of enunciation to the level of fiction. As a result of this, the code effectively disappears and the ideological effect of the film is thereby secured. The code, which *produces* an imaginary, ideological effect, is hidden by the message. Unable to see the workings of the code, the spectator is at its mercy. His imaginary is sealed into the film; the spectator thus absorbs an ideological effect without being aware of it. . . . [449]

Dayan's notion of ideology is very close to that advanced by Louis Althusser in the famous essay "Ideology and Ideological State Apparatuses," particularly in its deployment of the term "imaginary," and in its emphasis on invisibility. We will consequently turn to Althusser for a fuller exposition of the definition of ideology which informs the theory of suture.

Althusser defines ideology as a system of representations which promotes on the part of the subject an "imaginary" relation to the "real" conditions of its existence:

> . . . all ideology represents in its necessarily imaginary distortion not the existing relations of production (and the other

relations that derive from them), but above all the (imaginary) relationship of individuals to the relations of production and the relations that derive from them. What is represented in ideology is therefore not the system of real relations which govern the existence of individuals, but the imaginary relation of those individuals to the real relations in which they live.[12]

Althusser here uses two terms which are central to the Lacanian argument—"real" and "imaginary"—while implying a third—"symbolic." However, he attributes to each a slightly different meaning, and these differences are critical to our understanding of his ideological model.

Whereas within the Lacanian scheme "real" signifies the phenomenal world and the subject's organic being, in the Althusserean one it refers instead to the complex of economic "facts" which obtain at any given moment of history—to "the relations of production and to class relations" (166–67). Although he does not say so, Althusser would presumably include the apparatuses of cinematic enunciation in the category "means of production," and would agree with the theoreticians of suture that the viewer is encouraged to establish a relationship not with those apparatuses themselves, but with their fictional representation—i.e. that the viewer's real relation to the cinema is concealed by an imaginary one.[13]

The term "imaginary" occupies a much more ambiguous place within Althusser's writings. While designating the operations of identification associated with it by Lacan, it also refers to activities which the latter attributes to the symbolic. In other words, when Althusser uses the term "imaginary" he means identifications which have been culturally initiated. This important point requires a fuller exposition.

We recall that for Lacan the subject's first identification occurs prior to its entry into the symbolic order, during what he calls the "mirror stage." Although he describes this identification as involving the subject's confusion of itself with an ideal image—and although he claims that it in this respect anticipates the Oedipus complex—Lacan nevertheless insists that the mirror stage is spontaneous.

Althusser denies that identifications ever occur spontaneously or outside of the symbolic order. He argues that the subject is from the very outset within culture. To be more precise, Althusser states that the subject has "always-already" been inside ideology, has from the very beginning of its existence defined itself by means of historically specific ideal images. A passage from "Brecht and Bertolazzi," which relies heavily upon the metaphor of a mirror, helps to clarify the connection established by Althusser between the imaginary and the ideological:

> . . . what . . . is . . . ideology if not simply the "familiar," "well known," transparent myths in which a society or an age can recognize itself (but not know itself), the mirror it looks into for self-recognition, precisely the mirror it must break if it is to know itself? What is the ideology of a society or a period if it is not that society's or period's consciousness of itself, that is, an immediate material which spontaneously implies, looks for and naturally finds its forms in the image of a consciousness of self living the totality of its world in the transparency of its own myths? [144]

What Althusser describes in this passage is the process whereby the subject constantly rediscovers itself in the same ideological representations by means of which it first knew itself. Thus Emma Bovary reconfirms her masochistic subjectivity with each repetition of the romantic scenario whose confines she first made hers at the convent, and the male viewer aligns himself once again with the paternal position when he identifies with the protagonist of *Rebel Without a Cause*. They do so transparently, without any consciousness that the images and narratives with which they identify are historically and culturally specific.

When Althusser talks about breaking the mirror within which the subject finds a prefabricated identity, he does not mean to suggest that the subject thereby transcends ideology, but rather becomes aware of its operations. Not only does he argue that there is no moment during the early life of the subject when it is outside of ideology, but that there will be no such moment in the future. As he observes in "Marxism and Humanism," to posit such a moment would be to affirm an "essence" of man:

. . . ideology is as such an organic part of every social totality. It is as if human societies could not survive without these *specific formations*, these systems of representations (at various levels), their ideologies. Human societies secrete ideology as the very element and atmosphere indispensable to their historical respiration and life. Only an ideological world outlook could have imagined societies *without ideology* and accepted the utopian idea of a world in which ideology (not just one of its historical forms) would disappear without trace. . . . *historical materialism cannot conceive that even a communist society could ever do without ideology.* . . .[14]

Althusser thus eliminates both the notion of a pre-cultural alienation which anticipates later cultural alienations of the subject from being, and that of a revolutionary culture within which subjects at last know themselves in an unmediated way.

A final meaning which comes into play when Althusser uses the word "imaginary"—i.e. "illusory"—must presumably be understood as pertaining only to existing bourgeois ideologies. Since for Althusser the relations of production and class relations constitute the real, any ideology which clearly permitted us to conceptualize our own position within those relations would no longer function to conceal the real from us; that ideology would still promote a system of identification, still provide us with mirrors within which we would find ourselves, but they would more accurately reflect the material conditions of our lives. (It is important to note that although Althusser's definition of the real is congruent with Marxism, it is also by no means incompatible with our own semiotic argument, in that like the symbolic order it is a field of relationships.)

As we observed in Chapter 1, Althusser describes the operation whereby individuals are compelled to identify with the representations which their culture supplies as "interpellation." This concept is central not only to his discussion of ideology but to the whole system of textual identification:

. . . ideology "acts" or "functions" in such a way that it "recruits" subjects among the individuals (it recruits them all), or "transforms" the individuals into subjects (it transforms them all) by that very precise operation which I have called *interpel-*

lation or hailing, and which can be imagined along the lines of the most common everyday police (or other) hailing: "Hey, you there!"

Assuming that the theoretical scene I have imagined takes place in the street, the hailed individual will turn round. By this mere one-hundred-and-eighty-degree physical conversion, he becomes a *subject*. Why? Because he has recognized that the hail was "really" addressed to him, and that "it was *really him* who was hailed." . . .

Naturally for the convenience and clarity of my little theoretical theatre I have had to present things in the form of a temporal succession. . . . But in reality these things happen without any succession. The existence of ideology and the hailing or interpellation of individuals as subjects are one and the same thing.[15]

Interpellation designates the conjunction of imaginary and symbolic transactions which results in the subject's insertion into an already existing discourse. The individual who is culturally "hailed" or "called" simultaneously identifies with the subject of the speech and takes his or her place in the syntax which defines that subjective position. The first of these operations is imaginary, the second symbolic. The concept of interpellation would thus seem to be intimately related to that of suture.

Althusser distinguishes between what he calls concrete individuals and concrete subjects, but he admits that the distinction is purely theoretical. We are concrete individuals until we have been culturally interpellated as subjects, but each of us was from the beginning "always-already a subject, appointed as a subject in and by the specific familial ideological configuration in which [we were] 'expected' once [we had] been conceived."[16] This formulation would suggest that the family plays as central a role within the Althusserean scheme as it does in the Freudian or Lacanian ones. It remains to determine whether that role is seen as ideological or as transcultural, as it is in the other two models. Needless to say, this is a critical determination since it includes the all-important issue of sexual difference.

By making the phallus the central cultural signifier, and by universalizing the Oedipal experience (in short, by making it

synonymous with culture), Freud and Lacan effectively eliminate the category of the ideological. Culture is seen as the
product of the incest taboo, and is therefore necessarily patriarchal. It becomes quite simply impossible for the subject to transcend the Oedipal limitations; any attempt to do so results in
illness or regression.

In the body of his essay "Lacan and Freud," Althusser
accedes to the claims made by Freud and Lacan for the univer-
sality of the Oedipal experience, but in a footnote halfway
through that essay he argues that while there may be a transcendent "Law of Culture," it expresses itself through specific
ideological paradigms, "in which the persons inscribed in (real
kinship) structures live their functions":

> It is not enough to know that the Western family is patriar-
> chal and exogamic . . . we must also work out the ideological
> formations that govern paternity, maternity, conjugality and
> childhood: what are "husband-and-wife-being," "father-being,"
> "mother-being" and "child-being" in the modern world? A mass
> of research remains to be done on these ideological forma-
> tions. This is a task for *historical materialism*.[17]

In other words, Althusser perceives familial relations as elaborately mediated by ideological representations. At the conclusion of "Lacan and Freud," Althusser also proposes that the
functions served by the structures of kinship vary historically,
and that these variations will always be ideologically articulated
(199). Indeed, in the essay with which we began this discussion,
Althusser describes the family as an ideological state apparatus—as an agency for reproducing the existing cultural order
by supplying it with sexually differentiated subjects.

Althusser's emphasis upon the material forms which ideology always takes provides a final link between his writings and
the theory of suture. Althusser, Benveniste, and the theoreticians of suture all argue that it is only through discourse that
ideological identifications occur, and that the subject emerges.
They also agree that discourse can be activated only through
subjects who permit themselves to be spoken by it.

We have seen that the match of subject and cinematic dis-

Suture 221

course occurs not just at the level of the shot, but at that of the story—that films re-interpellate the viewer into pre-established discursive positions not only by effacing the signs of their own production, but through the lure of narrative. The standard format of the classic cinematic text duplicates within the fiction as a whole the paradigm of the shot/reverse shot, disrupting the existing symbolic order, dislocating the subject-positions within it, and challenging its ideals of coherence and fullness only in order subsequently to re-affirm that order, those positions, and those ideals.

Sometimes it is recognizably the same order which is restored at the end of the film. Thus *It's a Wonderful Life* calls into question the potency of George Bailey and the authenticity of the structures of the family and capitalism only so that it can re-validate them. In other cases a new order seems to replace one which has been fractured. For instance, in *Marnie* a "false" coherence (the coherence of a matriarchy) gives way to a "true" coherence (the coherence of a patriarchy). However, the new order always turns out to have been the original order, temporarily interrupted. The system of suture functions not only constantly to re-interpellate the viewing subject into the same discursive positions, thereby giving that subject the illusion of a stable and continuous identity, but to re-articulate the existing symbolic order in ideologically orthodox ways.

We observed earlier, in relation to *Psycho,* that the insertion of the viewer into the cinematic discourse is facilitated through the cuts by means of which films are articulated. That insertion also involves another cutting operation, that implied by sexual difference. It is imperative to note that the identifications and erotic investments of classic cinema—like those established during the Oedipus complex—produce a sexually differentiated subject. Not only are classic cinema's subject positions organized along sexual lines, but so is the desire it inaugurates. Indeed, the entire system of suture is inconceivable apart from sexual difference. As Claire Johnston points out in "Towards a Feminist Film Practice: Some Theses":

As a process, a practice of signification, suture is an ideological operation with a particular function in relation to paternal ide-

ology in that out of a system of differences it establishes a position in relation to the phallus. In so doing it places the spectator in relation to that position. . . . It is this imaginary unity,
the sutured coherence, the imaginary sense of identity set up
by the classic film which must be challenged by a feminist film
practice to achieve a different constitution of the subject in
relation to ideology.[18]

One of the chief mechanisms by which the system of suture
conceals the apparatuses of enunciation is by setting up a relay
of glances between the male characters within the fiction and
the male viewers in the theater audience, a relay which has the
female body as its object. Similarly, one of the most effective
strategies at its disposal for deflecting attention away from the
passivity and lack of the viewing subject's own position is by
displacing those values onto a female character within the fiction. (Needless to say, this displacement assuages the anxieties
only of the male viewer; it heightens those of the female viewer.)
Often the entire narrative is organized around a demonstration
and an interrogation of the female character's castrated condition, a demonstration and an interrogation which have as their
ultimate aim the recovery of a sense of potency and wholeness
for both the male character and the male viewer. This narrative
organization reflects the paradigm which suture establishes at
the level of the shot; in both cases an absence is first revealed,
and then covered over through a skillful displacement from the
level of enunciation onto that of the fiction. We will discuss the
relationship between suture and sexual difference in greater
detail in the following section.

D) SUTURE AND SEXUAL DIFFERENCE

In an extremely influential essay, "Visual Pleasure and Narrative Cinema," Laura Mulvey argues that the classic film text
distinguishes sharply between the male and the female subjects,
and that it does so on the basis of vision.[19] The former of these
is defined in terms of his capacity to look (i.e. as a voyeur) and
the latter in terms of her capacity to attract the male gaze (i.e.
as an exhibitionist). This opposition is entirely in keeping with

the dominant cultural roles assigned to men and women, since voyeurism is the active or "masculine" form of the scopophilic drive, while exhibitionism is the passive or "feminine" form of the same drive. As a means of emphasizing this point, Mulvey describes the male subject as the imagined source of the gaze, and the female subject as the imagined recipient of the gaze.

In fact, the only truly productive gaze in the cinema is that of the camera; that gaze produces the images with which the viewer identifies, and which he or she loves. In short, the camera "looks" the viewer as subject. However, just as a shot of a character within the fiction engaged in the activity of seeing functions to cover over the camera's coercive gaze, so the representation of the male subject in terms of vision has the effect of attributing to him qualities which in fact belong to that same apparatus—qualities of potency and authority.

The female subject of the speech or narrative—i.e. the female protagonist of the fiction—plays a crucial role in the second of these substitutions. She signifies the lack which properly belongs both to the male and the female viewers, who are spoken, not speaking, and whose gazes are controlled, not controlling. She also signifies lack within the fiction of the film, a fiction which inevitably duplicates dominant cultural values. She signifies, that is, the absence of the phallus (of control, power, privilege). As usual, her body provides the means for representing this deprivation. She simultaneously attracts the gaze— appeals to the senses—and represents castration.

The spectacle of classic cinema promotes a constant re-enactment of the primal "discovery" of the female subject's lack. As we have noted, this "discovery" helps to define the male subject as adequate, facilitates his identification with attributes which in fact belong to the apparatuses of enunciation. However, as Mulvey points out, the revelation of female lack can also have a very different effect upon the male subject, inducing in him the fear of a similar deprivation. In other words, the re-staging of the sexual division which determines subjectivity as we presently know it always threatens to trigger a castration crisis in the male viewer. A similar anxiety is often manifested at the level of the fiction, on the part of a male character, and drastic measures must be taken to exorcise it.

Mulvey suggests that there are two recurrent solutions to this problem. The first involves a demonstration that the woman's castrated condition is the result either of wrong-doing or of sickness. Thus, in Hitchcock's *Notorious,* Alicia's loss of control—a loss which finds its ultimate expression in a drugged and poisoned state verging on a coma—is attributed to her transgressive sexuality, the "promiscuity" of which Devlin is so censorious. Similarly, in *Marnie,* as we have already seen, the incapacity to which the heroine is finally reduced is shown by her husband to be the consequence of a psychic illness.

The second solution to the anxiety aroused by the spectacle of female lack involves the transformation of the female body into a fetish, substituting either one of its parts or the whole for the missing phallus. This privileged zone (legs, ankles, breasts, face, hair, general "shape") is subjected to an overvaluation, and in this way compensates for the deficiency which is always associated with the female genital region, although it is in fact broadly cultural. The mechanisms of fetishism function to reassure the male subject that the woman to whom his identity is keyed lacks nothing, that she has not been castrated after all. Examples of this second solution include not only the song-and-dance number, but the entire star system.

Mulvey's argument bears a striking resemblance to the suture theory. Both posit a cinematic adventure in which plenitude is fractured by difference and lack, only to be sealed over once again. For the theoreticians of suture, the salvage activity is carried out by means of the movement from one shot to the next. For Mulvey, as for the many feminist film theoreticians who have worked along similar lines,[20] the lack which must be both dramatized and contained finds its locus in the female body. The various absences upon which classic cinema turns, from the excluded real to the hidden camera and tape-recorder, are in effect signified *through* woman. As Jacqueline Rose observes in "The Cinematic Apparatus: Problems in Current Theory," the female subject

. . . is structured as image around this reference [to the excluded real] and . . . thereby *comes to* represent the potential

> loss and difference which underpins the whole system. . . .
> What classical cinema performs or "puts on stage" is this image
> of woman as other, dark continent, and from there what es-
> capes or is lost to the system; at the same time as sexuality is
> frozen into her body as spectacle, the object of phallic desire
> and/or identification.[21]

"Visual Pleasure and Narrative Cinema" suggests a kind of
"thematics" which complements and enriches that part of the
suture argument which is more strictly concerned with the level
of enunciation. It also demonstrates the impossibility of thinking about any part of the classic cinematic organization—including editing—apart from sexual difference. Indeed, the two
theoretical models achieve a particularly tight join at precisely
that point most stressed by Oudart and Dayan, i.e. the
shot/reverse shot formation. Not only can a metaphoric connection be established between the two halves of that formation on
the one hand, and the alignment of female spectacle with male
vision on the other, but the former provides the ideal vehicle
for the latter. Classic cinema abounds in shot/reverse shot formations in which men look at women. We will examine below
some of the other ways in which cinematic articulation relies
upon the female figure.

However, before doing so I would like to return to the two
representational strategies isolated by Mulvey for neutralizing
the anxiety aroused by female lack. The first of these, we recall,
involves an interrogation calculated to establish either the female subject's guilt or her illness, while the second negotiates
her erotic over-investment. Mulvey associates the former alternative with narrative progression, and the latter with narrative
interruption. In other words, whereas investigation of the guilty
or sick woman always entails a diegetic coercion, fetishism of
the female form sometimes serves to rupture the diegesis and
so to "dis-place" the viewer. These two very different resolu-
tions to the problem of castration anxiety warrant a careful
analysis, since the second contains the potential to subvert the
first. As we will see, the model described by Mulvey can give
rise to at least two transgressive representations. One of these

representations, brilliantly exploited by *Lola Montes,* transfers to woman qualities which are normally the exclusive property of the phallus, most notably the capacity to transcend narrative.

Max Ophuls's highly self-conscious film can almost be read as a disquisition about the status of the female image in classic cinema. Its elaborately orchestrated narrative unfolds through the interrogation of Lola, an interrogation which establishes that she is both "fallen" and unwell. In addition the film quite literally circles around Lola-as-spectacle, and although that spectacle is nothing if not fetishized, it is nonetheless fully contained within the narrative. It thus not only dramatizes both of the solutions cited by Mulvey for neutralizing the male viewer's anxiety, but shows how they can be combined.

At the same time, *Lola Montes* gives us another series of female images which remain much more fragmented, and which threaten the coherence not only of the diegesis but of the dominant symbolic order. Ultimately those images are consolidated within the main narrative, but the strain which they exert upon it suggests that they represent an important area of resistance to traditional power-relations.

Ophuls's film moves back and forth between two temporal planes, one of which situates the viewer in a continuous present tense, and the other of which locates the viewer in a discontinuous past. The sequences from the film's present tense all take place in a circus whose one and only theme is the rise and descent of a *femme fatale.* Lola's climb to fame and fall to ignominy are dramatized in a variety of ways, ranging from pantomime to trapeze acts. The show is written, directed and produced by the ringmaster, who is in the business of selling scandals. However, it is billed as "the whole truth and nothing but the truth," the real-life story of Lola Montes told in "her own inimitable words."

Parts of that story are narrated by the ringmaster. Other parts are extracted in the form of set speeches from Lola, who particularly toward the end of the film requires frequent prompting. However, portions of her past are also conveyed to us through flashbacks, and they are connected with her much more intimately than the lines she speaks. Not only do the usual conventions governing flashbacks serve to link them with Lola's consciousness, but they are invariably signaled by a lap dissolve of her face over a remote object or landscape.

The flashbacks differ from the circus performance in other important respects as well. Whereas Lola's movements are rigorously supervised in the latter, in the former they are characterized by an unusual freedom and spontaneity. Our first glimpse of her in the circus proves paradigmatic in this respect: she sits on a fixed base while the camera circles vertiginously around her. Later, dressed in a white wedding dress and bridal crown, Lola remains immobile in the middle of an even more dazzling display of movement; she is stationed on a rotating platform, surrounded by a second platform which rotates in the opposite direction. These two sequences underscore the fact that in the circus Lola does not so much move as submit to movement. They thus anticipate the film's final shot, in which a caged and altogether tamed Lola extends her hand through the bars to be kissed by a long line of male spectators.

This last enclosure contrasts strikingly with the carriage in which Lola travels in all but two of the flashbacks. Not only does that vehicle permit her to leave one country and enter another at will, but to break off one relationship and begin another whenever she chooses to do so; even when she travels in someone else's carriage her own follows closely behind. It is while seated in the latter that she makes her most revealing statement: "For me, life is movement."

That remark is borne out again and again in the flashback scenes. Lola repeatedly breaks away from or interrupts rituals within which she has been assigned a relatively passive place— a pre-arranged marriage, a marital union in which she is called upon to act the part of a martyr, a Spanish dance, a military procession, a royal audience. Indeed, she effects her dramatic ascent entirely through actions which defy the norm.

In each of these situations Lola makes a spectacle of herself. In other words, she invites the male gaze, draws visual attention to herself. However, it is important to note that the alignment of male look with female image does not here work in the usual way, since far from locating power on the male side that visual transaction confers it on the female side. Thus whereas in the circus episodes the scopic exchange functions to subordinate Lola, in the flashback scenes it provides the agency whereby she assumes power.

The very different status of the male gaze in the film's two temporal registers can be explained by the fact that in one instance Lola's exhibitionism is passive, but in the other active. In the circus scenes she is constrained by the ringmaster's look to conform to a pre-established representation, and obliged night after night to repeat the same part. In the flashback scenes, however, Lola exercises fascination and control over numerous male gazes through an elaborate masquerade, an on-going performance in which she both scripts and constantly changes the parts she plays. Her recourse to the principle of unpredictability is as vital as the artistic control she wields, and may indeed be synonymous with it, since as we suggested above it permits her to disrupt the many narratives which would otherwise contain her.

Lola's capacity to transgress the diegetic flow is inscribed into the film's formal operations as well as its fiction. The fluctuation between the sustained story-telling efforts of the ringmaster and the fragmented and non-linear memories which proceed from Lola's consciousness introduce into the film's structure a tension which is not neutralized until her literal and metaphoric fall. Like her scandals, those memories have the quality of a "cut-out or icon" which Mulvey associates with the fetishist solution, situating the film in a "no-man's land outside its own time and space"(12). In short, they run counter to the flow of the circus narrative. However, after her jump Lola entirely succumbs to the tyranny of the ringmaster's gaze, and her memories cease to function as a point of resistance to the passivity and masochism of her present plight. The flashbacks abruptly terminate, and she takes her place inside the gilded cage.

The one flashback which the ringmaster shares with Lola proves critical in determining the ultimate assimilation of past to present. That flashback also clarifies the very different terms under which Lola will be obliged to play to the male gaze once she joins the circus. In it the ringmaster pays Lola a private visit and offers to sell her as "the most scandalous woman in the world." Although she declines his offer, we know from certain other signs of acquiescence that she will eventually capitulate. For instance, he tells her to stop pacing and she does so—she submits, that is, to the restrictions which he verbally places on her movements, permits herself to be positioned by him. Similarly, when he informs her that she smokes too much, she throws away her cigar.

Even more significant is Lola's response to the ringmaster's assertion that men come to watch her dance only because of her beauty: she sits down in front of a mirror and regards her reflection, as if for the first time. In effect, she subordinates herself to his view of her. For the first time Lola submits to the look of another, is constituted through and dominated by the male gaze.

Lola Montes uses its governing circus metaphor as a means of foregrounding the centrality of a passive and compliant female representation to the operations of classic cinema. Not only does the ringmaster write his narrative across the surface of Lola's body, but the film shows itself to be dependent upon that same surface for its own articulation. Composition, *mise-en-scène,* lighting, camera movement and shot matches all function to display Lola, and that display in turn provides them with their formal coherence.

At the same time that Ophuls's film dramatizes the "ideal" relationship between the fetishized female image and narrative progression, it also suggests ways in which that image can be used to subvert or disrupt the diegesis. Like Sternberg's *Blonde Venus* or *Morocco, Lola Montes* indicates that the power relations which are inscribed into classic cinema through its scopic regime are by no means as stable as is the regime itself. In other words, the identification of the female subject with specularity and the male subject with vision does not necessarily assure the latter a dominant position. The construction of woman-as-fetish carries with it certain dangers for male subjectivity. Not only does that construction facilitate the detachment of the female image from narrative control, but it can challenge the very assumption upon which the existing symbolic order depends—the assumption, that is, that woman is castrated or lacking. In short, the fetish can become indistinguishable from the phallus. This is of course precisely what happens in some of the flashback sequences in *Lola Montes.*

Yet another "perverse" resolution of the castration anxiety discussed by Mulvey involves the privileging of lack and passivity over potency and aggressivity. This resolution, like the one in which the woman aspires to the position of the phallus, leaves intact the scopic regime of classic cinema. Indeed, both are only made possible by the preservation of that regime.

The famous strip sequence from Charles Vidor's 1946 film, *Gilda,* provides a particularly vivid dramatization of the second way in which the construction of woman-as-fetish can challenge the system of which it is a part. The episode in question represents the climactic moment in a plot which is notable for its masochistic excess: the title character has earlier made a toast to her own destruction, referred to herself as the "dirty laundry," married someone who frightens her, and encouraged Johnny Farrell, the man she loves, to imagine her a whore.

The strip sequence is in fact an extension of the last of these projects. It takes place after the assumed death of Gilda's first husband, and her remarriage to Johnny—a marriage which, due to Johnny's sexual jealousy, has never been consummated. Gilda goes to the casino, where he works, to assure him once again that her seeming promiscuity has only been a masquerade. When he casts renewed aspersions on her fidelity, she decides to play her assigned part to the hilt.

Like most of the other episodes of ritual self-humiliation engineered by Gilda, this one relies on the equation of female subjectivity with spectacle, and male subjectivity with the look. Here she does not play just to Johnny's gaze, but to those of the casino staff, a large group of predominantly male customers, and a detective. Initially she contents herself with singing and swaying to an erotically self-lacerating song, but when she is encouraged by the onlookers to remove her clothes she promptly complies, only stopping when she is dragged from the floor by one of Johnny's henchmen.

This song-and-dance number provides a classic example of what Mulvey calls the "fetishist" solution to the problem of female lack. However, it deviates from Mulvey's model in that the erotic overvaluation of Gilda's body (her arms, her face, her hair, the black sheath she wears, the necklace and gloves she tosses to the crowd) does not serve to conceal her castration, but to flaunt it. It also involves a rather noisy demonstration of female guilt, in that it is intended by Gilda to provide the final, irrefutable evidence of her promiscuity. Finally, that demonstration is not orchestrated by the male subject, but is "voluntarily" supplied by the female subject; Gilda not only engages in a self-incriminating strip-tease, but sings a song about the age-old evil of woman ("Put the Blame on Mame").

The film thus superimposes the two rather contradictory strategies isolated by Mulvey as calculated to neutralize the male subject's castration anxieties. The insufficient figure loudly proclaims her guilt, and through her song, dance, and strip-tease simultaneously fosters the overvaluation of her physical attributes. Confession and fetishism do not here work to deflect attention away from female lack to male potency, but to inspire in the viewer (fictional and actual) the desire to have it fully revealed—to have it revealed, moreover, not as a repellent but as a pleasurable sight.

Perhaps most remarkably, the conjunction of castration and overvaluation results in a kind of masochistic eroticism in which Johnny participates not only as viewer, but as spectacle. When Gilda is pulled away at the end of her act she says to Johnny: "You wanted that. Now you should be happy. You wanted everyone to know that Johnny Farrell's wife is a tramp." She thereby suggests that Johnny wants not only her exposure, but his own; that his position, like hers, is a passive and masochistic one. The viewing subject is no more exempt from this passivity and masochism than is Johnny; whether that subject identifies with Gilda or Johnny, the result is at least in this respect the same.

Suture can be understood as the process whereby the inadequacy of the subject's position is exposed in order to facilitate (i.e. create the desire for) new insertions into a cultural discourse which promises to make good that lack. Since the promised compensation involves an ever greater subordination to already existing scenarios, the viewing subject's position is a supremely passive one, a fact which is carefully concealed

through cinematic sleight-of-hand. This sleight-of-hand involves attributing to a character within the fiction qualities which
in fact belong to the machinery of enunciation: the ability to
generate narrative, the omnipotent and coercive gaze, the castrating authority of the law.

The shot/reverse shot formation merely constitutes one device for achieving this transfer. As Mulvey suggests, others include spying on the woman, diagnosing her illness, forcing her
to confess, or better yet (as in *Lola Montes*) writing a narrative
by means of which she is defined. It is no accident that in the
films described by Mulvey the woman is *made* to confess by a
male character.

Gilda threatens to reveal this cinematic sleight-of-hand when
she freely "confesses" to the crimes and natural disasters caused
by women throughout history. Perhaps even more disruptive is
the fact that she renders so transparent the degree to which
her guilt is culturally inherited and written. However, most remarkable is the way in which the film acknowledges and dwells
upon the lures of castration. Gilda exercises fascination precisely by virtue of those things she lacks—money, legal authority, power, the omnipotent and coercive gaze. She insists upon
her inadequacy, repeats words ("decent?") which might be used
to put her beyond the pale, drinks to her own downfall, invites
men to undress her, and sings lyrics which underscore female
guilt.

Vidor's film thus poses a temptation which suture is intended to overcome: the temptation to refuse cultural re-inte-
gration, to skid off-course, out-of-control, to prefer castration
to false plenitude. That danger, like the one suggested by *Lola
Montes,* is implicit in classic cinema's scopic regime. It represents a point of female resistance within the very system which
defines woman as powerless and lacking.

In "Paranoia and the Film System," Jacqueline Rose addresses yet another way in which suture can be seen as containing the potential for its own disruption. She describes the system as inherently paranoic, both because it subordinates the
viewing subject to the cinematic apparatus, obliging that subject
to define itself in relation to a symbolic Other, and because it
promotes an aggressive dialectic similar to that first experi-

enced at the mirror stage. The second of these paranoic inscriptions, which Rose finds potentially subversive, warrants our close attention.

Rose points out that the system of suture, particularly insofar as it relies upon the shot/reverse shot formation, engages the viewer in a series of irreducibly binary identifications—identifications which are characteristic not of the symbolic but of the imaginary register:

> The code occults the position of the camera by setting up an opposition between two terms: the observer and the observed. What is seen is the subject himself and what he sees. The opposition is however a lure *in its very structure*. Firstly, the camera has to identify not only with the subject . . . in order to show what he sees, but also with the object of vision in order to show the subject. The series can therefore only be structured by a partial activation of the potentially aggressive reversal of its system. Secondly, the fact that the camera must identify with both terms of the opposition, and in the place of one of them cannot be assimilated to a subjectivity, reveals its presence *prior* to the point at which it disengages from that opposition, cancels the observer's centrality and subjects the observer and the observed to a [transcendent] gaze. . . . The opposition shot/countershot therefore contains its own principle of instability prior to the moment of its activation.[22]

Rose here draws our attention to the fact that the second shot in a shot/reverse shot formation requires the viewer to take up a quite contrary position to that maintained in the first shot. In other words, the two shots foster irreconcilable points of view. A film like Hitchcock's *The Birds,* discussed at length by Rose in "Paranoia and the Film System," underscores the intense ambivalence encoded into the shot/reverse shot formation by situating the viewer first in Melanie's position, and then in that of the birds who attack her. This ambivalence is a feature of the imaginary register, and it speaks to a regressive potential within the system of suture. The editing procedure most closely associated with that system thus encourages a psychic operation which is at odds with its larger signifying activities.

Once again this point of resistance to symbolic structuration—a point of resistance internal to the film system which promotes that structuration—finds its locus in the female subject. Rose argues that woman as she is presently constituted not only has a negative relation to the symbolic, but a positive one to the imaginary, and hence to psychic constructions like paranoia. The first of these relations—her negative association with the symbolic—is determined by the fact that she is defined in opposition to the phallus, i.e. that she can only be signified through what she lacks. The second of these relations—her privileged association with the imaginary—is in part a corollary of the first, in that she never enters as fully as does her male counterpart into the symbolic order. However, it can also be seen as one of the effects of the very different Oedipal route which she is obliged to take.

We recall that whereas the male subject is encouraged at the Oedipal juncture to invest in the same object he has previously loved as the source of warmth and nourishment (i.e. the mother), and which has provided him with his most important objects (a), the female subject is obliged instead to substitute the father. Thus a libidinal continuity smoothes the little boy's transition from imaginary to symbolic, a continuity denied the little girl. She is required to renounce her imaginary love object for one located exclusively within the symbolic, with the additional complication that this second love object will also provide the means whereby she undergoes a negative definition.

There are consequently two powerful lures recalling the female subject to the imaginary—the original love object, and the desire to return to a space unmarked by castration and phallic difference. Rose suggests that the film system dramatizes this imaginary seduction through its shot/reverse shot formations. Those formations disrupt the stability of the symbolic order by calling into question the fixity of its subject positions. They introduce into the narrative progression an aggressivity and paranoia which—like the construction of woman-as-fetish—threaten to disrupt it. In other words, the shot/reverse shot paradigm speaks to the insecurity of the female subject's position within the symbolic order, dramatizes the principle of imaginary reversibility to which she remains to some degree bound.

Hitchcock's *The Birds,* which provides Rose with her central example, renders unusually clear both the female subject's symbolic insecurity and her imaginary reversibility. Melanie's uneasy residence within the symbolic order is indicated not only by her problematic relationship with the law, but by the fact that she is seen by the inhabitants of Bodega Bay as having brought with her the threat to their town.

"Paranoia and the Film System" urges theoreticians to take the female subject much more fully into account when discussing classic cinema's scopic regime. It points out that neither cinema's imaginary nor its symbolic can be treated in isolation from sexual difference, and that it is only by foregrounding the part played by the latter in each of the former terms that alternative film practices can be articulated:

> . . . the emphasis on the imaginary in the discussion of film as a specific ideological form must address itself to the relation of woman to that register, since that relation is itself a comment on the impossibility of stabilising positions in the symbolic. It is therefore crucial when talking of the film's constant replay of loss and retrieval and the possibility of articulating that loss to transform the position of the spectator in film, to remember that the negativity in question is now only accessible through the sexual differentiation which has overlaid the primary severance. [102]

Rose's own notion of how we can best transform the position of the viewing subject involves maximizing the disruptive potential of the imaginary excess which always haunts the system of suture—and which does so most fully precisely at the shot/reverse shot juncture. She sees in that excess not only the return of a repressed "femininity," but the possibility for destabilizing the symbolic order, for throwing into jeopardy its Oedipal identifications. Rose's argument, like Mulvey's, suggests the centrality of the female subject not only to any description of the existing film system but to any alternative formulation. It also indicates that even within the former there are already ruptures and contradictions.

As the preceding discussion indicates, suture is not so much one theory as a group of overlapping theories. Whereas for some theoreticians it can be isolated in the shot/reverse shot formation, for others it is inherent in all of the operations which constitute narrativity. However, the theoreticians of suture agree that it provides the agency whereby the subject emerges within discourse, and (at least ideally) takes up a position congruent with the existing cultural order. Feminist writers like Mulvey, Rose, and Johnston also suggest that whether suture is taken in its most specialized or its broadest sense it always implies a sexual differentiation. Moreover, they suggest that it is precisely at the point where suture joins with female subjectivity that it is most vulnerable to subversion.

The theory of suture has yet to be extended to literary discourse, although it has obvious relevance to that discourse. First-person narration and other indicators of point-of-view would seem to be the equivalents for novels and poems of the shot/reverse shot formation in cinema, and like the latter would seem both to conceal all signs of actual production, and to invite identification. The narrative organization of the classic novel even more closely conforms to that of the classic film. However, this is not the place to suggest a full-fledged theory of literary suture. We will content ourselves with these brief remarks, particularly since the next chapter will be as single-minded in its scrutiny of literary discourse as this chapter has been of cinematic discourse.

Chapter 6 is devoted to Roland Barthes's *S/Z*, a theoretical model which is ideally suited to the task of revealing the disembodied cultural voices which speak not only the books we read and the films we view, but our own subjectivity and the world in which we live.

6

Re-Writing the Classic Text

In the two preceding chapters we have focused a good deal of attention upon discourse as the agency whereby the subject is produced, and the existing cultural order sustained. We have also spoken at length there about the central role played by sexual difference in the organization of all three. In short, we have tried to demonstrate the imbrication of subject, discourse, and symbolic order.

However, the emphasis has fallen more consistently upon the first two of these categories than it has upon the last. This chapter will address a theoretical model which is calculated to introduce the symbolic order more fully into our treatment of subjectivity and discursivity, that provided by Roland Barthes in *S/Z*. Although *S/Z* is generally considered to be a study of prose narrative, we will discover that its most remarkable achievement is to have articulated an interpretive strategy which permits the reader (or viewer) to uncover the symbolic field inhabited by a given text, and to disclose the oppositions—sexual and other—which structure that field.

Despite the fact that *S/Z* moves its argument forward through the segmentation of a short story by Honoré de Balzac ("Sarrasine"), it is less concerned with those features which are specific to prose narrative than it is with a group of codes which can be activated by a number of textual systems (prose narrative, lyric poetry, epic poetry, narrative film, drama, comic-strips, etc.). These codes manifest themselves through connotation.

As we observed in Chapter 1, connotation has always been an important element within Barthes's semiotics. In *Mythologies,* where he treats the issue most exhaustively, Barthes defines connotation as a secondary operation, one which builds on denotation. In other words, he has recourse to the Hjelmslevian paradigm, in which the entire denotative sign becomes a signifier in a new signifying transaction, that of connotation. We illustrated this commutation in our earlier discussion of Barthes with the photograph of the black soldier saluting a French flag, a denotative sign which generates the secondary meanings "colonialism," "nationalism," and "militarism." However, Barthes supplements the paradigm which he appropriates from Hjelmslev in one important respect: he identifies connotation as an agency of ideology, or what he in his early writings calls "myth."

In other words, Barthes argues that connotation naturalizes history, that it makes a given culture seem eternal and inevitable. It encourages on the part of the reading, viewing, or listening subject a constant mis-recognition, both of the world and of itself. In short, it re-interpellates the subject into familiar positions, positions which constitute an important part of a larger symbolic matrix. In *Mythologies* Barthes writes that connotation

> . . . has an imperative, buttonholing character: stemming from an historical concept, directly springing from contingency . . . it is *I* whom it has come to seek. It is turned toward me, I am subjected to its intentional force, it summons me to receive its expansive ambiguity. . . . this interpellant speech is at the same time a *frozen* speech: at the moment of reaching me, it suspends itself, turns away and assumes the look of a generality: it stiffens, it makes itself look neutral and innocent.[1]

Like the cinematic apparatuses responsible for the enunciation of a film, the "voices" behind connotation remain anonymous, off-stage. In both cases that anonymity and that representational removal function to conceal the production of meaning, to obscure the operations of discourse. (However, the strategies devised by Barthes for foregrounding this surreptitious signifying activity differ from those devised by the theoreticians of suture. Whereas the former focus on editing procedures and a technological complex specific to cinema, Barthes turns his attention to the production of what might be designated a "portable" meaning—to a signifying phenomenon that occurs in a wide variety of textual systems.)

Barthes makes clear at the outset of *S/Z*, a book published thirteen years after *Mythologies*, that connotation still implies for him an ideological event. Indeed, he brings the ideological dimensions of connotation into even sharper relief through the emphasis which he there places upon codes. *S/Z* describes connotation as simultaneously the "invasion" of a text by a code, and a digression away from the text toward the larger discursive field—as a incursion that results in an excursion. Connotation is thus an operation which both originates outside of and extends beyond any individual signifying instance.

As Barthes explains in *S/Z*, a code represents a sort of bridge between texts. Its presence within one text involves a simultaneous reference to all of the other texts in which it appears, and to the cultural reality which it helps to define—i.e. to a particular symbolic order:

> The code is a perspective of quotations, a mirage of structures; we know only its departures and returns; the units which have resulted from it (those we inventory) are themselves, always, ventures out of the text, the mark, the sign of a virtual digression toward the remainder of a catalogue (*The Kidnapping* refers to every kidnapping ever written); they are so many fragments of something that has always been *already* read, seen, done, experienced; the code is the wake of that *already*. Referring to what has been written, i.e. to the Book (of culture, of life, of life as culture), it makes the text into a prospectus of this Book.[2]

The codes which manifest themselves through connotation function endlessly to repeat what has been written in other books and portrayed in other films, and so to reproduce the existing cultural order. Repetition does the same thing for that order as constant re-interpellation does for the subject: it creates the illusion of stability and continuity.

While *S/Z* still distinguishes connotation from denotation, referring to them as different systems, it rejects the chronological model advanced by *Mythologies*. In the later book Barthes abandons the notion that denotation always comes first, and that it has an authenticity and innocence which connotation lacks. Instead he proposes that denotation is the agency of closure—that it represses the play of meaning by insisting upon "true" and "literal" signifieds. In this respect it can better be understood as producing the last rather than the first meaning:

> . . . denotation is not the first meaning, but pretends to be so; under this illusion, it is ultimately no more than the *last* of the connotations (the one which seems both to establish and to close the reading), the superior myth by which the text pretends to return to the nature of language, to language as nature: doesn't a sentence, whatever meaning it releases, subsequent to its utterance . . . appear to be telling us something simple, literal, primitive: something *true*, in relation to which all the rest (which comes *afterwards, on top*), is literature? That is why, if we want to go along with the classic text we must keep denotation, the old deity, watchful, cunning, theatrical, foreordained to *represent* the collective innocence of language. [9]

S/Z draws our attention to the way in which a logo-centric semiotics tends to establish the denotative signified as a privileged and authoritative term, one which moreover results in impoverished texts. Connotation is there seen as the means whereby that privileged and authoritative term can be contested, and a signifying diversity promoted. Barthes tells us, in what is a complete reversal of his earlier position on the matter, that connotation offers us "the way into the polysemy of the classic text, to that limited plural on which the classic text is based" (8).

The rather paradoxical attitude taken by *S/Z* toward connotation can only be understood in the light of Barthes's claim that no text is ever reducible to a single code—that even the most classic of texts is the point of convergence for numerous codes. Thus although every connotation is an ideological event, that event is by no means unchallenged; it is obliged to compete with others which may or may not be congruent with it. Barthes defines textuality as a process carried out simultaneously at five different levels which intersect at multiple points, and he uses the metaphor of a braid to illustrate their intersection:

> The grouping of codes, as they enter into the work, into the movement of the reading, constitute a braid (*text, fabric, braid:* the same thing); each thread, each code, is a voice; these braided—or braiding—voices form the writing: when it is alone, the voice does no labor, transforms nothing; it *expresses;* but as soon as the hand intervenes to gather and intertwine the inert threads, there is labor, there is transformation. [160]

This passage insists on the distinction between expression and production. The first of these is seen as the passive repetition of something which has already been formulated, whereas the second involves an active transformation of existing materials through new combinations of them. It is by means of these new combinations that texts always exceed the sum of their component codes, that they are never entirely predictable. Moreover, the greater the number and diversity of the codes which participate in the production of a given text, the more contradictory and unstable will be its play of signification. Connotation is thus the agency both of ideological consistency and ideological inconsistency; it will serve the first of these goals if only a few codes are activated by a given text, and the second if a wide variety are brought into service.

As we noted a moment ago, Barthes isolates five different kinds of codes or levels of connotation. He refers to these five levels of connotation as the semic, the hermeneutic, the proairetic, the symbolic, and the cultural. The semic code functions to define persons and places, while the hermeneutic code is entrusted with the responsibility of articulating and resolving enigmas. The proairetic code establishes fixed sequences of actions, and the symbolic code unresolvable oppositions. The cultural codes, which are extremely numerous and heterogeneous, to a very large degree subsume all the other categories. They speak the familiar "truths" of the existing cultural order, repeat what has "always been *already* read, seen, done, experienced." We will return to these codes later in this chapter, but before doing so we need to confront the interpretive strategy devised by Barthes for revealing their presence in classic texts, and for maximizing their signifying resources.

One of the more interesting and important features of this interpretive strategy is that it does not serve merely to reveal and to maximize the codes which operate on the premises of the classic text, but to transform that text into what Barthes calls a "writerly" one. In other words, it not only discloses the symbolic field inhabited by a given novel, poem, or film, making manifest its latent contradictions, but engages the reader or viewer in the production of a different sort of text.

S/Z defines the writerly text and the reading or viewing relationship which it entails in opposition to the "readerly" text and the reading or viewing relationship which it promotes. The readerly approach stresses all of the values implicit in the paradigmatic classic text—unity, realism, and transparency—and is therefore virtually synonymous with it. By means of this approach the reader or viewer is reduced to an involuntary rehearsal of what has already been culturally written. These two very different sets of relationships with the classic text require a much fuller explanation, but before embarking upon that explanation I would like to comment briefly on the status of that text.

The term "classic text" refers not so much to any actual text as to the model of the classic text, a model which can only be derived from a process of abstraction from numerous textual instances, much the way that *langue* can only be derived from numerous instances of *parole*. It is important to stress that no actual text ever conforms at all points to the classic model; the actual text always contains a surplus of meaning, signifying elements which are incompatible with the abstract model. It is this excess which makes possible the conversion of the classic text into a writerly text.

A) THE READERLY TEXT

As we have just indicated, the readerly text is the result of so smooth a match of the reader or viewer with the classic textual model that the two are for all intents and purposes identical. Consequently, "readerly" and "classic" will here be used as interchangeable terms, with the understanding that it is only through the readerly approach that an individual classic text can be made fully to approximate its model.

The readerly or classic text strives above all for homogeneity. It organizes its materials according to the "principle of non-contradiction," stressing at all points the "compatible nature of circumstances." This is not to say that the readerly text eliminates oppositions; on the contrary, it uses them as a major structuring device. However, it rigorously limits the number of oppositions which can come into play at any juncture, and the manner in which they can be articulated.

The exemplary classic text projects the same oppositions onto every level of the fiction (character, action, setting, theme, etc.). Moreover, it does so in ways which admit of no integration, and hence no change in the existing cultural order. It shows a marked preference for paradox (most theological of oppositional tropes) and antithesis (most ideological), but it steers clear of contradiction, which would challenge the imperative of inevitability.

The readerly text purports to be a transcript of a reality which pre-exists and exceeds it, and it tightly controls the play of signification by subordinating everything to this transcendental meaning. It encourages the reader or viewer to move away from its signifiers, which are understood as secondary, toward a privileged and originating signified:

> . . . it is the *direction* of meaning which determines the two major management functions of the classic text: the *author* is always supposed to go from signified to signifier, from content to form, from idea to text, from passion to expression; and, in contrast, the *critic* goes in the other direction, works back from signifiers to signified. The *mastery* of *meaning*, a veritable semiurgism, is a divine attribute, once this meaning is defined as

the discharge, the emanation, the spiritual effluvium overflowing from the signified toward the signifier: the *author* is a god (his place of origin is the signified); as for the critic, he is the priest whose task is to decipher the Writing of the god. [174]

The readerly text thus attempts to conceal all traces of itself as a factory within which a particular social reality is produced through standard representations and dominant signifying practices. Reflexivity provides one of the most successful means of effecting this concealment. The readerly text often foregrounds its own stylistic operations as a means of deflecting attention away from the more broadly cultural pressures at work upon it. Through this strategy the text seems to refer primarily to the reality of a "private consciousness," a category which dictates the terms of its own analysis, and so escapes any probing scrutiny. Texts of this sort, which include such illustrious novels as Vladimir Nabokov's *Pale Fire* and James Joyce's *Portrait of an Artist as a Young Man,* as well as a cinematic corpus within which the films of Federico Fellini centrally figure, have been dubbed "self-conscious." They generally enjoy critical esteem precisely because they seem to issue from an author who conforms to the paradigm of the Cartesian subject: autonomous, self-knowing, capable of thinking worlds into existence. Reflexive texts feature the author as transcendental signified.

Another way in which many nineteenth- and twentieth-century novels and short stories efface the signs of their actual production resembles the shot/reverse shot formation within classic cinema: a voice within the fiction claims responsibility for the discourse, thus covering over the cultural enunciation. This can be done obliquely, through a third person narrative of the sort found in many Henry James stories, such as *What Maisie Knew,* where events are filtered through a single and rather obtrusive point of view; through a framing technique of the kind used in Joseph Conrad's *Heart of Darkness,* where attention is constantly drawn to the fictional process of narrating; or through a first person narrative, continuous as in Vladimir Nabokov's *Lolita,* or intermittent as in Henry Fielding's *Tom Jones.*

Barthes emphasizes that the classic text depends upon a linear reading or viewing; any deviation from that norm threatens its existence. This is because the classic text is finally nothing more than a large-scale predication, i.e. a statement which defines and situates a subject. As we noted in the preceding chapter, discourse requires readers and viewers who will identify with the subjects it projects, who will agree to be spoken through them. In other words, it requires readers and viewers who will accede to the terms of its (linear) unfolding. It enlists those readers and viewers by fostering in them a desire for closure, and a belief in the revelatory nature of endings. Narrative represents a particularly powerful syntagmatic lure, affirming the coherence of the text and binding the reader or viewer to it in a relationship of pleasurable dependence. However, poetry also has its syntagmatic lures—rhyme, meter, structural expectations (the couplet, the refrain). What Barthes writes of narrative thus holds equally true for all classic texts, except that in the case of a lyric poem there will be a higher degree of compression:

> The dramatic narrative is a game with two players: the snare and the truth. At first a tremendous indetermination rules their encounters, the wandering is wide of the mark; gradually however, the two networks move closer together, co-penetrate, determination is completed and with it the subject . . . the game is ended, the drama has its *dénouement,* the subject correctly "predicated" (fixed): the discourse can do nothing more than fall silent. [188]

At the moment of closure toward which every readerly experience moves, the reader or viewer enjoys an illusory sense of liberation—illusory because through that closure his or her subjectivity has been reconfirmed. Subjectivity must be constantly re-activated in this way; hence the readerly text is a disposable product, designed to be consumed during one encounter. More always wait on the shelf:

> Rereading [is] an operation contrary to the commercial and ideological habits of our society, which would have us "throw away" the story once it has been consumed ("devoured"), so

> that we can then move on to another story, buy another book,
> and . . . is tolerated only in certain marginal categories of
> readers (children, old people, and professors). . . . [15–16]

(Barthes's point obviously pertains less to poetry than it does to
narrative forms. Poetry is itself "marginal" in our culture, and
on those rare occasions when it is read at all it is almost always
reread or memorized.)

As we shall see, the writerly text engages the reader or
viewer in a productive rather than a consumptive capacity. It
opts for heterogeneity rather than unity, and instead of the
familiar it looks for the alien and the unpredictable. Finally, far
from striving for transparency, it attempts to foreground the
traces of its cultural inscription.

B) THE WRITERLY TEXT

The writerly text comes into existence as an archaeological dig
at the site of a classic text. It exhumes the cultural voices or
codes responsible for the latter's enunciation, and in the process it discovers multiplicity instead of consistency, and signifying flux instead of stable meaning. The writerly text is one which
the reader or viewer has obliged to reveal the terms of its own
construction, one which has been made available as discourse
instead of as a transparent poetic, novelistic, or cinematic fiction.

No "glue" holds together the disparate pieces of the writerly
text; in it heterogeneity and contradiction are multiplied as
much as possible. None of its codes is subordinated to any
other—on the contrary, the writerly text strives for anarchy and
incoherence. Barthes insists that even irony must be banished
from that text's premises since it enacts a repressive discourse
in which the voice of implied criticism dominates all others. Here
numerous codes signify simultaneously, without regard to the
rules of precedence or sequentiality.

The writerly text promotes an infinite play of signification;
in it there can be no transcendental signified, only provisional
ones which function in turn as signifiers. It thus denies the pos-

sibility of closure. The writerly text has no syntagmatic order, but can be "entered" at any point. Barthes proposes that within it "everything signifies ceaselessly and several times, but without being delegated to a final great ensemble, to an ultimate structure" (12). The writerly text replaces the concepts of "product" and "structure" with those of "process" and "segmentation."

These substitutions effect a profound transformation in the experience of textuality. Whereas the notion of the text as product implies a reader or viewer who functions as a passive consumer, that of process suggests instead a reader or viewer who participates in an on-going manufacture of meaning, an activity without a final goal or resting point. Similarly, whereas the notion of structure implies a kind of seamlessness or transparency, that of segmentation draws attention not only to the seams which join together the pieces which make up the whole, but to the ways in which the former exceed the latter. In short, it emphasizes the relative autonomy of each of the "*lexia*" or textual segments.

Segmentation provides the agency whereby the text as product yields to the text as process. It fragments the structure of the classic text in order to reveal the cultural voices which speak it, the codes which constitute its "reality." Segmentation first cuts up the text into its smallest units of signification, and then demystifies those units by demonstrating their coded status. Barthes describes that operation as a series of interruptions which serve to isolate signifying units from each other. It is thus the converse of suture; whereas the latter involves the stitching together of signifiers in such a way as to induce a forward movement, the former divides one signifier from another so as to impede linear progression:

> We shall . . . star the text, separating, in the manner of a minor earthquake, the blocks of significance of which reading grasps only the smooth surface, imperceptibly soldered by the movement of sentences, the flowing discourse of narration, the "naturalness" of ordinary language. The tutor signifier will be cut up into a series of brief, contiguous fragments, which we shall call *lexias*, since they are units of meaning. [13]

It is important to note that segmentation not only demystifies the classic text, but enriches it enormously. The "starred"
text has been expanded to four or five times its original size.
Its play of signification now occurs in slow motion, and it accommodates endless digressions and interpolations. These
digressions and interpolations open up a whole new field of
meaning—one which was there all along, but whose existence
was hidden behind the linear organization of the text.

We commented above on the fact that point of view functions in novels and short stories much the way the look does in
cinematic narrative; in both cases the discourse seems to proceed from a source within the fiction which serves to conceal
the real apparatuses of enunciation. The writerly text, on the
contrary, draws attention to itself as a series of cultural utterances. It does this by permitting all of the voices on its premises
to be heard, i.e. by tolerating a veritable Babel. It also attempts
whenever possible to identify the code responsible for each
emission. Barthes encourages us to listen to the classic text as
"an iridescent exchange carried on by multiple voices, on different wavelengths and subject from time to time to a sudden
dissolve, leaving a gap which enables the utterance to shift from
one point of view to another, without warning," and in so doing
to transform it into a writerly text (41–42). Here too the writerly project seems ideally suited to challenge the operations of
suture. Not only does it disrupt the smooth join of adjacent
signifiers, but it shows them to proceed from a source external
to the fiction.

Segmentation opposes yet another of the closures effected
by suture—the closure of the reader or viewer within a predetermined subject-position. As we observed in Chapter 5, the
classic text requires concrete individuals as its support; it is activated only at those moments when someone occupies its subjective space. In so doing that person or collectivity not only
assumes the "place" from which the classic text's signifying operations become intelligible and seemingly natural, but "agrees"
to be constituted through them. By fragmenting the classic text
and revealing the codes responsible for its enunciation, the
writerly project "dis-places" the reader or viewer, alienates him
or her from the all-too-familiar subject-positions of the existing

cultural regime. The deconstructive strategies outlined by
Barthes in *S/Z* call upon us to speak rather than to be spoken,
encourage us to participate in the production not only of
meaning but of subjectivity and the larger symbolic order.

This last point warrants a restatement: *S/Z* suggests that we
can escape from the symbolic field which we presently inhabit
by first mastering its codes, and then recombining them to form
a new one—by moving from a passive to an active discursive
position, from repetition to innovation. Segmentation thus provides more than an agency of *de*construction; it also offers the
possibility of a radical *re*construction. We by no means diminish
the importance of *S/Z* when we acknowledge that it finally helps
us much more with the first of these tasks than it does with the
second; after all, the former is a necessary prelude to the latter.

Before proceeding any farther in our discussion of *S/Z*, we
must take cognizance of the fact that a considerable distance
separates the rewritten classic text from the writerly ideal.
Whereas the former is characterized only by a limited polysemy, the second offers the image of a "triumphant plural,"

> unimpoverished by any constraint of representation (of imita-
> tion). In this ideal text, the networks are many and interact,
> without any one of them being able to surpass the rest; this
> text is a galaxy of signifiers, not a structure of signifieds; it has
> no beginning; it is reversible; we can gain access to it by several
> entrances, none of which can be authoritatively declared to be
> the main one; the codes it mobilizes extend *as far as the eye can
> reach*, they are indeterminable (meaning here is never subject
> to a principle of determination, unless by throwing dice); the
> systems of meaning can take over this absolutely plural text,
> but their meaning is never closed, based as it is on the infinity
> of language. [5–6]

The definition which Barthes here supplies can perhaps best
be understood as a description of the goals toward which the
writerly project aims, goals which can never be perfectly realized. Indeed, we will discover that far from always disclosing
heterogeneity and contradiction, the writerly approach to the
classic text often serves to reveal a startling degree of cultural
overdetermination.

In the pages that follow we will attempt to account for the operations of each of the codes enumerated by Barthes, codes which enter the classic text through connotation, and whose discovery transforms that text into a writerly one. Since the preceding chapter focused so exclusively on cinematic texts, this one will concentrate on literary examples. It will not limit itself to narrative forms; on the contrary, it will have recourse as frequently to lyric poems as to short stories or novels, indicating the portability of the codes tabulated by *S/Z*, and the wide relevance of its interpretive strategy.[3]

C) THE CODES

Barthes claims that his five codes resist reconstitution—that they escape any effort to chart their activities. In spite of that assertion, he later provides a quite definitive map of the hermeneutic code, indicating not only its constituent parts, but the rough order in which they generally appear. He also gives a rather explicit account of the semic code.

Barthes's reluctance similarly to systematize the symbolic, proairetic, and cultural codes, as well as disclaimers of the kind just mentioned, can be attributed to his desire to preserve at all costs the irreducibility of the classic text to any absolute meaning. His concentration in *S/Z* on coding operations may seem somewhat at odds with the impulse to avoid systematization, but he sees in the stratification of the textual field the possibility for an ever greater complexity of signifying transactions—a kind of "jamming" of the interpretive machine so as to prevent transcendental meaning from emerging.

The codes enumerated by Barthes would seem capable of invading the classic text on multiple levels, ranging from individual signifiers to larger syntactic and narrative constructions. The semic code, which functions to define character and place, relies upon the specificity of the proper name for its central term. However, the attributes which it clusters around that name may be conveyed either through adjectives or through larger conceptual formations, like metaphor and metonymy. Similarly, the hermeneutic code, which assumes responsibility for the formulation and resolution of enigmas, finds expression through half-sentences, questions, and silences as well as through narrative delay or equivocation. The proairetic or action code determines not only narrative but syntactic progression. In an analogous fashion the symbolic code generates rhetorical antitheses along with the oppositions which structure major conflicts within the fiction.

Finally, the cultural codes organize linguistic segments of novels, short stories, and poems in the form of proverbial statements and commonplaces, but they also dictate the range of possible narratives, character types, and conflicts, as well as the sorts of knowledge likely to be repressed, and the conditions under which that knowledge will ultimately be divulged. While there is a good deal of interaction between all five codes the cultural codes extend their influence farthest. Indeed, in many classic texts a single powerful cultural code subordinates the proairetic, semic, symbolic, and hermeneutic activities.

i. *The semic code.* The semic code represents the major device for thematizing persons, objects, or places. It operates by grouping a number of signifiers around either a proper name, or another signifier which functions temporarily as if it were a proper name, like the red wheel barrow in the William Carlos Williams poem:

> so much depends
> upon
>
> a red wheel
> barrow
>
> glazed with rain
> water
>
> beside the white
> chickens

The signifiers so grouped function like a collective signified to the proper name or its surrogate—thus the red wheel barrow signifies "to have so much depend upon it," "to be glazed with rain water" and "to be beside white chickens." The verb "depends," which has the meanings "to be suspended from" and "to belong to something as subordinate," nicely expresses the semic relationship.

Barthes refers to the signifiers which provide another signifier with its semantic value as "semes." He insists that the same signifiers must attach themselves to a proper name more than once before the connection becomes permanent ("When identical semes traverse the same proper name several times and appear to settle upon it, a character is created" (67)). Obviously this stipulation does not obtain in the case of a poem like the one just cited, where everything "depends" upon brevity and simplicity, but John Milton's "L'Allegro" and "Il Penseroso" make clear the degree of redundancy which the semic code generally requires.

These two poems are virtual exercises in semic coding and re-coding, whereby the qualities associated with the signifier "Melancholy" in the first poem are reversed in the second, and a similar operation carried out in relation to "Mirth." Lines 11–16 of "Il Penseroso" connect Melancholy three times with the attribute of divinity, and twice with that of wisdom. A number of ancillary terms ("holiness," "saintliness," "brightness," "staidness," "blackness of hue") fortify and extend these associations, creating an ever larger semantic field:

> But hail thou goddess, sage and holy,
> Hail divinest Melancholy.
> Whose saintly visage is too bright
> To hit the sense of human sight;
> And therefore to our weaker view,
> O'erlaid with black staid wisdom's hue.

Redundancy provides the means whereby even a complex group of semes can be stabilized. That stabilization permits one signifier in the group to stand in for the others in their absence— thus once the attributes of divinity and darkness have been linked through their common relationship to Melancholy, the former implies the latter, and the latter the former. Moreover, additional terms which connect metaphorically with one also refer to the other; thus "sad leaden downward cast (43)" indicates a demeanor appropriate to a divinity as well as one sugggestive of gloom.

The semic code operates in an even more overt fashion in a text like the anonymous *Everyman*, where the single quality by which a character is defined actually coincides with that character's name. However, it is one of the conventions of nineteenth-century narrative, still the dominant tradition, that the semic code should operate unobtrusively. Attributes are seldom openly distributed around characters in novels by George Eliot or Honoré de Balzac; instead, they are implied by clothes, gestures, patterns of speech. The qualities which constitute a character emerge gradually, over the course of the story, and seemingly under the pressure of the reader's investigation.

The fragmentation of the semic field fosters the illusion that the "truth" precedes its enunciation, and that character exceeds the sum total of its attributes (i.e. that it is a mysterious and finally uncalculable entity):

> This fleeting citation, this surreptitious and discontinuous way of stating themes, this alternating flux and outburst, create together the allure of the connotation; the semes appear to float freely, to form a galaxy of trifling data in which we read no order of importance . . . the greater the syntagmatic distance between two data, the more skillful the narrative. . . .[22]

The indirection which Barthes here describes—an indirection which involves a heavy reliance upon connotation rather than denotation, and which requires the dispersal of semes over a large textual territory—creates that impression of reality for which the nineteenth-century novel has been so celebrated. However, as *S/Z* makes clear, it is only as the result of intense cultural coding that the qualities associated with a given name can come to seem "natural," or as if they are spontaneously discovered by the reader.

In other words, the semic code can only operate invisibly to the degree that signification has already intimately invaded speech, appearance, clothing, gesture, and action. The fact that these things can be trusted to carry the information which would otherwise require a direct authorial statement indicates how fully even the private and quotidian have been coded. Consequently, far from revealing a reality previously neglected by literature, the nineteenth-century novel can be said to have created that reality by radically extending the human subject's discursive potential: within its confines not even the slightest verbal lapse or twitch of an eye can escape surveillance and meaning.

The gaze which the narrator focuses on Durbeyfield at the opening of Thomas Hardy's *Tess of the D'Urbervilles*, for instance, defines the latter through a discourse in which place, time, sex, age, clothing, equipment, posture, manner of walking, and absence of concentrated thought all signify:

> On an evening in the latter part of May a middle-aged man was walking homeward from Shaston to the village of Marlott, in the adjoining Vale of Blakemore or Blackmoor. The pair of legs that carried him were rickety, and there was a bias in his gait which inclined him somewhat to the left of a straight line. He occasionally gave a smart nod, as if in confirmation of some opinion, though he was not thinking of anything in particular. An empty egg-basket was slung upon his arm, the nap of his hat was ruffled, a patch being quite worn away at its brim where his thumb came in taking it off.[4]

Before the proper name is even supplied, the semes have been assembled: poverty ("middle-aged man walking," "empty egg-basket"), decrepitude ("rickety" legs, shabby hat), aimlessness ("bias in his gait," "not thinking of anything in particular"), social insignificance ("a patch being quite worn away at his brim where his thumb came in taking it off"). The time of year (late May) promises change, which is inaugurated by the parson several sentences later when he informs Durbeyfield about his illustrious ancestors.

Because its function is to define, the semic code operates as an agency for inscribing what Foucault would call "power-relations" into literary and cinematic texts. It makes available certain strategies for understanding persons and places which are really ways of signifying and controlling those persons and places. Those epistemological strategies also determine the position from which power is exercised, and therefore must be seen as exceeding the agent who occupies that position. In other words, they constitute the speaking as well as the spoken subject.[5]

As we will discover later in this chapter, the semic code always operates in close conjunction with the cultural codes. Indeed, it is to a large degree an adjunct code, defining person and place in ideologically symptomatic ways. For example, in a text in which Christianity functioned as the dominant cultural code the semic code would delineate characters and settings which were indicative of such oppositions as body/soul, pride/humility, evil/good, etc. Thus the semic code does not so much initiate as express those power-relations which are fundamental to knowledge.

So far we have stressed the repressive dimensions of the semic code. Barthes dwells much more on the play of signification which that code makes possible, and hence on connotation. He defines the seme as a *connotative signified,* a device for delaying rather than facilitating the revelation of "truth." This interesting but puzzling notion requires clarification.

In the section of *S/Z* entitled "Signified and Truth," Barthes writes that within the hermeneutic system,

> . . . the connotative signified occupies a special place: it brings into being an insufficient half-truth, powerless to name itself: it is the incompleteness, the insufficiency, the powerlessness of truth . . . a hermeneutic morpheme, whose function is to thicken the enigma by outlining it: a powerful enigma is a dense one, so that, provided certain precautions are taken, the more signs there are, the more the truth will be obscured, the harder one will try to figure it out. The connotative signified is literally an index: it points but it does not tell . . . it is both the temptation to name and the impotence to name. . . .[62]

Barthes's use of the term "connotative signified" may be a bit misleading since it indicates signifieds which themselves connotate or "point to" further meaning, and not necessarily signifieds which are the result of connotation, although that is almost always the case as well. The examples which he lists in the same passage ("the Empty, the Inanimate, the Feminine, the Superannuated, the Monstrous, the Wealthy") have been deduced from the mass of signifiers clustered around the old man in the opening section of Balzac's story. For instance, "Empty" has been extrapolated from such textual details as "a form without substance, a being without life, or a life without action," and "Feminine" from Zambinella's ruffles, his "fabulous" diamond and the watch-chain which shimmers "like the brilliants of a choker around a woman's neck." In short, these signifieds derive from what the Barthes of *Mythologies* would call "connotative signifiers," i.e. from the entire denotative sign. However, what makes them "connotative signifieds" within Barthes's later system is the fact that they themselves connote. For instance, "Empty" signifies "lacking the penis," while "Feminine" signifies "other than masculine."

A connotative signified or seme perpetuates the play of signification. It represents the antithesis of a transcendental signified, like "God" within the Christian code, which provides the final meaning to which every other term points, but never points beyond itself. The connotative signified *always* refers beyond itself, appears, as Barthes puts it, "pregnant" with additional disclosures. It constitutes a hermeneutic as well as a semic element since it prolongs the search for "truth," deepens the mystery. It functions as a passage or doorway through which we must pass, and never as the final destination.

The writerly project involves a relentless pursuit of new signifieds—a ceaseless slippage from one connotation to another:

> . . . if we are told that Sarrasine had *"one of those strong wills that know no obstacle,"* what are we to read? *will, energy, obstinacy, stubbornness,* etc.? The connotator refers not so much to a name as to a synonymic complex whose common nucleus we sense even while the discourse is leading us toward other possibilities, toward other related signifieds: thus, reading is absorbed in a kind of metonymic skid, each synonym adding to its neighbor some new trait, some new departure: the old man who was first connoted as *fragile* is soon said to be *"of glass"*: an image containing signifieds of rigidity, immobility, and dry, cutting frangibility. This expansion is the very movement of meaning: the meaning skids, recovers itself, and advances simultaneously. . . . [92]

Reading or viewing according to the model proposed by Barthes is thus a process of "skidding" from one signified to another, related one. This dizzying movement is halted only by further supplementations at the syntagmatic level (i.e. the provision of additional denotative signs), supplementations which indicate new connotative signifieds and eliminate others already considered. Meaning undergoes a series of constant transformations, remains in a state of perpetual flux. The writerly goal is to sustain this flux indefinitely, to postpone forever the castrating decision "this, not that" by supporting all of the signifying possibilities, no matter how manifold and contradictory.

ii. *The hermeneutic code.* Barthes observes that "semic space is glued to hermeneutic space" in that what the hermeneutic code moves toward (i.e. a "profound or final space") is nothing other than a signified which refuses to connote. The hermeneutic code inscribes the desire for closure and "truth."

However, this code provides not only the agency whereby a mystery is first suggested and later resolved, but a number of mechanisms for delaying our access to the desired information:

> . . . the problem is to *maintain* the enigma in the initial void of its answer; whereas the sentences quicken the story's "unfolding" and cannot help but move the story along, the hermeneutic code performs an opposite action: it must set up *delays* (obstacles, stoppages, deviations) in the flow of the discourse; its structure is essentially reactive, since it opposes the ineluctable advance of language with an organized set of stoppages: between question and answer there is a whole dilatory area whose emblem might be named "reticence," the rhetorical figure which interrupts the sentence, suspends it, turns it aside. . . .[75]

Barthes divides the hermeneutic code into ten constituent parts or "morphemes," many of which overlap in practice, and whose order can be considerably varied: thematization, proposal of the enigma, formulation of the enigma, request for an answer, snare, equivocation, jamming, suspended answer, partial answer, and disclosure. These morphemes can be combined in assorted ways to make up what might be called the hermeneutic "sentence."

The first of the hermeneutic morphemes is *thematization,* or "an emphasizing of the object which will be the subject of the enigma" (209). Thematization involves a quite complex operation, in which the semic code plays an important role. It is in effect the definition of character, object or place in ways which signify "mystery." Stevenson's *Dr. Jekyll and Mr. Hyde*, for example, simultaneously defines the central character and establishes that there is an enigma. Mr. Utterson's name implies that he has something to tell, but the opening sentences of the narrative indicate that he will not relinquish any information easily:

> Mr. Utterson the lawyer was a man of rugged countenance that was never lighted by a smile; cold, scanty and embarrassed in discourse; backward in sentiment; lean, long, dusty, dreary, and somehow lovable. At friendly meetings, and when the wine was to his taste, something eminently human beaconed from his eye; something which indeed never found its way into his talk, but which spoke not only in these silent symbols of the afterdinner face, but more often and loudly in the acts of his life. He was austere with himself; drank gin when he was alone, to mortify a taste for vintages; and though he enjoyed the theater, had not crossed the doors of one for twenty years.[6]

The predominant attribute suggested by these two sentences, remarkable for the circuitousness of their syntax, is that of repression—repression of the taste for wine, the impulse to smile, fondness for the theater and, above all, verbal communication. The passage contains as well two references to wine-drinking, one of which promises that the bar of repression will only be lifted through the intervention of that liquid, and the other of which counteracts the promise by announcing that Utterson has forced himself to renounce wine in favor of gin. A conflict thus emerges at the very outset between self-indulgence and self-denial, a conflict which finds its locus in a mind-altering substance akin to the potion which we later learn transforms Jekyll into Hyde.

No overt reference to the central enigma occurs until several pages later, when Utterson's comrade, Enfield, decides to tell the former about a "very odd story" which is connected with the street through which they happen to be walking. However, immediately prior to Enfield's remark that street is thematized in ways which elaborately anticipate the formulation of the enigma. This thematization proceeds not only through the assistance of the semic code, but that of the symbolic code, whose function is to structure textual materials in oppositional terms:

> Even on Sunday, when it veiled its more florid charms and lay comparatively empty of passage, the street shone out in contrast to its dingy neighbourhood, like a fire in a forest; and with its freshly-painted shutters, well-polished brasses, and general cleanliness and gaiety of note, instantly caught and pleased the eye of the passenger.
>
> Two doors from the corner, on the left side going east, the line was broken by the entry of the court, and just at that point, a certain sinister block of building thrust forward its gable on the street. It was two stories high; showed no window, nothing but a door on the lower story; and a blind forehead of discoloured wall on the upper; and bore in every feature the marks of prolonged and sordid negligence. [9]

"Feature," "blind forehead" and "florid charms" all establish a metaphoric relationship between architectural forms and their human inhabitants. As a consequence, the signifiers "freshly-painted," "cleanliness," "discoloured," "blind," and "sordid negligence" provide a moral commentary as well as a physical description. They set up an opposition not just between a group of brightly-lit and carefully groomed buildings and one which is dark and dingy, but between industry and slovenliness, moral hygiene and moral lassitude. In short, the street connotes a human conflict which will not be revealed until the conclusion of the narrative—the conflict of body and soul. (Clearly, yet another code is at work here—the cultural code of Christianity. We will comment further on the last point below.)

The second hermeneutic morpheme isolated by Barthes is the *proposal* that there is an enigma. When Enfield draws Utterson's attention to the door of what is later shown to be Hyde's house, and remarks: "It is connected in my mind . . . with a very odd story," he overtly proposes the enigma. However, myriad details have already made us aware of the fact that there is a mystery, ranging from the emphasis placed on Utterson's taciturnity to the description of Hyde's house as windowless and sinister.

The story which Enfield subsequently tells illustrates Barthes's third "hermeneuteme," the *formulation* of the enigma. This formulation receives frequent supplementations as the larger narrative progresses. Utterson elicits it from Enfield by asking to hear the story. This *request for an answer* constitutes the fourth of Barthes's hermeneutic elements, and here facilitates narrative movement.

The *snare* represents the most intricate of the hermeneutic morphemes, and the one richest in possible variations. Barthes explains it as "a pretense which must be defined . . . by its circuit of destination (by one character for another, for himself, the discourse for the reader)" (210). The snare can thus involve three sorts of deception, only two of which—those involving either a set of characters or the discourse and the reader—would seem to require a deliberate evasion of the truth.

Dr. Jekyll and Mr. Hyde demonstrates that there are even situations in which the first of the snares enumerated by Barthes—the deception of one character by another—can be innocent. For instance, when Utterson queries Poole about Hyde, the butler unwittingly misleads both Utterson and the reader. Ignorant of the connection between Jekyll and Hyde, he responds:

> "O, dear no, sir. He never *dines* here. . . . Indeed we see very little of him on this side of the house; he mostly comes and goes by the laboratory." [25]

The double identity of the title character makes this kind of snare the most prevalent in Stevenson's story, although Jekyll does occasionally deliberately misrepresent himself to his friends and servants (at one point he disingenuously tells Utterson: "I cannot say that I care what becomes of Hyde; I am quite done with him. I was thinking of my own character, which this hateful business has rather exposed" (38). It should be added that the third kind of snare described by Barthes—the deception of the reader by the discourse—often coexists with the other two.

Poole's unintentional snare constitutes an intentional one at the level of the story's enunciation, as does Jekyll's deliberate lie.

A related hermeneutic device, *equivocation,* combines a snare and a truth; it is a statement which can be understood in two quite different ways. Again, because of the "split personality" of the Jekyll/Hyde character, Stevenson's story provides numerous examples. One such example occurs at the moment of apparent disclosure, when the body of Hyde is discovered. Utterson remarks: "Hyde is gone to his account; and it only remains for us to find the body of your master" (63). The second part of his statement is correct in one sense—nothing is left of Jekyll but his body. However, it is incorrect in another sense: Utterson is already in the presence of that body, and so has no need to search for it.

Two of the four remaining hermeneutic elements enumerated by Barthes—*suspended answer* and *partial answer*—are self-explanatory, but the other two, *jamming* and *disclosure,* warrant a brief discussion. Jamming involves an acknowledgment of the apparent failure of the hermeneutic activity, usually because of the exhaustion of all available resources (the death of a key witness, the destruction of vital evidence, someone's stubborn refusal to talk, etc.), and is intended to induce in the reader a frenzy of epistemophilia. *Dr. Jekyll and Mr. Hyde* contrives an interesting variation on this theme by featuring characters who refuse knowledge in one way or another, and by portraying knowledge as something threatening, evil, to be avoided. When Enfield finishes his tale about the child who was viciously attacked by Hyde in the middle of the night, Utterson queries him about the afore-mentioned house. Enfield responds:

> "I feel very strongly about putting questions; it partakes too much of the style of the day of judgment. You start a question, and it's like starting a stone. You sit quietly on the top of a hill; and away the stone goes, starting others; and presently some bland old bird (the last you would have thought of) is knocked on the head in his own back garden and the family have to change their name. No sir, I make it a rule of mine; the more it looks like Queer Street, the less I ask."
> "A very good rule, too," said the lawyer. [13–14]

We will attempt to account for this attitude toward knowledge in *Dr. Jekyll and Mr. Hyde* later in this chapter through recourse to the category of cultural coding, and through a demonstration of some of the ways in which it coerces the other codes isolated by Barthes.

Barthes defines the tenth hermeneutic component, *disclosure*, as "a final nomination, the discovery and uttering of the irreversible word" (210)—as the moment of closure and the end of signification. He thereby associates it much more fully with the semic operation—i.e. with prediction—than with any of the other hermeneutemes, all of which impede or delay predication.

Because the hermeneutic code moves toward disclosure, it, like the semic code, projects a stable subject about whom things can ultimately be discovered although the process may be painstaking and full of delays—a subject, in short, who can be defined and known. This code, described by Barthes as "reducible to a dyadic unity of subject and predicate," operates in tandem with the semic code to inscribe and re-inscribe a culturally determined position or group of positions to which the reader or viewer is expected to conform.

iii. *The proairetic code.* Barthes does not offer a great deal of information about the proairetic code. He tells us that its organization is intensely syntagmatic, and that consequently it forms "the strongest armature of the readerly" (i.e. the classic text); that it has no logic other than that of the "already-done" or "already-written"; and that its basis is "more empirical than rational" (19, 203–4). The proairetic code determines the sequence of events within a story. It is the "glue" which makes certain that clusters of events will follow each other in a predictable order:

> Actions (terms of the proairetic code) can fall into various sequences which should be indicated merely by listing them, since the proairetic sequence is never more than the result of an artifice of reading: whoever reads the text amasses certain data under some generic titles for actions (*stroll, murder, rendezvous*), and this title embodies the sequence; the sequence exists when and because it can be given a name, it unfolds as this process

of naming takes place, as a title is sought or confirmed. . . .
[19]

These sequences emerge most clearly from fixed generic
forms, like the western film or the gothic novel, where there is
a high degree of what Michael Riffaterre would call "previsibil-
ity"—i.e. where it is possible to predict from one event what the
next one will be.[7] Within such genres we can anticipate not only
the ultimate outcome, but the order in which actions will occur,
and the kind of dialogue which will accompany them. Thus
when a line like "This town isn't big enough for you and me"
is spoken in a western film, it invariably forecasts a showdown
at sunset on the main street of a frontier town; the odds are
usually on the side of the figure who represents illicit power,
yet he almost always loses to the figure of greater moral authority. Jane Austen's *Northanger Abbey* parodies the similar narrative inflexibility of the gothic novel.

One of the most amusing climaxes of that parody occurs
during the carriage ride to the estate after which the novel is
named. Henry, Austen's hero, recounts to Catherine, an invet-
erate reader of gothic romances, the adventures which await
her at his country home. Those adventures conform with comic
precision to the severe proairetic imperatives of her beloved
narrative form; Henry is not content merely to sketch in the
broad outlines of the classic Gothic plot, but accounts for every
gesture Catherine will make and every emotion she will experience once her personal romance begins:

> "Nothing further to alarm, perhaps, may occur the first
> night. After surmounting your *unconquerable* horror of the bed,
> you will retire to rest, and get a few hours' unquiet slumber.
> But on the second, or at farthest the *third* night after your
> arrival, you will probably have a violent storm. Peals of thun-
> der so loud as to seem to shake the edifice to its foundation
> will roll around the neighbouring mountains; and during the
> frightful gusts of wind which accompany it, you will probably
> think you discern (for your lamp is not extinguished) one part
> of the hanging more violently agitated than the rest. Unable
> of course to repress your curiosity in so favorable a moment
> for indulging it, you will instantly arise, and, throwing your

dressing-gown around you, proceed to examine this mystery. After a very short search, you will discover a division in the tapestry so artfully constructed as to defy the minutest inspection, and on opening it, a door will immediately appear, which door being only secured by massy bars and a padlock, you will, after a few efforts, succeed in opening, and, with your lamp in your hand, will pass through it into a small vaulted room."[8]

This passage provides a vivid dramatization of the ways in which the proairetic code functions to interpellate the reading, viewing or listening subject. Henry does not only give to the actions he recounts an obligatory sequence, but he recounts them in the form of a series of grammatical imperatives addressed to Catherine. In short, he hails her. He does this so successfully that she spends the night searching for objects which conform to the ones in his narrative, and attempting to match her behavior to its dictates.

In addition to stressing the syntagmatic organization of the proairetic code, and the repetition which it always promotes, Barthes notes its inevitable subordination to the other four. In the section of *S/Z* entitled "How an Orgy Is Created," he observes that "What we have called the proairetic code is . . . itself made up of other diverse codes based on different disciplines" (158). Although this is not a point to which Barthes elsewhere returns, it is of critical importance to any understanding of the proairetic code. Like the semic and hermeneutic codes, the proairetic code never operates in isolation from a range of other signifying activities.

The excerpt just quoted from *Northanger Abbey* suggests that the proairetic code both impels and derives impetus from the hermeneutic code. It dramatizes the way in which certain events (e.g. the storm which moves the curtain) can create a sense of mystery, and how that mystery can in turn promote additional action (e.g. the search for a secret door). That passage also indicates the interdependence of the proairetic and semic codes; by inserting Catherine into his Gothic narrative, Henry inspires in her—i.e. attaches to her name—the qualities of restlessness and extreme curiosity.

However, this example is not adequate to the task of revealing the complex interplay not only between the proairetic, semic, and hermeneutic codes within the classic text, but the symbolic and cultural ones as well. Another prose narrative— F. Scott Fitzgerald's *The Great Gatsby*—is perhaps better suited to illustrate the wide range of possible interactions between the five codes enumerated by Barthes.

The first two references to Gatsby after the narrator's preliminary remarks locate him semically, hermeneutically, culturally, and symbolically. They also anticipate the story which follows. The earlier of these passages thematizes Gatsby through his house, the latter functioning as a systematic metonymy for the former:

> I lived at West Egg, the—well, the less fashionable of the two, though this is a most superficial tag to express the bizarre and not a little sinister contrast between them. My house was at the very tip of the egg, only fifty yards from the Sound, and squeezed between two huge places that rented for twelve or fifteen thousand a season. The place on my right was a colossal affair by any standard—it was a factual imitation of some Hotel de Ville in Normandy, with a tower on one side, spanking new under a thin beard of raw ivy, and a marble swimming pool, and more than forty acres of lawn and garden. It was Gatsby's mansion.[9]

The phrase "Not a little sinister contrast" introduces the novel's central symbolic opposition—East Egg/West Egg—along with the qualifying subset "more fashionable" and "less fashionable." This opposition structures the description which follows, so that everything we learn about Gatsby's house emerges in relation to the very different houses on the other side of the bay, specifically Tom Buchanan's. We thus grasp the character of Gatsby from the very beginning in terms of what he isn't, i.e. the attributes he lacks. The semes which "gravitate" to his name even before it has been supplied, and which remain a permanent constellation, include *nouveau riche* ("places that rented for twelve or fifteen thousand a season," "spanking new," "marble swimming pool"), cultural pretentiousness ("imitation of some Hotel de Ville in Normandy"), callowness ("thin beard of raw ivy"), and seriousness ("factual"). These semes derive their value from their opposites—inherited wealth, breeding, physical ripeness, and an indifference to facts (a quality suggested by the subsequent speech about Nordic superiority). Nick associates these attributes with Tom Buchanan a page later, but they are already present through their absence. The opposition East Egg/West Egg, which controls the operations of the semic code, is itself the product of intense social and economic coding.

The second reference to Gatsby adds to his signifying network; it also adds the master to his house. Nick has just returned from an evening visit to the Buchanans, and he looks around as he gets out of his car:

> . . . I saw that I was not alone—fifty feet away a figure had emerged from the shadow of my neighbor's mansion and was standing with his hands in his pockets regarding the silver pepper of the stars. Something in his leisurely movements and the secure position of his feet upon the lawn suggested that it was Mr. Gatsby himself, come out to determine what share was his of our local heavens.
>
> I decided to call to him. . . . But I didn't . . . for he gave a sudden intimation that he was content to be alone—he stretched out his arms toward the dark water in a curious way, and, far as I was from him, I could have sworn he was trembling. Involuntarily I glanced seaward—and distinguished nothing except a single green light, minute and far away, that might have been the end of a dock. When I looked once more for Gatsby he had vanished, and I was alone in the unquiet darkness. [24]

This passage associates Gatsby with mystery ("a figure . . . emerged from the shadow," "curious way," "When I looked . . . he had vanished," "unquiet darkness"), and in the process sets the hermeneutic code in motion. (Since Gatsby is himself the main enigma of the story, much like the old man at the beginning of "Sarrasine," the semic and hermeneutic codes frequently overlap in Nick's narrative.) This passage also connects him with the solitude ("he gave a sudden intimation that he wanted to be alone") of the visionary romantic ("he stretched out his arms toward the dark water").

Gatsby's entrepreneurial relationship with the stars represents the intersection of this romantic coding with the economic coding of the earlier passage. However, the easy collaboration of these codes falters after the first paragraph, leaving Gatsby alone with his green light. The sense of isolation which Nick notes proceeds from the abrupt elimination of any but romantic signifiers—by the exclusion of social and economic coding.

Both the brief coexistence of the cultural codes of capitalism and romantic love, and the triumph of the latter over the former anticipate the events which are subsequently revealed. Thus we discover over the course of the novel that Gatsby's economic success was entirely motivated by his romantic obsession—that he accumulated money only as a means of securing Daisy. When that latter quest proves unsuccessful, Gatsby abandons the scenario of the successful businessman, but follows the romantic scenario to its ultimate conclusion.

The same narrative is implicit in the shift from qualifiers like "secure and "leisurely" to "trembling" a few lines later. That shift suggests that no matter how confident Gatsby may be as a businessman, his position *vis-à-vis* Daisy (and by extension "high" society) can never be anything but insufficient—that he will always function as the deprivileged subject in the masochistic scenario of desire, a scenario whose final point is death. That scenario is also indicated by the distance which separates him from the green light, and the dark water toward which he reaches.

The events which make up the novel are in this way already mapped out, determined through the earliest activities of the semic, symbolic, and cultural codes. The alignment of certain culturally coded and symbolically opposed semes to Gatsby's name places a given set of proairetic wheels in motion, wheels whose movements thereafter become inseparable from the hermeneutic code. (Nick knows the entire story all along, and refers cryptically to its conclusion. However, he insists on maintaining in his account the strict chronological order of the events he has witnessed. Thus in this situation the linear logic of the proairetic code doubles as a hermeneutic "sentence," simultaneously postponing and progressing toward disclosure.)

These brief discussions of *Northanger Abbey* and *The Great Gatsby* have indicated a few of the possible interactions between the proairetic code on the one hand, and the semic, hermeneutic, symbolic, and cultural codes on the other. Whereas the passage quoted from the former novel has shown that the proairetic code can organize actions in such a manner as to define character and place, and to express and assist in the resolution of an enigma, those cited from the latter have suggested that the code of action is often at the service of the others—that its operations can be anticipated and indeed coerced through a preliminary conjunction of semic, hermeneutic, symbolic, and cultural elements. Before turning to the symbolic code, we should give some consideration to the role played by the proairetic code in a literary form which is generally considered to be non-narrative—lyric poetry.

Although the proairetic code would seem to provide a more regular feature of novels, short stories, and films, it plays an important role as well in lyric poetry, interjecting bits and pieces of established sequences into even the briefest of verses. A lyric poem can supply an invitation to engage in a certain action (Herrick's "To the Virgins To Make Much of Time"); it can manipulate or distort a familiar narrative (Donne's "The Relic"); it can hold up to scrutiny a series of events which occur with absolute regularity (Plath's "Lady Lazarus"); it can suspend and examine one part of a proairetic sequence (Keats's "Ode on a Grecian Urn"); it can pit one syntagm against another (Marvell's "To His Coy Mistress"); or it can locate itself within a narrative which admits of no escape.

Shakespeare's Sonnet 129 ("The expense of spirit") is probably the most famous dramatization of syntagmatic entrapment, in which the past, present, and future tenses of lust all confine the lover to the same "extreme" condition. However, the less familiar Sonnet 105 also records a narrative impasse, and it does so in ways which are of particular relevance to the present discussion. The jamming of the proairetic code is here shown to effect a similar paralysis of the semic, hermeneutic, and symbolic activities, reminding us once again of the intimate relationship between the various signifying operations discussed by *S/Z:*

Let not my love be called idolatry,
Nor my beloved as an idol show.

Since all alike my songs and praises be
To one, of one, still such, and ever so.
Kind is my love today, tomorrow kind,
Still constant in a wondrous excellence;
Therefore my verse, to constancy confined,
One thing expressing, leaves out difference.
"Fair, kind, and true" is all my argument,
"Fair, kind, and true," varying to other words;
And in this change is my invention spent,
Three themes in one, which wondrous scope affords.
Fair, kind, and true have often lived alone,
Which three till now never kept seat in one.

The Petrarchan narrative, from which this poem consciously deviates in more ways than the sex of the beloved,*
derives its contours from an intransigently inconsistent lady. Her
apparent indifference to the lover is variously interpreted by
him as devotion to God (i.e. true religion) and self-love (i.e.
idolatry). The psychic condition of the Petrarchan lover fluc-
tuates on a daily basis, in keeping with his most recent interpretive effort. The elaborate use of oxymoron and paradox in his
poetry expresses the irreducible contradictions of that lover's
amorous life.

Shakespeare's Sonnet 105, on the contrary, rules out the
possibility of change, contradiction or even "difference." It is
inspired by a beloved whose qualities never vary, and who because he has only one guise inspires in the lover a kind of mon-
otheism (the Petrarchan lady usually encourages idolatry
through her narcissism, and polytheism through her many
"faces"). The sonnet is the product of an absolutely inflexible
semic operation. The beloved always signifies the same three
attributes: fairness, kindness, and truth. Because the poem seeks
to duplicate the beloved, it is "confined" to the same three
"themes" or attributes, which it enumerates in a fixed order,
and with increasing frequency in the sestet. By leaving out difference—i.e. by eliminating all symbolic opposition—the narrative undergoes a radical truncation; it consists only of the same
abstract prediction (the beloved is fair, kind, and true) end-

* Sonnet 20 suggests that the preponderance of Shakespeare's *Sonnets* celebrate
a male rather than—as is customary—a female beloved.

lessly repeated, in every conceivable tense. Needless to say, the hermeneutic code is entirely banished from the premises of this poem; to admit it would be to concede the possibility of change on the part of the beloved.

The concluding assertion ("Which three till now never kept seat in one"), with its theological implications, does not generate much tension since such compatible attributes as "fair," "kind," and "true" easily coexist. The real paradox of the poem is the notion that these "three themes in one" afford a "wondrous scope" to the poet—the notion that there can be a play of signification with so little difference. Sonnet 105 not only dramatizes a kind of "stalling" of the proairetic, hermeneutic, and semic codes, but the virtual collapse of the symbolic code. As we will see in a moment, it is the responsibility of that last code to assert culturally coded oppositions, such as that between the Petrarchan lady's two guises.

iv. *The symbolic code.* Barthes consistently links the symbolic code to the fomulation of antitheses, especially that variety which admits of no mediation between its terms. In other words, he associates it with the articulation of binary oppositions, with the setting of certain elements "ritually face to face like two fully armed warriors" (27). These oppositions are represented as eternal and "inexpiable." Any attempt to reconcile them is seen as "transgressive."

The symbolic code inscribes into literary and cinematic texts antitheses which are central to the organization of the cultural order to which they belong. Indeed, it could be said that the symbolic code is entrusted with the maintenance of that order's dominant binary oppositions. Its failure to do so thus has ramifications far beyond the boundaries of any individual text.

As we have had repeated occasion to note, the most dominant and sacrosanct of all binary oppositions is that between the male and female subjects. *S/Z* makes Balzac's "Sarrasine" the object of its writerly experiment because that story challenges precisely this most rudimentary of antitheses. Since Barthes's definition of the symbolic code is so intimately tied to "Sarrasine" (he offers virtually no general theoretical statements about that code), and since it provides an extraordinarily interesting investigation not only of sexual difference but of other related oppositions, we will also make it the locus of our discussion.

"Sarrasine" articulates the usual conflict between the terms "active" and "passive," and "castrating" and "castrated," but it abolishes that between the terms "male" and "female." In the process it shows that the symbolic field always exceeds biological difference—that the phallus designates a cluster of privileges which are as fully capable of finding their locus in a female subject as in a male. Barthes observes that Mme de Lanty is "endowed with all the hallucinatory attributes of the Father: power, fascination, instituting authority, terror, power to castrate" (36)—that she in effect occupies the paternal position.

Not only does "Sarrasine" not establish the conventional connections between the terms "active," "castrating," and "male," and "passive," "castrated," and "female," but it declines the opportunity systematically to reverse the usual relationship. Such a reversal would of course preserve the symbolic value of sexual difference; it would permit "Sarrasine" to be read as a witty inversion of cultural norms, a sort of "holiday" from an orthodoxy which would instantly reassert itself at the story's end.

Instead, "Sarrasine" attributes symbolic qualities to characters irrespective of their sexual identity. It depicts two women (Mme de Lanty and Sappho) and one man (Bouchardon) as actively castrating, and three men (Sarrasine, Monsieur de Jaucourt, and the narrator) as passively castrated. Other characters, such as Marianina, Filippo, and Clothilde, defy classification. Finally, the figure who obliges the symbolic code to operate in the absence of sexual determinants—Zambinella—mediates between the extremes represented by Mme de Lanty and Sarrasine:

> As for the castrato himself, we would be wrong to place him of necessity among the castrated: he is the blind and mobile flaw in this system; he moves back and forth between active and passive: castrated, he castrates. . . . [36]

Ironically, it is by ideally conforming to the visual image of a woman that Zambinella gains access to the paternal heritage.

The operation which he undergoes, and which strips him of biological potency, supplies him with power, wealth, musical prowess, and artistic fame. It also initiates a cultural regime in which these things can be passed on to women as well as to men, a regime in which the lack of a penis does not translate into the lack of the phallus. Certain other qualities—cunning, the ability to manipulate one's appearance, talent—emerge as far more important than gender in determining who will enjoy the privileges of the symbolic. Significantly, these qualities are much more difficult to locate and to define; it is no longer possible to predict which characters will be valorized.

Barthes describes the disequivalence between sexual and symbolic differentiation in Balzac's tale as a "scandal," and attributes to it the failure of a number of other economies, including that of representation:

> . . . the story *represents* . . . a generalized collapse of economies: the economy of language, usually protected by the separation of opposites, the economy of genders (the neuter must not lay claim to the human), the economy of the body (its parts cannot be interchanged, the sexes cannot be equivalent), the economy of money (Parisian Gold produced by the new social class, speculative and no longer land-based—such gold is without origin, it has repudiated every circulatory code, every rule of exchange, every line of propriety. . . . This catastrophic collapse always takes the same form: that of an unrestrained metonymy. By abolishing the paradigmatic barriers, this metonymy abolishes the power of *legal substitution* on which meaning is based: it is then no longer possible regularly to contrast opposites, sexes, possessions; it is no longer possible to safeguard an order of just equivalence; in a word, it is no longer possible to *represent*, to make things *representative*, individuated, separate, assigned; *Sarrasine* represents the very confusion of representation, the unbridled (pandemic) circulation of signs, of sexes, of fortunes. [215–16]

"Sarrasine" dramatizes how dependent the usual operations of the symbolic code are upon sexual difference, and the radical transformations which are registered within the larger cultural order when that difference is belied. All of the systems of exchange most basic to that order, from the familial to the monetary and the linguistic, are threatened by the disruption of sexual difference. That tale suggests that the relation of voyeurism to exhibitionism, and narrative to silence also undergoes a startling readjustment when the male subject is no longer privileged over the female. Both the aesthetically knowledgeable gaze which Sarrasine directs toward Zambinella and the narrative control which the storyteller attempts to exercise over the Marquise prove ineffectual. Sarrasine's voyeurism does not subjugate its object; instead, it reduces him to a state of helplessness and loss.

Balzac's text is very explicit about this last point—Zambinella's music converts Sarrasine from an active to a passive condition. It not only robs him of his symbolic legacy ("Fame, knowledge, future, existence, laurels, everything collapsed"), but hollows him out from within. That music creates a vacuum within Sarrasine, relocates the lack from female to male, outside to inside:

> He was presently obliged to leave the theater. His trembling legs almost refused to support him. He was limp, weak as a sensitive man who has given way to overwhelming anger. He had experienced such pleasure, or perhaps he had suffered so keenly, that his life had drained away like water from a broken vase. He felt empty inside, a prostration similar to the debilitation that overcomes those suffering from serious illness. [239]

And once the narrator has communicated his information to the Marquise, she lapses into a self-absorbed silence; her refusal to speak—to be heard and known—triumphs over his garrulousness.

The plurality of meaning which Barthes finds in "Sarrasine" derives from what he calls its "scandalous" features, i.e. from its subversion of one of the most dominant of its culture's binary oppositions. In it the symbolic code functions atypically, in violation rather than in support of the larger social matrix. We will find that situations of this sort are always the result of some conflict at the level of the cultural codes. It is at that level that the homogeneity or heterogeneity of the classic text is decided, and that coincidences or contradictions occur. The symbolic code is really no more than an extension or subset of the cultural codes, whose structuring oppositions it articulates. We will consequently continue our discussion of the symbolic code concurrently with that of the cultural codes.

v. *The cultural codes.* Barthes establishes a direct connection between the cultural codes and that larger discursive field which we have identified with the symbolic order. He suggests that the cultural codes function not only to organize but to naturalize that field—to make it seem timeless and inevitable. They also assure that future textual production will be congruent with what has gone before.

Barthes underscores the discursive basis of the "reality" to which the cultural codes refer by equating it with "the set of seven or eight handbooks accessible to a diligent student in the classical bourgeois educational system," and he indicates what some of those handbooks might be:

> . . . a History of Literature (Byron, *The Thousand and One Nights,* Ann Radcliffe, Homer), a History of Art (Michelangelo, Raphael, the Greek miracle), a History of Europe (the age of Louis XV), an Outline of Practical Medicine (disease, convalescence, old age, etc.), a Treatise on Psychology (erotic, ethnic, etc.), an Ethics (Christian or Stoic: themes from Latin translations), a Logic (for syllogisms), a Rhetoric, and an anthology of maxims and proverbs about life, death, suffering, love, women, ages of man, etc. [205–6]

The cultural codes provide the means whereby the "information" contained in the authoritative texts of a given symbolic order finds its way into the novels, poems, and films which perpetuate that order.

S/Z sees proverbial statements as one of the most conspicuous symptoms or manifestations of cultural coding. Those statements, which are described by Barthes as "fragments of ideology," not only address the reader or viewer with particular insistence but make possible the writerly deconstruction of the classic text:

The utterances of the cultural code are implicit proverbs: they are written in that obligative mode by which the discourse states a general will, the law of a society, making the proposition concerned ineluctable or indelible. Further still: it is because an utterance can be transformed into a proverb, a maxim, a postulate, that the supporting cultural code is discoverable: stylistic transformation "proves" the code, bares its structure, reveals its ideological perspective. [100]

Barthes comes closer here than anywhere else in *S/Z* to formulating a theoretical model which has specific and indeed exclusive relevance to literary texts, since he insists that it is only through certain stylistic groupings that the presence of cultural codes can be detected.

However, more careful consideration indicates that cultural codes make their effect felt everywhere in a classic text—not just through style, but through the activity of the semic, hermeneutic, proairetic, and symbolic codes. We attempted to demonstrate this point earlier, through selected passages of *Dr. Jekyll and Mr. Hyde.* We will turn to that text once again in order to facilitate a further clarification of cultural coding.

Stevenson provides us with a densely coded narrative, whose obsessive antitheses and preoccupations would enable us to exhume Christianity even if the latter were not still as fully operative as it is. That cultural code can be traced in *Dr. Jekyll and Mr. Hyde* not only through certain rhetorical formulas, but through its coercion of all of the other codes isolated by Barthes. Stevenson's tale reveals the extraordinary interdependence of semic, hermeneutic, proairetic, symbolic, and cultural elements.

Dr. Jekyll and Mr. Hyde is organized at every level by mutually reinforcing antitheses, of which light/darkness, groomed/ungroomed, day/night, soul/body, humanity/bestiality, Jekyll/Hyde, and good/evil are only the most evident. The last of these represents the central symbolic opposition, that which gives rise to and supports the others.

This fundamental Christian antithesis finds frequent rhetorical expression through parallelisms of the sort noted by Barthes in "Sarrasine." Thus on one occasion the narrator tells us that just as "good shone upon the countenance" of Jekyll, "evil was written broadly and plainly on the face of the other."

Elsewhere we learn that Jekyll "was slowly losing hold of [his] original and better self, and becoming slowly incorporated with [his] second and worse" (90).

The same cultural code motivates the activities of the semic code in Stevenson's story. The characters of Jekyll and Hyde dramatize a Christian commonplace, the notion that man is a house divided against itself. In the letter he leaves behind for Utterson, Jekyll writes that

> . . . man is not truly one, but truly two. . . . If each, I told myself, could be housed in separate identities, life would be relieved of all that was unbearable; the unjust might go his way, delivered from the aspirations and remorse of his more upright twin; and the just could walk steadfastly and securely on his upward path, doing the good things in which he found his pleasure, and no longer exposed to disgrace and penitence by the hands of this extraneous evil. It was the curse of mankind that these incongruous faggots were thus bound together—that in the agonised womb of consciousness these polar twins should be continuously struggling. [79–80]

The dilemma against which Jekyll protests—i.e. the dilemma of duality—manifests itself whenever the symbolic code appears, and is always implicit in the operations of the semic code since the attributes it clusters around a proper name derive their value from opposing ones (the phallus can only be defined through female lack, the law through criminality, the gaze through the object which it subjugates, and good through evil). Here the Christian, the symbolic, and the semic codes intersect to produce a character with two names linked to two conflicting sets of attributes (physical as well as psychological), each of which can materialize only in the absence of the other. The sense of crisis which permeates Stevenson's tale is generated by the frequency with which the same unnegotiable antitheses are articulated.

The proairetic configuration in *Dr. Jekyll and Mr. Hyde* is also Christian in nature; it reflects the dominant symbolic oppositions of that cultural code, and it reinforces its semic activity. It suggests, that is, that just as man is shown to contain two ruling impulses, one rational and the other instinctual, so two roads are shown to be open to him: that which leads to heaven, and that which leads to hell. By giving priority to one or other of those impulses, he automatically chooses the complementary path.

Finally, the distrust of knowledge which pervades *Dr. Jekyll and Mr. Hyde,* and which we noted above as a device for hermeneutic delay, also has its origin in the Christian code. The potion which Jekyll drinks, and which gives him access to the guilty consciousness of Hyde, duplicates the Christian fall. Jekyll observes that after swallowing the liquid he experienced a complete moral transformation, akin to that induced in Adam and Eve by the forbidden fruit:

> I felt younger, lighter, happier in body; within I was conscious of a heady recklessness, like a current of disordered sensual images running like a millrace in my fancy, a solution of the bonds of obligation, an unknown but not an innocent freedom of the soul. I knew myself, at the first breath of this new life, to be more wicked, tenfold more wicked, sold a slave to my original evil; and the thought, in that moment, braced and delighted me like wine. I stretched out my hands, exulting in the freshness of these sensations; and in the act, I was suddenly aware that I had lost stature. [81–82]

Christianity entertains so profound a mistrust of knowledge that it always treats epistemological ambition as a moral descent, and increase in consciousness as a spiritual loss. Utterson's reluctance to penetrate mysteries can only be understood in the context of this very negative attitude toward discovery; it is the correlative of Adam and Eve's prelapsarian condition, which could best be described as the acquiescence to a hermeneutic impasse.

Dr. Jekyll and Mr. Hyde suggests the degree to which the cultural codes determine every aspect of textuality. Far from being confined to proverbial formulas, they find expression through character, action, symbolic opposition, and epistemological patterning. Indeed, the semic, proairetic, symbolic, and hermeneutic codes can perhaps best be described as branches of the cultural codes.

In the textual example we have just explored, cultural coding functions to impede the play of signification, to make every detail yield the same meaning. As Barthes would say, "because of its cultural codes, it stales, rots, excludes itself from writing (which is always a contemporary task): it is the quintessence, the residual condensate of what cannot be rewritten" (98). In other words, Stevenson's tale permits us to identify the voices which speak it, but not to disrupt their harmony. It enables us to scrutinize the symbolic order to which it belongs, but not to dislocate it from that order.

However, this is not always the case. Many classic texts owe a not inconsiderable diversity to cultural coding. The complexity of "Sarrasine," for instance, derives from the forced cohabitation of a large and heterogeneous assortment of cultural codes, including those of homosexuality, heterosexuality, the supernatural, the natural, free enterprise, landed wealth, art, music, and piracy. The incompatibility of many of these codes results in a high degree of signifying flexibility, and the temporary collapse of the major structuring opposition in the present symbolic order: sexual difference.

The same flexibility can be introduced into a classic text by the playful deployment of even a few cultural codes. Sir Philip Sidney's *Astrophil and Stella*, Sonnet 52, is a case in point. This poem represents one of the many will/wit dialogues in Sidney's sequence, a dialogue that revolves around the opposition between body and soul, passion and reason, and poetic ingenuity and humorless morality. Other sonnets work out these conflicts through a variety of codes and signifying transactions, but here it is elaborated through the sophisticated alignment of only two distinctly antipathetic cultural codes—Petrarchanism and Ovidianism:

> A strife is grown between Virtue and Love,
> While each pretends that Stella must be his:
> Her eyes, her lips, her all, saith Love, do this
> Since they do wear his badge, most firmly prove.
> But Virtue thus that title doth disprove:
> That Stella (oh dear name) that Stella is
> That virtuous soul, sure heir of heav'nly bliss,
> Not this fair outside, which our hearts doth move;

> And therefore, though her beauty and her grace
> Be Love's indeed, in Stella's self he may
> By no pretense claim any manner place.
> Well, Love, since this demur our suit doth stay,
> Let Virtue have that Stella's self; yet thus,
> That Virtue but that body grant to us.

As we shall see, the slippage between the two cultural codes which organize this poem has as one of its effects a constant oscillation between two definitions of the lover, two definitions of the lady, and two contradictory sets of subject-positions for the reader.

"Love" refers to the speaker in his Ovidian guise, while "Virtue" refers to him in his Petrarchan guise. As a consequence of the pretense that these signifiers designate companions rather than aspects of the speaker's self, the pronouns "we" and "us" take the place of "I" and "me." Significantly, these pronouns are employed only in relation to Love, suggesting that the poem's real center of gravity is Ovidian rather than Petrarchan. The speaker never manifestly identifies himself with Virtue.

Some clarification of the lover's status in each of these cultural codes would seem appropriate. Ovidianism projects a phallocentric system which gives the male lover the power of possession over the female beloved, a beloved whose value is entirely physical. (If you look carefully, says Ovid, you will see that every woman has at least one good anatomical feature; concentrate on that feature.) Petrarchanism, on the contrary, delineates the female beloved in terms of her spiritual attributes, and hence maintains a fixed distance between her and the male lover. (If you look carefully, says Petrarch, you will understand that the lady is a divine signifier, pointing beyond herself to God; concentrate on that thing toward which she leads.) Within each of these codes the desired object implies a particular desiring subject, and *vice versa*.

Although the lady is consistently associated with the name "Stella," like the lover she enjoys a dual status in this poem. Lines 3–4 define her according to the semic code of Ovidianism, i.e. according to her "fair outside." There is a little hesitation on the speaker's part at this juncture, since "eyes" and "lips" can function as Petrarchan attributes as well. However, "all" retrospectively assumes an exclusively Ovidian meaning through its syntactic relation with the phrase "do wear his [Love's] badge." The Petrarchan lady never wears the lover's insignia; she always signifies either herself, in which case she is accommodated within Petrarchanism's negative, narcissistic paradigm, or God, in which case she illustrates that code's exemplary and ultimately Christian paradigm. However, the Ovidian lady is often depicted as branded in one way or another. In John Donne's "To His Mistress Going to Bed," for instance, one of the most frankly Ovidian of Renaissance lyrics, the speaker announces to his lady: "Then where my hand is set, my seal shall be."

This trope always signals the cession of the female body to the Ovidian lover. Thus in Sidney's poem, as in Donne's, the proairetic code of Ovidianism supplements the semic one with a copulatory syntagm—the claiming of a place "in Stella's self." In other words, the speaker asserts the right of physical residence within the lady.

However, what is "proved" (i.e. predicated) about Stella by means of the code of Ovidianism is "disproved" by means of the code of Petrarchanism. Her name is restored to her—the name which was supplanted by love's badge a few lines earlier—and with it her independence from the lover. Stella is positioned within Petrarchanism's exemplary narrative; she now signifies "virtuous soul," and the speaker prophesies that she will be "sure heir of heavn'ly bliss."

The symbolic oppositions—body/soul, outside/inside—of the poem emerge from the conflict between its two central cultural codes, which endorse contrary values. It is important to understand, however, that while these oppositions play a critical role within Petrarchanism, which is a deeply repressive code, they are entirely absent from Ovidianism, whose dichotomies all issue from sexual difference. Thus while the Petrarchan lover is obsessed with his lady's body, even though he knows that it is off-limits to him, the Ovidian lover remains absolutely indifferent to that part of the lady which is excluded from his dealings with her—i.e. the soul. Sonnet 52 of *Astrophil and Stella* brings together two codes which are not so much contradictory as asymmetrically oppositional. One privileges the soul over the body, while the other privileges the body over the soul. However, whereas Petrarchanism defines the soul in relation to the body, Ovidianism defines the body in relation to sexual pleasure.

Not surprisingly, the conflicts upon which Astrophil insists are ultimately resolved around line 12, when he unequivocally allies himself with the code of Ovidianism, and cheerfully surrenders Stella's soul to the competing code. It is clear that those conflicts were set in motion earlier in the poem through the intrusion of Petrarchan signifiers into an Ovidian reverie, and by the speaker's willingness intermittently to adopt a corresponding point of view.

Despite its formal resolution of the will/wit debate, Sonnet 52 ends on a note of profound irresolution. It is not possible in the concluding three lines, any more than it was earlier in the poem, to make any definitive statements about the identity either of the lady or of the lover. Both remain "in pieces"; Stella has undergone a radical surgery calculated to detach her soul from her body, while Astrophil has been obliged to renounce a subject-position for which he still feels considerable nostalgia. The sonnet breaks off at a semic impasse, implicitly acknowledging its own inability to provide satisfactory predications.

Barthes's writerly approach enables us not only to uncover the symbolic field inhabited by Sonnet 52 of *Astrophil and Stella*, but to produce at its site an irreducible conflict of meaning. As a result of the first of these achievements, the poem recovers its discursive "visibility"; it refers away from itself toward the cultural voices which speak it. By means of the second of these achievements the relationship of the reader to the text is radically altered. The production of a limited but nonetheless unresolvable polysemy leaves the reader without a stable point of identification, and while indicating two possible erotic transactions alienates him or her from both. That alienation—that disruption of the system of suture—has its complement in a much more intimate association with the means of discursive production. It leads to a better understanding of how both texts and subjects are constructed, an understanding which can be translated into the constitution of new textual forms, new subject-positions, and a new symbolic order.

Like "Sarrasine," Sonnet 52 of *Astrophil and Stella* shows that it is at the level of cultural coding that the classic text achieves signifying plurality, just as it is there that closure is effected. To the degree that a single cultural code dominates a text, or that only compatible ones are granted admission to its premises, the writerly project will uncover nothing there but redundancy. However, to the degree that a classic text brings together contradictory cultural codes, the writerly project will approach the triumphant plural celebrated by Barthes. As we have just seen, even the forced coexistence of two such codes frustrates a linear reading, draws attention to the cultural voices responsible for a text's enunciation, "splits" the reader or viewer between two subject-positions, and points to potential rifts within the broader symbolic field.

The foregoing chapters have attempted to demonstrate, through a variety of approaches and interpretative strategies, that signification cannot be studied apart from discourse, discourse from subjectivity, or subjectivity from the symbolic order. Chapter 1 suggested a "history" of semiotics within which the subject assumes priority, both as the concrete support for discourse and as a critical discursive category. Chapters 2 and 3 indicated the importance of the unconscious to semiotic investigation, first by isolating those signifying processes which are internal to the psyche but which reflect the external cultural order, and then by examining some of the signifying formations which result from their interaction. Chapter 4 outlined both the Freudian and Lacanian models of subjectivity, emphasizing the semiotic dimensions of each. Thus we noted the irreducible distance which separates being from signification, the determinative role played by the paternal signifier in the organization of the unconscious, and the forced identification of the subject with sexually differentiated representations. We also examined the dominant symbolic order within which the Western subject emerges, and the unequal relationship of the two sexes to that order. Chapter 5 explored a theory of textuality which was only made possible by the convergence of semiotics and psychoanalysis. It dealt with some of the means by which cinematic texts function constantly to re-interpellate viewers into familiar subject-positions, and thereby to maintain the existing cultural order. That chapter also elaborated upon some vital points of "feminine" resistance within the system of suture. Finally, Chapter 6 discussed a textual model which permits us not only to disclose the symbolic field within which a given text resides, but to maximize the contradictions within that field. It indicated some of ways in which the implementation of that model can help us to alter our own relationship to texts, assist us in the project of re-speaking both our own subjectivity and the symbolic order.

Notes

CHAPTER 1: FROM SIGN TO SUBJECT, A SHORT HISTORY

1. *Course in General Linguistics*, trans. Wade Baskin (New York: McGraw-Hill, 1966), p. 16.

2. *A Theory of Semiotics* (Bloomington: Indiana Univ. Press, 1976), pp. 9–14.

3. *Ferdinand de Saussure*, ed. Frank Kermode (New York: Penguin Books, 1977), p. 15.

4. *Course in General Linguistics*, p. 120.

5. Fredric Jameson provides a more extended discussion of the relationship between synchrony and diachrony in *The Prison-House of Language: A Critical Account of Structuralism and Russian Formalism* (Princeton: Princeton Univ. Press, 1972), pp. 18–22.

6. *Within a Budding Grove*, trans. G.K. Scott Moncrieff (New York: Vintage Books, 1970), pp. 66–67.

7. *The Collected Papers of Charles Sanders Peirce*, ed. Charles Hartshorne and Paul Weiss (Cambridge: Harvard Univ. Press, 1931), Vol. II, p. 135.

8. *Signs and Meaning in the Cinema* (Bloomington: Indiana Univ. Press, 1972), pp. 116–54.

9. *Le Signifiant imaginaire: Psychanalyse et cinéma* (Paris: Union Générale d'Éditions, 1977), pp. 7–109. This chapter of Metz's book is available in English as "The Imaginary Signifier," trans. Ben Brewster, *Screen*, Vol. XVI, no. 2 (1975), 14–76.

10. *Selected Writings* (The Hague: Mouton Press, 1971), Vol. II, p. 132.

11. "Quest for the Essence of Language," *Selected Writings*, Vol. II, p. 353.

12. *Prolegomena to a Theory of Language,* trans. Francis J. Whitfield (Madison: Univ. of Wisconsin Press, 1969), p. 119.

13. *Mythologies,* trans. Annette Lavers (New York: Hill and Wang, 1972), p. 115.

14. *For Marx,* trans. Ben Brewster (New York: Pantheon Books, 1969), pp. 221–47.

15. *S/Z,* trans. Richard Miller (New York: Hill and Wang, 1974), p. 9.

16. *Writing and Difference,* trans. Alan Bass (Chicago: Univ. of Chicago Press, 1978), pp. 278–80.

17. *Of Grammatology,* trans. Gayatri Chakravorty Spivak (Baltimore: Johns Hopkins Univ. Press, 1976), p. 20.

18. *Course in General Linguistics,* p. 119.

19. *Of Grammatology,* p. 7.

20. *Bleak House* (London: Oxford Univ. Press, 1948), p. 10.

21. *Of Grammatology,* p. 159.

22. *The Archaeology of Knowledge,* trans. A.M. Sheridan Smith (New York: Pantheon Books, 1972), p. 23.

23. *Problems in General Linguistics,* trans. Mary Elizabeth Meek (Coral Gables: Univ. of Miami Press, 1971), p. 226.

24. Colin MacCabe has consistently organized his cinematic writings around these two categories. See "Realism and the Cinema: Notes on Some Brechtian Theses," *Screen,* Vol. XV, no. 2 (1974), 7–29; "Principles of Realism and Pleasure," *Screen,* Vol. XVII, no. 3 (1976), 7–29; "The Discursive and the Ideological in Film: Notes on the Condition of Political Intervention," *Screen,* Vol. XIX, no. 4 (1978/79), 29–42; and "On Discourse," in *The Talking Cure: Essays in Psychoanalysis and Language* (New York: St. Martin's, 1981), pp. 188–217.

25. *Lenin and Philosophy,* trans. Ben Brewster (London: Monthly Review Press, 1971), p. 174.

CHAPTER 2: PRIMARY AND SECONDARY PROCESSES

1. *The Standard Edition of the Complete Psychological Works of Sigmund Freud,* trans. James Strachey (London: Hogarth Press, 1953), Vol. V, p. 541. All future Freud citations will be from this edition.

2. *Death in Venice and Seven Other Stories,* trans. H.T. Lowe-Porter (New York: Vintage Books, 1930), p. 21.

3. *Swann's Way,* trans. G.K. Scott Moncrieff (New York: Vintage Books, 1970), pp. 35–36.

4. In "Instincts and Their Vicissitudes" (1915), Freud writes: "An 'instinct' appears to us as a concept on the frontier between the mental

and the somatic, as the psychical representative of the stimuli originating from within the organism and reaching the mind, as a measure
of the demand made upon the mind for work in consequence of its
connection with the body" (*Standard Edition,* Vol. XIV, pp. 121–22).

5. *The Language of Psycho-Analysis,* trans. Donald Nicholson-Smith
(New York: Norton, 1973), p. 339.

6. *Standard Edition,* Vol. IV, p. 461n; Vol. XVII, pp. 14–17.

7. *Elementary Structures of Kinship,* trans. James Harle Bell, John
Richard von Stumer, and Rodney Needham (Boston: Beacon Press,
1969). Another important contribution to the anthropological account
of the Oedipus complex is provided by Marie-Cécile and Edmond
Ortigues in *Oedipe africain* (Paris: Plon, 1966). The Ortigues argue that
within Senegalese society the Oedipus complex involves lateral, generational relationships rather than hierarchical, cross-generational ones.

8. *Anti-Oedipus: Capitalism and Schizophrenia,* trans. Robert Hurley,
Mark Seem, and Helen R. Lane (New York: Viking, 1977).

9. *Course in General Linguistics,* p. 120.

10. Freud first makes this point in *Interpretation of Dreams* (*Standard
Edition,* Vol. IV, p. 303), returning to it in his case study of little Hans
(X, p. 59n). He also remarks upon a similar phenomenon in jokes
(VII, p. 120).

CHAPTER 3: SIMILARITY AND CONTIGUITY

1. Before proceeding any further, some clarification of the position of Christian Metz both within semiotic theory and this book would
seem in order. Metz's early work, which is represented in English by
Film Language: A Semiotics of the Cinema, trans. Michael Taylor (New
York: Oxford Univ. Press, 1974) and *Language and Cinema,* trans.
Donna Jean Umiker-Sebeok (The Hague: Mouton Press, 1974), is
largely concerned with cinematic language, and with the related issues
of denotation and connotation. It does not touch on questions of subjectivity, nor does it otherwise incorporate psychoanalysis. In effect,
that work is an attempt to extend the findings of linguistic semiotics
into the area of film analysis—to define the nature of the cinematic
sign, and of those codes which govern its operations.

Le Signifiant imaginaire marks a departure from the rigorous formalism of Metz's early work both in its attentiveness to the cinematic
subject and in its incorporation of material drawn from Freud and
Lacan. The first chapter of that book was translated in *Screen* in 1975
as "The Imaginary Significer" (see Chapter 1, note 9) and helped to
establish the centrality of psychoanalytic semiotics to much of the writ-

ing which appeared there during the subsequent five years. That chapter returns once again to the topic of cinematic signification, but it does so in ways radically different from those in *Film Language* or *Language and Cinema*. The cinematic signifier is now defined as "imaginary," a word which supports three different meanings: it is used by Metz to emphasize the perceptual base of filmic signification, to stress the profoundly fictive nature of the cinematic spectacle, and—most importantly—to align film with Lacan's imaginary register, the register within which identifications are sustained. The section of *Le Signifiant imaginaire* which is most relevant to the present discussion is "Metaphore/Metonymie, ou le référent imaginaire."

Since the writing of this book a complete English translation of *Le Signifiant imaginaire* has been published under the title *The Imaginary Signifier*, trans. Celia Britton, Annwyl Williams, Ben Brewster, and Alfred Guzzetti (Bloomington: Indiana Univ. Press, 1982).

2. See "Agency of the letter in the unconscious," *Ecrits: A Selection,* trans. Alan Sheridan (New York: Norton, 1977), pp. 146–78; and "The function and field of speech and language in psychoanalysis," *Ecrits,* pp. 30–113.

3. In *Discours/figure* (Paris: Klincksieck, 1971), Lyotard associates the unconscious with figural representation, and the preconscious with language, much as we did in the preceding chapter. However, whereas we stressed that all signification must be understood as a compromise between the two, Lyotard argues that figural representation is sharply antagonistic to language. The latter is on the side of censorship and repression, while the former is on the side of desire and transgression.

4. Metz observes at one point in *Le Signifiant imaginaire* that the distinction between the primary and secondary processes cannot even be maintained—that there are only degrees of secondarization (p. 325).

5. On pp. 224–29, Metz distinguishes between the discursive and the referential axes. The first of these involves relationships of similarity and contiguity at the level of the sign, whereas the latter refers to relationships of similarity and contiguity at the level of the referent. Paradigm and syntagm represent the outcome of the discursive operation, while metaphor and metonymy derive from the referential operation. Metz sees four possible combinations of the discursive and the referential: referential comparability and discursive contiguity (the syntagmatic elaboration of metaphor), referential comparability and discursive comparability (the paradigmatic elaboration of metaphor), referential contiguity and discursive comparability (the syntagmatic elaboration of metonymy), and referential contiguity and discursive contiguity (the syntagmatic elaboration of metonymy).

6. *Standard Edition,* Vol. VIII, pp. 12–21.

7. *Course in General Linguistics,* p. 121.

8. Jean-Louis Baudry, "The Apparatus," trans. Jean Andrews and Bertrand Augst, *Camera Obscura,* no. 1 (1976), 104–28. See also "Ideological Effects of the Basic Cinematographic Apparatus," trans. Alan Williams, *Film Quarterly,* Vol. XXVIII, no. 2 (1973/74), 39–47.

9. *Within a Budding Grove,* pp. 300–301.

10. *Aristotle, Horace, Longinus: Classical Literary Criticism,* trans. T.S. Dorsch (Baltimore: Penguin, 1965), p. 61.

11. For a much more elaborate and extended treatment of metaphor and metonymy in *Pursued,* see Paul Willemen, "The Fugitive Subject" in *Raoul Walsh,* ed. Phil Hardy (Edinburgh Film Festival, 1974), pp. 63–92.

12. *Madame Bovary,* trans. Paul de Man (New York: Norton, 1965), pp. 105–106.

CHAPTER 4: THE SUBJECT

1. *The Method, Meditations and Philosophy,* trans. John Vietch (Washington: Walter Dunne, 1901), pp. 170–71.

2. *The Order of Things: An Archaeology of the Human Sciences* (New York: Pantheon, 1971), pp. 379–80.

3. See *Structural Anthropology,* trans. Claire Jacobson and Brooke Grundfest Schoepf (Garden City, N.Y.: Doubleday, 1967); *Elementary Structures of Kinship;* and *The Raw and the Cooked,* trans. John and Doreen Weightman (New York: Harper and Row, 1969).

4. One of the most thoroughgoing, albeit highly idiosyncratic, critiques of the Western Oedipus complex and its economic and political determinants is Gilles Deleuze and Felix Guattari's *Anti-Oedipus,* a book which draws freely on a wide range of theoretical materials, from the psychoanalytic to the Marxist. This is perhaps the occasion to mention as well several more rigorously Marxist texts which offer a necessary supplement to the present study: Terry Eagleton, *Criticism and Ideology: A Study in Marxist Literary Theory* (London: Verso Edition, 1978) and *Marxism and Literary Criticism* (Berkeley: Univ. of California Press, 1976); and Fredric Jameson, *Marxism and Form: Twentieth Century Dialectical Theories of Literature* (Princeton: Princeton Univ. Press, 1972), and *The Political Unconscious: Narrative as a Socially Symbolic Act* (Ithaca: Cornell Univ. Press, 1981). Two other works which combine Marxism and semiotics in rather controversial ways, but which warrant mention,

are Jean Baudrillard, *The Mirror of Production* trans. Mark Poster (St. Louis: Telos Press, 1976), and Paul Hirst, *Law and Ideology* (London: Macmillan, 1979).

5. See *Standard Edition,* Vol. XII, pp. 59–80, both for the diagram and Freud's account of it.

6. "The Ego and the Id," *Standard Edition* Vol. XIX, p. 17.

7. In *Lenin and Philosophy* Althusser isolates the family as one of the most important of what he calls the "ideological state apparatuses" (pp. 149–70). For a more extended discussion of the imbrication of the family and the state within Western culture see Wilhelm Reich, *The Mass Psychology of Fascism,* trans. Vincent R. Carfagno (New York: Farrar, Straus and Giroux, 1970).

8. Deutsch summarizes the "feminine" woman as "a harmonious interplay between narcissistic tendencies and masochistic readiness for painful giving and loving," and the "motherly" woman as one in whom "the narcissistic wish to be loved is [partially] transferred from the ego to the child or his substitute," *The Psychology of Women* (New York: Grune and Stratton, 1945), Vol. II, p. 17.

9. "The Symposium," trans. Michael Joyce, in *Collected Dialogues of Plato,* ed. Edith Hamilton and Huntington Cairns (New York: Pantheon, 1961), pp. 542–44.

10. *The Four Fundamental Concepts of Psycho-Analysis,* trans. Alan Sheridan (New York: Norton, 1978), pp. 204–5.

11. *T Zero,* trans. William Weaver (New York: Harcourt Brace, 1969), pp. 59–60.

12. "The mirror stage," *Ecrits,* p. 2.

13. Fredric Jameson provides an excellent account of these imaginary oscillations in "Imaginary and Symbolic in Lacan: Marxism, Psychoanalytic Criticism, and the Problem of the Subject," *Yale French Studies,* nos. 55/56 (1977), 338–95.

14. Anika Lemaire, *Jacques Lacan,* trans. David Macey (London: Routledge and Kegan Paul, 1977), pp. 60–61.

15. *Ecrits,* p. 126.

16. *Ecrits,* p. 65.

17. *Ecrits,* p. 170.

18. *Four Fundamental Concepts,* p. 62.

19. "The Subject and the Other: Alienation," *Four Fundamental Concepts,* p. 218.

20. "Analysis and Truth or the Closure of the Unconscious," *Four Fundamental Concepts,* p. 144.

21. *Four Fundamental Concepts,* p. 252.

22. "The Subject and the Other: Alienation," *Four Fundamental Concepts,* p. 218.
23. *Ecrits,* p. 265.
24. *Ecrits,* p. 264.
25. *Ecrits,* p. 66.
26. "Desire and the Interpretation of Desire in *Hamlet,*" trans. James Hulbert, *Yale French Studies,* nos. 55/56 (1977), p. 28.
27. *Ecrits,* p. 67.
28. *Discipline and Punish: The Birth of the Prison,* trans. Alan Sheridan (New York: Vintage Books, 1979), p. 202.
29. *Le Séminaire livre XX: Encore,* ed. Jacques-Alain Miller (Paris: Editions du Seuil, 1975).
30. Stephen Heath offers a valuable critique of this formulation in "Difference," *Screen,* Vol. XIX, no. 3 (1978), 51–112.
31. "Inquiry into Femininity," trans. Parveen Adams, *m/f,* no. 1 (1978), 83–101. This essay is taken from *L'Ombre et le nom: Sur la feminité* (Paris: Editions de Minuit, 1977), which otherwise remains untranslated, but which contains a very interesting reading of hysteria as well as a number of unusual juxtapositions of literary and cinematic texts with psychoanalytic materials.
32. I will discuss this point at much greater length in my forthcoming *Woman in Cinema: Body and Voice.*
33. "On the possible treatment of psychosis," *Ecrits,* p. 200.

CHAPTER 5: SUTURE

1. *Problems in General Linguistics,* p. 224.
2. Both Baudry in "The Apparatus" and Metz in "The Imaginary Signifier" have argued for this understanding of the cinematic apparatus, and the essays published in *The Cinematic Apparatus,* ed. Teresa de Lauretis and Stephen Heath (New York: St. Martin's Press, 1980), have extended the meaning of that term even farther.
3. I say "most exemplarily" because there are situations in which the viewer refuses to take up residence within any of the positions projected by a given text, choosing instead to activate his or her subjectivity within another discourse. Thus a viewer might distance him or herself from a given classic film by taking up residence within the discourse of Marxism or feminism. It should also be noted that even though the director is always located on the speaking side, he or she may also be simultaneously spoken through the cinematic discourse.

4. MacCabe argues for an approach to cinematic texts which maximizes their discursive contradictions in "Principles of Realism and Pleasure": "film is constituted by a set of discourses which . . . produce a certain reality. The emphasis on production must be accompanied by one on another crucial Marxist term, that of contradiction. There is no one discourse which produces a certain reality. . . . A film analysis is dealing with a set of contradictory discourses transformed by specific practices. Within a film these may be different 'views' of reality which are articulated together in different ways" (p. 11).

5. "Suture (elements of the logic of the signifier)," *Screen*, Vol. XVIII, no. 4 (1977/78), 25–26.

6. *Theory of Film Practice*, trans. Helen R. Lane (New York: Praeger, 1973), p. 12.

7. "Notes on Suture," *Screen*, Vol. XVIII, no. 2 (1977/78), 65–66.

8. "The Tutor-Code of Classical Cinema," in *Movies and Methods*, ed. Bill Nichols (Berkeley: Univ. of California Press, 1976), p. 448.

9. "Narrative Space," *Screen*, Vol. XVII, no. 3 (1976), 107.

10. "Narrative Space," p. 91–92.

11. "Narrative Space," p. 99.

12. *Lenin and Philosophy*, p. 164–65.

13. Terry Eagleton provides a very sophisticated discussion of artistic modes of production and ideology and their relationship to general modes of production and ideology in *Criticism and Ideology*, pp. 44–101.

14. *For Marx*, p. 232.

15. *Lenin and Philosophy*, p. 174–75.

16. *Lenin and Philosophy*, p. 176.

17. *Lenin and Philosophy*, p. 211.

18. "Towards a Feminist Film Practice: Some Theses," *Edinburgh Magazine*, no. 1 (1976), 56.

19. "Visual Pleasure and Narrative Cinema," *Screen*, Vol. XVI, no. 3 (1975), 6–18.

20. See Mary Ann Doane, "Misrecognition and Identity," *Ciné-Tracts*, Vol. III, no. 3 (1980), 25–32, and "Woman's Stake: Filming the Female Body," *October*, no. 17 (1981), 23–31; Teresa de Lauretis, "Through the Looking Glass," in *The Cinematic Apparatus*, pp. 187–202, and "Woman, Cinema and Language," *Yale Italian Studies*, Vol. I, no. 2 (1980), 5–21; Sandy Flitterman, "Woman, Desire and the Look: Feminism and the Enunciative Apparatus in Cinema, *Ciné-Tracts*, Vol. II, no. 1 (1978), 63–68; Leslie Stern, "Point of View: The Blind Spot," *Film Reader*, no. 5 (Evanston, Ill.: Northwestern Univ. Film Division/School of Speech, 1977), 214–36; and Linda Williams,

"Film Body: An Implanation of Perversions," *Ciné-Tracts,* Vol. III, no. 4 (1981), 19–35, and "When the Woman Looks" (unpublished talk).
21. "The Cinematic Apparatus: Problems in Current Theory," in *The Cinematic Apparatus,* p. 182.
22. "Paranoia and the Film System," *Screen,* Vol. XVII, no. 4 (1976/77), 92.

CHAPTER 6: RE-WRITING THE CLASSIC TEXT

1. *Mythologies,* pp. 124–25.
2. *S/Z,* pp. 20–21.
3. There have, needless to say, been cinematic "appropriations" of Barthes's model. The film journal *Camera Obscura,* for instance, has consistently promoted analyses based upon the deconstructive principles of *S/Z.* See in particular Thierry Kuntzel, "The Film-Work, 2," *Camera Obscura,* no. 5 (1980), 7–68, and "Sight, Insight, and Power: Allegory of a Cave," *Camera Obscura,* no. 6 (1980), 92–110.
4. *Tess of the d'Urbervilles* (New York: Modern Library, 1951), p. 3.
5. On pp. 27–28 of *Discipline and Punish,* trans. Alan Sheridan (New York: Vintage Books, 1979), Foucault writes: "power and knowledge directly imply one another . . . there is no power relation without the correlative constitution of a field of knowledge, nor any knowledge that does not presuppose and constitute at the same time power relations. These 'power-knowledge relations' are to be analysed, therefore, not on the basis of a subject of knowledge who is or is not free in relation to the power system, but, on the contrary, the subject who knows, the objects to be known and the modalities of knowledge must be regarded as so many effects of these fundamental implications of power-knowledge and their historical transformations. In short, it is not the activity of the subject of knowledge that produces a corpus of knowledge, useful or resistant to power, but power-knowledge, the processes and struggles that traverse it and of which it is made up, that determines the forms and possible domains of knowledge."
6. "Dr. Jekyll and Mr. Hyde," *The Works of Robert Louis Stevenson* (Edinburgh: Longmans, Green, 1895), p. 7.
7. *Essais de stylistique structurale,* trans. Daniel Delas (Paris: Flammarion, 1971).
8. *Northanger Abbey* (New York: Frank S. Holby, 1906), pp. 204–5.
9. *The Great Gatsby* (New York: Charles Scribner's Sons, 1925), p. 10.

Selected Bibliography
in English

Althusser, Louis. *For Marx*. Trans. Ben Brewster. New York: Pantheon, 1969.

⎯⎯⎯. *Lenin and Philosophy*. Trans. Ben Brewster. London: Monthly Review Press, 1971.

Barthes, Roland. *Elements of Semiology*. Trans. Annette Lavers and Colin Smith. New York: Hill and Wang, 1968.

⎯⎯⎯. *Writing Degree Zero*. Trans. Annette Lavers and Colin Smith. New York: Hill and Wang, 1968.

⎯⎯⎯. *Critical Essays*. Trans. Richard Howard. Evanston, Ill.: Northwestern Univ. Press, 1972.

⎯⎯⎯. *Mythologies*. Trans. Annette Lavers. New York: Hill and Wang, 1972.

⎯⎯⎯. *S/Z*. Trans. Richard Miller. New York: Hill and Wang, 1974.

⎯⎯⎯. *Pleasure of the Text*. Trans. Richard Miller. New York: Hill and Wang, 1975.

⎯⎯⎯. *Sade, Fourier, Loyola*. Trans. Richard Miller. New York: Hill and Wang, 1976.

⎯⎯⎯. *Image, Music, Text*. Trans. Stephen Heath. New York: Hill and Wang, 1977.

Baudrillard, Jean. *The Mirror of Production*. Trans. Mark Poster. St. Louis: Telos, 1976.

Baudry, Jean Louis. "Ideological Effects of the Basic Apparatus." Trans. Alan Williams. *Film Quarterly*, vol. xxviii, no. 2 (1973/74), 39–47.

⎯⎯⎯. "Writing, Fiction, Ideology." Trans. Diane Matias, *Afterimage*, no. 5 (1974), 23–39.

⎯⎯⎯. "The Apparatus." Trans. Jean Andrews and Bertrand Augst. *Camera Obscura*, no. 1 (1976), 104–28.

Benveniste, Emile. *Problems in General Linguistics*. Trans. Mary Elizabeth Meek. Coral Gables: Univ. of Miami Press, 1971.

Chatman, Seymour. *Story and Discourse: Narrative Structure in Fiction and Film.* Ithaca, N.Y.: Cornell Univ. Press, 1978.

Coward, Rosalind, and John Ellis. *Language and Materialism: Developments in Semiology and the Theory of the Subject.* London: Routledge and Kegan Paul, 1977.

Culler, Jonathan. *Structuralist Poetics.* Ithaca, N.Y.: Cornell Univ. Press, 1975.

———. *Ferdinand de Saussure.* Ed. Frank Kermode. New York: Penguin Books, 1977.

Dayan, Daniel. "The Tutor Code of Classical Cinema." *Movies and Methods.* Ed. Bill Nichols. Berkeley: Univ. of Calif. Press, 1976, pp. 438–51.

Deleuze, Gilles. *Proust and Signs.* Trans. Richard Howard. New York: George Braziller, 1972.

Deleuze, Gilles, and Felix Guattari. *Anti-Oedipus: Capitalism and Schizophrenia.* Trans. Robert Hurley, Mark Seem, and Helen R. Lane. New York: Viking, 1977.

Derrida, Jacques. *Of Grammatology.* Trans. Gayatri Chakravorty Spivak. Baltimore: Johns Hopkins Univ. Press, 1976.

———. *Writing and Difference.* Trans. Alan Bass. Chicago: Univ. of Chicago Press, 1978.

———. *Dissemination.* Trans. Barbara Johnson. Chicago: Univ. of Chicago Press, 1981.

Doane, Mary Ann. "Misrecognition and Identity." *Ciné-Tracts,* vol. iii, no. 3 (1980), 25–32.

———. "Woman's Stake: Filming the Female Body." *October,* no. 17 (1981), 23–36.

Eagleton, Terry. *Marxism and Literary Criticism.* Berkeley: Univ. of Calif. Press, 1976.

———. *Criticism and Ideology: A Study in Marxist Literary Theory.* London: Verso Editions, 1978.

Eco, Umberto. *A Theory of Semiotics.* Bloomington: Indiana Univ. Press, 1976.

Flitterman, Sandy. "Woman, Desire and the Look: Feminism and the Enunciative Apparatus in Cinema," *Ciné-Tracts,* vol. ii, no. 1 (1978), 63–68.

Foucault, Michel. *The Order of Things: An Archaeology of the Human Sciences.* New York: Pantheon, 1971.

———. *Archaeology of Knowledge.* Trans. A.M. Sheridan Smith. New York: Pantheon, 1972.

———. *The History of Sexuality.* Trans. Robert Hurley. New York: Pantheon, 1978.

Discipline and Punish: Birth of the Prison. Trans. Alan Sheridan. New York: Vintage, 1979.

Freud, Sigmund. *The Standard Edition of the Complete Psychological Works,* Vols. I–XXIII. Trans. James Strachey. London: Hogarth Press, 1953.

Guiraud, Pierre. *Semiology.* Trans. George Gross. London: Routledge and Kegan Paul, 1975.

Hawkes, Terence. *Structuralism and Semiotics.* Berkeley: Univ. of California Press, 1977.

Heath, Stephen. "Lessons from Brecht." *Screen,* vol. xv, no. 2 (1974), 103–28.

"On Screen, in Frame: Film and Ideology." *Quarterly Review of Film Studies,* vol. i, no. 3 (1976), 251–65.

"Narrative Space." *Screen,* vol. xvii, no. 3 (1976), 66–112.

"Notes on Suture." *Screen,* vol. xviii, no. 2 (1977/78), 48–76.

"Difference." *Screen,* vol. xix, no. 3 (1978), 51–112.

"The Turn of the Subject." *Ciné-Tracts,* vol. ii, nos. 3/4 (1979), 32–48.

Henderson, Brian. *Critique of Film Theory.* New York: Dutton, 1980.

Hirst, Paul. *On Law and Ideology.* London: Macmillan, 1979.

Hjelmslev, Louis. *Prolegomena to a Theory of Language.* Trans. Francis J. Whitfield. Madison: Univ. of Wisconsin Press, 1969.

Jakobson, Roman, and Morris Halle. *Fundamentals of Language.* The Hague: Mouton Press, 1956.

Selected Writings. The Hague: Mouton Press, 1971, Vols. I–IV.

Jameson, Fredric. *The Prison-House of Language: A Critical Account of Structuralism and Russian Formalism.* Princeton: Princeton Univ. Press, 1972.

Marxism and Form: Twentieth Century Dialectical Theories of Literature. Princeton: Princeton Univ. Press, 1972.

"Imaginary and Symbolic in Lacan: Marxism, Psychoanalytic Criticism, and the Problem of the Subject." *Yale French Studies,* nos. 55/56 (1977), 338–95.

The Political Unconscious: Narrative as a Socially Symbolic Act. Ithaca, N.Y.: Cornell Univ. Press, 1981.

Johnston, Claire. "Towards a Feminist Film Practice: Some Theses." *Edinburgh Magazine,* no. 1 (1976), 50–59.

Kristeva, Julia. *Desire in Language: A Semiotic Approach to Literature and Art.* Trans. Thomas Gora, Alice Jardine, and Leon S. Roudiez. Ed. Leon Roudiez. New York: Columbia, Univ. Press, 1980.

Lacan, Jacques. *The Language of the Self: The Function of Language in Psychoanalysis.* Trans. Anthony Wilden. New York: Dell, 1968.

"Of Structure as an Inmixing of Otherness Prerequisite to Any
Subject Whatsoever." *The Structuralist Controversy.* Eds. Richard
Macksey and Eugenio Donato. Baltimore: Johns Hopkins Univ.
Press, 1970, pp. 186–95.

"Seminar on 'The Purloined Letter.' " Trans. Jeffrey Mehlman. *Yale
French Studies,* no. 48 (1972), 39–72.

"Desire and the Interpretation of Desire in *Hamlet.*" Trans. James
Hulbert. *Yale French Studies,* nos. 55/56 (1977), 11–52.

Ecrits: A Selection. Trans. Alan Sheridan. New York: Norton, 1977.

The Four Fundamental Concepts of Psycho-Analysis. Trans. Alan Sheridan. Ed. Jacques-Alain Miller. New York: Norton, 1978.

Laplanche, Jean. *Life and Death in Psychoanalysis.* Trans. Jeffrey Mehlman. Baltimore: Johns Hopkins Univ. Press, 1976.

Laplanche, Jean, and Serge Leclaire. "The Unconscious: A Psychoanalytic Study." *Yale French Studies,* no. 48 (1972), 118–78.

Laplanche, J., and J.-B. Pontalis. *The Language of Psycho-Analysis.* Trans.
Donald Nicholson-Smith. New York: Norton, 1973.

de Lauretis, Teresa. "Through the Looking-Glass." *The Cinematic Apparatus.* Eds. Teresa de Lauretis and Stephen Heath. New York:
St. Martin's Press, 1980, pp. 187–202.

"Woman, Cinema and Language." *Yale Italian Studies,* vol. I, no. 2
(1980), 5–21.

Lemaire, Anika. *Jacques Lacan.* Trans. David Macey. London: Routledge and Kegan Paul, 1977.

Lévi-Strauss, Claude. *Structural Anthropology.* Trans. Claire Jacobson and
Brooke Grundfest Schoepf. Garden City, N.Y.: Doubleday, 1967.

The Elementary Structures of Kinship. Trans. James Harle Bell, John
Richard von Sturmer, Rodney Needham. Boston: Beacon Press,
1969.

The Raw and the Cooked. Trans. John and Doreen Weightman. New
York: Harper and Row, 1969.

From Honey to Ashes. Trans. John and Doreen Weightman. New
York: Harper and Row, 1973.

MacCabe, Colin. "Realism and the Cinema: Notes on Some Brechtian
Theses." *Screen,* vol. xv, no. 2 (1974), 7–29.

"Principles of Realism and Pleasure." *Screen,* vol. xvii, no. 3 (1976),
7–29.

"The Discursive and the Ideological in Film: Notes on the Condition of Political Intervention." *Screen,* vol. xix, no. 4 (1978/79), 29–
43.

"On Discourse." *The Talking Cure: Essays in Psychoanalysis and Language.* Ed. Colin MacCabe. New York: St. Martin's, 1981.

Mehlman, Jeffrey. "The Floating Signifier: From Lévi-Strauss to Lacan." *Yale French Studies,* no. 48 (1972), 10–37.

Metz, Christian. *Language and Cinema.* Trans. Donna Jean Umiker-Sebeok. The Hague: Mouton Press, 1974.

Film Language: A Semiotics of the Cinema. Trans. Michael Taylor. New York: Oxford Univ. Press, 1974.

"The Imaginary Signifier." Trans. Ben Brewster. *Screen,* vol. xvi, no. 2 (1975), 14–76.

"History, Discourse: Note on Two Voyeurisms." Trans. Susan Bennett. *Edinburgh Magazine,* no. 1 (1976), 21–25.

"The Fiction Film and Its Spectator: A Metapsychological Study." Trans. Alfred Guzzetti. *New Literary History,* vol. viii, no. 1 (1976), 75–105.

Miller, Jacques-Alain. "Suture (elements of the logic of the signifier)," *Screen,* vol. xviii, no. 4 (1977/78), 24–34.

Mitchell, Juliet. *Psychoanalysis and Feminism: Freud, Reich, Laing and Women.* New York: Vintage, 1975.

Montrelay, Michèle. "Inquiry into Femininity." *m/f,* no. 1 (1978), 83–101.

Mulvey, Laura. "Visual Pleasure and Narrative Cinema." *Screen,* vol. xvi, no. 3 (1975), 6–18.

"Afterthoughts . . . Inspired by *Duel in the Sun.*" *Framework,* nos. 15/16/17 (1981), 12–25.

Peirce, Charles Sanders. *Collected Papers.* Eds. Charles Hartshorne and Paul Weiss. Cambridge: Harvard Univ. Press, 1931, Vols. I–VIII.

Riffaterre, Michael. *Semiotics of Poetry.* Bloomington: Indiana Univ. Press, 1978.

Rose, Jacqueline. "Paranoia and the Film System." *Screen,* vol. xvii, no. 4 (1976/77), 85–104.

"The Cinematic Apparatus: Problems in Current Theory." *The Cinematic Apparatus.* Eds. Teresa de Lauretis and Stephen Heath. New York: St. Martin's Press, pp. 172–86.

de Saussure, Ferdinand. *Course in General Linguistics.* Trans. Wade Baskin. New York: McGraw-Hill, 1966.

Scholes, Robert. *Structuralism in Literature: An Introduction.* New Haven: Yale Univ. Press, 1974.

Stern, Leslie. "Point of View: The Blind Spot." *Film Reader,* no. 5. Evanston, Ill.: Northwest Univ. Film Division/School of Speech, 1979, pp. 214–36.

Todorov, Tzvetan. *The Poetics of Prose.* Trans. Richard Howard. Ithaca, N.Y.: Cornell Univ. Press, 1977.

Wilden, Anthony. *System and Structure: Essays in Communication and Exchange.* London: Tavistock Publications, 1972.

Williams, Linda. "Film Body: An Implantation of Perversions. *Ciné-Tracts,* vol. iii, no. 4 (1981), 19–35.

Willemen, Paul. "The Fugitive Subject." *Raoul Walsh.* Ed. Phil Hardy. Edinburgh Film Festival, 1974, pp. 63–92.

Wollen, Peter. *Signs and Meaning in the Cinema.* Bloomington: Indiana Univ. Press, 1972.

Index